CHURCHILL
and
Spain

The Cañada Blanch / Sussex Academic Studies on Contemporary Spain

General Editor: Professor Paul Preston, London School of Economics

Published

Cristina Palomares, *The Quest for Survival after Franco: Moderate Francoism and the Slow Journey to the Polls, 1964–1977.*

Soledad Fox, *Constancia de la Mora in War and Exile: International Voice for the Spanish Republic.*

Isabelle Rohr, *The Spanish Right and the Jews, 1898–1945: Antisemitism and Opportunism.*

Richard Wigg, *Churchill and Spain: The Survival of the Franco Regime, 1940–1945* (paperback edition).

Forthcoming

Michael Eaude, *Triumph at Midnight in the Century: A Critical Biography of Arturo Barea*

Gareth Stockey, *Gibraltar: "A Dagger in the Spine of Spain?"*

Published by the Cañada Blanch Centre for Contemporary Spanish Studies in conjunction with Routledge / Taylor & Francis

1 Francisco J. Romero Salvadó, *Spain 1914–1918: Between War and Revolution.*
2 David Wingeate Pike, *Spaniards in the Holocaust: Mauthausen, the Horror on the Danube.*
3 Herbert Rutledge Southworth, *Conspiracy and the Spanish Civil War: The Brainwashing of Francisco Franco.*
4 Angel Smith (editor), *Red Barcelona: Social Protest and Labour Mobilization in the Twentieth Century.*
5 Angela Jackson, *British Women and the Spanish Civil War.*

CHURCHILL
and
Spain

THE SURVIVAL OF THE FRANCO REGIME, 1940–1945

RICHARD WIGG

Cañada Blanch Centre
for Contemporary
Spanish Studies

sussex
ACADEMIC
PRESS

BRIGHTON • PORTLAND

2 4 6 8 10 9 7 5 3 1

*First published 2005 by Routledge/Taylor & Francis in hardcover; this revised
paperback edition published in Great Britain by*
SUSSEX ACADEMIC PRESS
PO Box 139
Eastbourne BN24 9BP

and in the United States of America by
SUSSEX ACADEMIC PRESS
920 NE 58th Ave   Suite 300
Portland, Oregon 97213-3786

British Library Cataloguing in Publication Data
A CIP catalogue record for this book is available from the British Library.

Library of Congress Cataloging-in-Publication Data
Wigg, Richard, 1928–
Churchill and Spain : the survival of the Franco regime, 1940–1945 /
Richard Wigg. — Rev. pbk. ed.
    p. cm.
Includes bibliographical references and index.
ISBN 978-1-84519-283-9 (pbk. : acid-free paper)
1. Great Britain—Foreign relations—Spain. 2. Spain—Foreign
relations—Great Britain. 3. World War, 1939–1945—Diplomatic
history. 4. Churchill, Winston, Sir, 1874–1965. 5. Franco,
Francisco, 1892–1975. 6. Great Britain—Foreign relations—
1936–1945. 7. Spain—Foreign relations—1939–1975. I. Title.

DA47.8.W54 2008
327.41046—dc22   2008000115

FSC
Mixed Sources
Product group from well-managed
forests and other controlled sources
Cert no. SGS-COC-2482
www.fsc.org
© 1996 Forest Stewardship Council

Typeset and designed by SAP, Brighton & Eastbourne.
Printed by TJ International, Padstow, Cornwall.
This book is printed on acid-free paper.

Contents

The Cañada Blanch Centre for Contemporary Spanish Studies

In the 1960s, the most important initiative in the cultural and academic relations between Spain and the United Kingdom was launched by a Valencian fruit importer in London. The creation by Vicente Cañada Blanch of the Anglo-Spanish Cultural Foundation has subsequently benefited large numbers of Spanish and British scholars at various levels. Thanks to the generosity of Vicente Cañada Blanch, thousands of Spanish schoolchildren have been educated at the secondary school in West London that bears his name. At the same time, many British and Spanish university students have benefited from the exchange scholarships which fostered cultural and scientific exchanges between the two countries. Some of the most important historical, artistic and literary work on Spanish topics to be produced in Great Britain was initially made possible by Cañada Blanch scholarships.

Vicente Cañada Blanch was, by inclination, a conservative. When his Foundation was created, the Franco regime was still in the plenitude of its power. Nevertheless, the keynote of the Foundation's activities was always a complete open-mindedness on political issues. This was reflected in the diversity of research projects supported by the Foundation, many of which, in Francoist Spain, would have been regarded as subversive. When the Dictator died, Don Vicente was in his seventy-fifth year. In the two decades following the death of the Dictator, although apparently indestructible, Don Vicente was obliged to husband his energies. Increasingly, the work of the Foundation was carried forward by Miguel Dols whose tireless and imaginative work in London was matched in Spain by that of José María Coll Comín. They were united in the Foundation's spirit of open-minded commitment to fostering research of high quality in pursuit of better Anglo-Spanish cultural relations. Throughout the 1990s, thanks to them, the role of the Foundation grew considerably.

In 1994, in collaboration with the London School of Economics, the Foundation established the Príncipe de Asturias Chair of Contemporary Spanish History and the Cañada Blanch Centre for Contemporary Spanish Studies. It is the particular task of the Cañada Blanch Centre for

Contemporary Spanish Studies to promote the understanding of twenti-eth-century Spain through research and teaching of contemporary Spanish history, politics, economy, sociology and culture. The Centre possesses a valuable library and archival centre for specialists in contemporary Spain. This work is carried on through the publications of the doctoral and post-doctoral researchers at the Centre itself and through the many seminars and lectures held at the London School of Economics. While the seminars are the province of the researchers, the lecture cycles have been the forum in which Spanish politicians have been able to address audiences in the United Kingdom.

Since 1998, the Cañada Blanch Centre has published a substantial number of books in collaboration with several different publishers on the subject of contemporary Spanish history and politics. A fruitful partner-ship with Sussex Academic Press began in 2004 with the publication of Cristina Palomares's fascinating work on the origins of the Partido Popular in Spain, *The Quest for Survival after Franco. Moderate Francoism and the Slow Journey to the Polls, 1964–1977*. More recently, this was followed in 2007 by the deeply moving biography of one of the most intriguing women of 1930s Spain, Constancia de la Mora, in *War and Exile. International Voice for the Spanish Republic* by Soledad Fox and *The Spanish Right and the Jews, 1898–1945* by Isabelle Rohr, a path-breaking study of anti-Semitism in Spain. The series is now consolidated by the publication of a revised edition of Richard Wigg's penetrating study of Churchill's relationship with General Franco.

PAUL PRESTON
Series Editor
London School of Economics

Series Editor's Preface

One of the most salutary elements of Richard Wigg's elegant and perceptively critical account of Churchill's policy towards Spain during the Second World War is to remind us of the great war leader's pragmatism and his cynicism. As is demonstrated amply by Wigg – a one-time correspondent in Madrid of *The Times* – that pragmatism, combined with the fact of Churchill's innate conservatism, was to contribute significantly to Franco's survival of Axis defeat in 1945. In contrast, ample tribute is paid to the ironic fact that Sir Samuel Hoare, sent as a notorious appeaser to please Franco, was so revolted by the regime that he put considerable effort into encouraging its monarchist enemies.

Churchill was an anti-fascist principally in terms of defending British imperial interests. During the Spanish Civil War, Winston Churchill believed that Britain should remain neutral. In his very first article on the Spanish crisis, published in the *Evening Standard* on 10 August 1936 and entitled "The Spanish Tragedy," Churchill wrote: "Meanwhile it is of the utmost consequence that France and Britain should act together in observing the strictest neutrality themselves and endeavouring to induce it in others. Even if Russian money is thrown in on the one side, or Italian and German encouragement is given to the other, the safety of France and England requires absolute neutrality and non-intervention by them."

Less than two months later, in an *Evening Standard* article, published on 2 October 1936 and entitled "Spain: Object Lesson For Radicals," he claimed: "The massacre of hostages falls to a definitely lower plane; and the systematic slaughter night after night of helpless and defenceless political opponents, dragged from their homes to execution for no other crime than that they belong to the classes opposed to Communism, and have enjoyed property and distinction under the Republican constitution, ranks with tortures and fiendish outrages in the lowest pit of human degradation. Although it seems to be the practice of the Nationalist forces to shoot a proportion of their prisoners taken in arms, they cannot be accused of having fallen to the level of committing the atrocities which are the daily handiwork of the Communists, Anarchists, and the POUM, as the new and most extreme Trotskyist organization is called. It would be a mistake alike in truth and wisdom for British public opinion to rate both sides at the same level."

In these early months of the war, Churchill was happy to believe, rather naïvely, that if Franco won, the Axis would have far less influence over him than would the Russians over the Republicans in the event of their victory. He wrote in an *Evening Standard* article entitled "No Intervention In Spain For Us", published on 8 January 1937, "Also there may be the feeling, whoever wins in Spain that Great Britain, which has intervened only upon errands of mercy, and which possesses at the time overwhelming sea power without coveting anything, is probably a country with which Spain would like to live on exceptionally friendly terms. This at any rate is a reasonable hope." Even more naïve was his view that: "It does not, however, follow that if General Franco wins he will be grateful to his Nazi and Fascist allies."

However, representations from Republican officials and from Katherine, the Duchess of Atholl, eventually provoked him into a re-think. By 1938, Churchill had come to believe that Franco's victory would pose a serious threat to the British Empire. In an article entitled "Can Franco Restore Unity and Strength to Spain?" in the *Daily Telegraph*, 23 February 1939, he questioned the likely neutrality of Franco's post-war foreign policy. Indeed, he had come to fear that Francoist Spain might become an Axis satellite largely as a result of a report by his son-in-law, Duncan Sandys, who had visited Barcelona in the spring of 1938. Churchill told a Buenos Aires newspaper: "Franco has all the right on his side, because he loves his country. Also Franco is defending Europe against the communist danger – if you wish to put it in those terms. But I – I am English, and I prefer the triumph of the wrong cause. I prefer that the other side wins because Franco would be an upset to British interests."

In "Let The Spaniards Make Peace Lest Spain Lose All", an article that appeared in the *Daily Telegraph*, 30 December 1938, Churchill wrote: "It must be admitted that if at this moment the Spanish Government were victorious they would be so anxious to live on friendly terms with Great Britain, they would find so much sympathy among the British people for them, that we should probably be able to dissuade them from the vengeance which would have attended their earlier triumph in the struggle. On the other hand, if Franco won, his Nazi backers would drive him to the same kind of brutal suppressions as are practiced in the Totalitarian States. The victory of the Spanish Republic would, therefore, not only be a strategic security for British Imperial communications through the Mediterranean, but gentler and reconciling forces would play a larger part." Elsewhere in the article, he wrote: "It would seem that today the British Empire would run far less risk from the victory of the Spanish Government than from that of General Franco."

As Richard Wigg's lucid account demonstrates, a similar element of single-minded patriotism, not to say cynical pragmatism, would dominate Churchill's attitude towards Franco during the Second World War. Based on impressively thorough research in British archives, the book goes a long way to revindicating the reputation of Sir Samuel Hoare, denigrated by Churchill as 'Slimey Sam' yet much more of a thorn in Franco's side because of his sympathies for the Spanish monarchists.

In the House of Commons on 24 May 1944, Churchill made what seemed to be a speech in praise of General Franco. Referring to the dangers from Spain in 1940, he spoke of "the Spanish resolve to keep out of the war". With regard to Operation Torch, his gratitude to the Spanish government was even more fulsome. Churchill considered that, during Torch, Spain had made full amends for her earlier acts of assistance to Germany and concluded that "as I am here today speaking kindly words about Spain, let me add that I hope she will be a strong influence for the peace of the Mediterranean after the war. Internal political problems in Spain are a matter for the Spaniards themselves. It is not for us – that is, the Government – to meddle in them."

Churchill's words certainly sprang from motives other than disinterested admiration for Franco. In the short term, he was trying to neutralize him during the forthcoming Normandy landings. Foreseeing the Cold War, he also had the longer term purpose of sanitizing Franco to be able to use him as a future bulwark of Western Mediterranean policy. At the time, however, there was considerable furore in English and American political circles, and dismay within the anti-Franco opposition. The impact of the speech was intensified by the Madrid propaganda machine which presented it as a full-scale endorsement both of Franco's foreign policy and of his regime. Spanish newspapers were jubilant.

Churchill's speech was a hostage to fortune from which Franco was to squeeze the last ounce of benefit both domestically and internationally. Hugh Dalton thought it an ill-judged, romantic gesture, "it was all totally unnecessary, but he made it up at 2.30 a.m. on the morning of his speech and the Foreign Office didn't see the draft until about an hour before it was to be delivered. They did their best to tone it down, but with hardly any success." Churchill wrote, in justification, to Roosevelt, "I see some of your newspapers are upset at my references in the House of Commons to Spain. This is very unfair, as all I have done is to repeat my declaration of October 1940. I only mention Franco's name to show how silly it was to identify Spain with him or him with Spain by means of caricatures. I do not care about Franco but I do not wish to have the Iberian Peninsula hostile to the British after the war." It was a feeble excuse for a cynical act aimed at preparing public opinion for the eventual collusion in the survival of Franco. The Caudillo could not have been more delighted. One of the many priceless gems in Richard Wigg's sparkling account is his discovery that, for fifty years the Foreign Office hid reports that Franco carried a copy of the speech wherever he went and pulled it from his pocket to read to doubters.

Acknowledgments

I have to acknowledge much help with this book. First and foremost, I wish to thank Sir Raymond Carr, doyen of British historians of Spain and former Warden of St Antony's College, Oxford, for his generous encouragement from the start, now more than a dozen years ago. In many conversations in Oxford and in Devon he allowed me to feel that there might be fresh conclusions to draw from studying Britain's relations with Spain during the Second World War. Hardly less is my debt to Professor Paul Preston of the London School of Economics and Political Sciences, historian of modern Spain and biographer of Franco, for his invaluable help as the book neared its completion.

Distinguished contemporaries of the period, now all dead, gave me many insights, even when I found I could not accept all their conclusions: Sir Frank Roberts, a key figure in the war-time Foreign Office concerned with Spain and Portugal; Tom Burns, Snr, in the Madrid embassy at the time, and Eugenio Vegas Latapie, from 1942 to 1947 the political secretary to the Spanish Pretender, Don Juan de Borbón. I had long conversations in Madrid in the 1980s with this monarchist opposed to Franco; it was these conversations which perhaps started my interest in that often murky period of world war, much of which he passed in exile in Switzerland. I have to thank here his daughter, Leonor Vegas-Latapie, for kind permission to quote from his personal archive. To a fourth contemporary of those events my debt is of long-standing: Professor Herbert Nicholas, Fellow of New College, Oxford and my politics tutor when at Oxford, who remembered well the United States of the Second World War from his visits to Washington for the Ministry of Information following the American press.

I benefited too from many conversations on Spain's modern history with Professor Borja de Riquer, of Barcelona Autonomous University, who first introduced me to the figure of the financier and politician, Francesc Cambó, and with Josep Manye ("Jorge Marin"), close observer for so many years of Britain's relations with Spain.

To many institutions and libraries my debt is fundamental: the National Archives, Kew, the Spanish Ministry of Foreign Affairs Archive, Madrid, the British Library, the Churchill Archives Centre, Churchill College, and the University Library, Cambridge, the Bodleian Library, Oxford, the

Biblioteca de Catalunya, Barcelona, the economics faculty library of Barcelona University, the library of Chatham House (Royal Institute of International Affairs), London, and the Staatsbibliotek, Berlin.

Any errors of fact – and, of course, judgment – are mine alone.

For Mercedes
Who Asked the First Questions

Prologue

> "History is lived forwards but it is written in retrospect. We know the end before we consider the beginning and we can never wholly recapture what it was to know the beginning only."
> (C. V. Wedgwood, *William the Silent, Prince of Orange*)

Shortly after the Second World War Gerald Brenan, the best-known English writer on Spain of the day, wrote a letter of praise to Lord Templewood who, as Sir Samuel Hoare, had been Britain's war-time special ambassador in Madrid. "If a book could bring down Franco's regime yours would do it," the author of *The Spanish Labyrinth* observed. "But I am afraid that the days of Joshua and Jericho have gone for ever." Hoare had just published his memoirs of his four and a half difficult years in Franco Spain, *Ambassador on Special Mission*. "My object," he had informed the Foreign Office, "is to make the complete case against Franco as quickly as possible." Concern was indeed growing by mid 1946 when the book appeared over the stubborn, and then puzzling, survival of the regime of General Franco. Hoare had wished to get his public indictment out earlier – a full draft had been ready as the year began – for he sensed that Franco's position was strengthening, contrary to initial post-war expectations throughout Europe that the Spanish dictator's fate had been decided with the Allied unconditional victory over Hitler in 1945.

Hoare had been told by Brenan in that letter that he personally held "great pressure" should have been applied on Spain during the winter of 1945–46 by the British, United States and French governments as the way to end Franco's rule. This book will, however, argue that the decisive phase for the Allied governments to bring their influence to bear upon Spain had been earlier, especially during the months of October 1944 to May '45, as the world war was ending victoriously for them in Europe. If the will exists at the apex of power, conditions can often be obtained in wartime, even from neutrals well aware the earth is moving, which are impossible in peace. This is not to maintain, and it must be made clear from the outset, that had such pressure been applied sincerely it would have been either fully or partially successful. But such pressure would have been in accord with the democratic ideals of personal liberty which had been constantly proclaimed as fundamentally underlying the Allies' war effort against Fascist tyranny. The exact reasons why this course of action was not tried will form the subject of this book. The might-have-beens of history are not popular with historians, but why something did not happen may be a proper subject of historical inquiry.

The role of Winston Churchill, at the zenith of his power and influence as Britain's victorious leader during those last months of the Second World War, and a beacon of hope for personal freedom for millions of Europeans, was, it will be argued, crucial in deciding General Franco's fate. This was so both in the councils of Britain's war-time coalition government and in Churchill's determined avoidance of working out a joint policy with the Roosevelt Administration towards Franco Spain. Churchill chose, it will be maintained, not to play a moral role, mixed with national interest, when he was uniquely equipped by the European war's triumphant outcome to do so. In the final phase of a prolonged debate within the British government the Prime Minister stubbornly rejected advice consonant with the proclaimed war-time aims, notably from Hoare whose evolution en poste in Madrid deserves, it will be argued, much more attention than has been given Neville Chamberlain's colleague and fellow appeaser in the infamous 1930s. A re-appraisal of the outstanding intelligence and sensitivity of Samuel Hoare will, it is hoped, be one of the fruits of this detailed study of his Madrid years.

Spain is, with France, Britain's closest big neighbour and historically has been an important player in Europe. It was the long night of the Franco era and his regime's isolation which caused this fact to be overlooked. Only with the advent of democracy after the dictator's death has an awareness of Spain's presence gradually returned. The underlying triangular relationship with Spain for Britain was spectacularly demonstrated in 1940 with the Fall of France. All the phases of the Second World War, and Britain's fortunes in it, were mirrored in Spain. Britain's decline, as the inexorable cost of waging that war, led to its being supplanted in influence in Spain by the United States. Churchill was a *Realpolitiker*, yet he failed to take account of the strategic changes brought about by the Allied successes in the war in Europe to exploit Franco Spain's isolation. What could be justified, and amply in Britain's hour of need in 1940, could no longer serve in 1944–45. Churchill's perception of Britain's strategic interests ignored the other strand of Allied war policy, the fight for democratic values. He held to outdated British imperial interests alone.

It is the fate of weaker nations, or those with a weak regime, as that of Franco during the Second World War, that their foreign policies must often bow to the dictates of stronger neighbours. Franco Spain had to change its declared foreign policy three, if not four, times during that conflict. In September 1939 the Franco government hastily declared for strict neutrality between Germany and Britain; that was changed in June 1940, as the power of the Axis nations reached its zenith, to a policy of non-belligerency in the Axis' favour. One year later, as Hitler attacked the Soviet Union, Franco dispatched the Blue Division to fight against "God-less Communism" alongside the German armies. In October 1943, as the Allies were beginning to harvest their victory, it was back to neutrality once again, though this time the foreign policy was dubbed "vigilant neutrality". It often appeared to Britain and the United States as *malevolent* neutrality.

This book studies primarily Churchill's responsibility for making policy towards Franco Spain and an eventual return of the Spanish monarchy. But there was, of course, a role to be played by his Foreign Secretary. "Eden was not very positive about Spain. He was not interested in a king's return, that was Churchill," Sir Frank Roberts observed when reminiscing about Spain and his Second World War years in the Foreign Office's central department.[1] Yet equally Eden's first reaction to the Franco regime was usually a negative one. "He was always wanting to be tough with Spain," the veteran British diplomat thought, confessing how the department had difficulty getting him to come round to the policy they were recommending. "It was not a country he was normally sympathetic about," Roberts summed up. Eden's failure in the final analysis, as we shall see, was a lack of will to pursue resolutely any policy towards Spain. Churchill's supreme confidence in himself in the closing stages of the war, and will power, came quickly to fill that void.

The quotation from the English historian, C. V. Wedgwood, which heads this Prologue, but which should be remembered throughout this book, helps us, hopefully, to attempt a better understanding of the early years of the Franco regime during the Second World War, which were so uncertain, and not view things from the perspective of the end we know – the 30 years' rule of Spain by General Franco from 1945 to 1975 when Europe was at peace.

1

In the Hour of Britain's Need
1940

When Winston Churchill took up the offices of Prime Minister and Defence Minister in that awesome May of 1940 Spain was not among his immediate priorities. He was busy elsewhere with the Fall of France imminent and with home matters including a real prospect of invasion of Britain's shores. To read the abundant literature available now on those overloaded and heroic days, or to study those days' events through the flood of signals daily from him on so many aspects of the war at the Churchill Archives, is to understand that the demands on the Prime Minister's time and energies could not be expected to make his attention to Spain anything but intermittent. This was so even when he did turn to the unavoidable strategic issues the Iberian peninsula threw up for Britain as a sea-power with an empire. Longer concentration was impossible: the demands of the war machine simply would not have permitted it him.

It was thus only in September 1940 that a considered policy by Churchill on how to handle Franco Spain appears as a personal minute in the archives.[1] He is answering Lord Halifax, still in place as Foreign Secretary in the coalition government Churchill now led, though a holdover from the previous Chamberlain administration. He was urging a measure of leniency towards the Spanish government. This concerned the British Navy's stringent blockade against Hitler's conquered Europe. A certain degree of trade with Spain, so long as it did not actually join the Axis camp and declare war against Britain, was a principal element of British policy at that juncture. The new Prime Minister endorsed this approach and set his own bold stamp on how far he saw it might serve Britain's war purposes.

"I entirely agree with you that we should delegate authority to our embassy at Madrid to smooth the economic path and settle minor blockade points out of hand," Churchill wrote. But raising bigger issues he went on: "I would far rather we should pay our way with Spain by economic favours, and other favours, than by promises of giving up Gibraltar after we have won the war." The British Cabinet had just considered what steps might be taken in the face of the Spanish government's, and the Falange's noisy public agitation, to recover the Rock for Spain that summer, but Churchill's argument against such thoughts had prevailed. "I do not mind if the

Spaniards go into French Morocco . . . I would far rather the Spaniards in Morocco than the Germans and if the French have to pay for their abject attitude it is better that they should pay in Africa to Spain than in Europe to either of the guilty powers {Germany and Italy}. Indeed I think you should let them {Spain} know that we shall be no obstacle to their Moroccan ambitions provided they preserve their neutrality in the war." "Must we always wait till a disaster has occurred?" Churchill had asked Halifax, revealing his most personal feelings after taking over in the darkest days of the war.

Gibraltar as the gateway to the Mediterranean would always excite Churchill's interest; it is often from this perspective alone that we see him early in the war taking Spain into account. Gibraltar, and one of the Navy's battle cruisers, HMS Hood in the harbour there, had characteristically caught his eye much earlier on. He person-ally minuted the First Sea Lord to get the Hood to sea on July 20; it should join the aircraft-carrier Ark Royal to avoid the risk of *"a surprise bombardment"*[2] by the enemy. Churchill added urgency with the words *"provided the Spanish situation has not further deteriorated."* Churchill's vigilance on details for a sea-power, the product of his long career, is obvious as well as his keen political uncertainty then as to which way Franco Spain might go.

On trade as a means to entice Franco Spain not to throw in its lot with the Axis powers, and still barely emerging from the devastation of the Civil War, Churchill was only giving his impetus to a policy which had been followed ever since the Anglo-Spanish War Trade agreement (WTA) of March 1940. The Prime Minister was content to leave the details to the Foreign Office, to Hoare after he reached Madrid in June, to the Admiralty and to that special wartime creation the Ministry of Economic Warfare (MEW). But Churchill's endorsement was important during 1940 for a policy struggle was going on whether any concessions could really be justi-fied. Could not vital items for Spain, such as petrol and cereals, be used as a build-up of supplies prior to joining the Axis? The detailed evidence could be read at the time either way – and often was by the rival ministers and their officials.

A consequence of Churchill's lack of time to attend to Spain, enhanced that summer and early autumn of 1940 by the Caudillo's ambiguity and manoeuvrings, was the Prime Minister's reliance upon selected individuals who enjoyed direct access to him – a rare privilege. Chief among these was Captain Alan Hillgarth, naval attaché at the British embassy in Madrid from 1939 to the autumn of 1943, but in fact much more regarding Britain's wartime dealings with Spain. "I know this officer, he is very good," Churchill once minuted a Cabinet minister. It is clear the Prime Minister enjoyed, and trusted, this naval officer's perception of Britain's strategic interests in the Western Mediterranean as well as personal knowledge of Spain. Churchill's liking for service types, and particularly those from the Royal Navy, allowed Hillgarth undoubted influence. His views and his entrée with the Spanish regime formed an essential element in the Prime Minister's highly personalized *approach to that country. Churchill felt rarely comfortable with Hoare's views and sympathies. Hillgarth's were always clear, bold and concise, just as the Prime Minister desired from his subordinates. Hillgarth could also keep a watch on Hoare. Hillgarth had retired early from the Navy possessing independent means and, having "married well" (as Churchill himself once noted to Eden), gone to live in Majorca. Bored, he decided to take the post of honorary British consul – though there must be a strong suspicion that Hillgarth appreciated its strategic position in the western Mediterranean made it interesting for intelligence purposes. Hillgarth became involved when the Spanish Civil War broke out. Majorca sided with the Nationalists becoming their chief naval base and Hillgarth made his first contacts there with senior Spanish naval and army commanders, soon to form the backbone of the Franco regime.*

Hillgarth settled the details on the spot of the Navy's wartime blockade regarding Spain as Churchill had directed. Even more important he was the artificer, with the Majorcan banker and free-booting trader Juan March, of the operation mounted to bribe a number of Spanish generals to strengthen opposition to Spain's going to war with the Axis, or, as a Foreign Office memorandum put it, to encourage "elements in Spain desiring to maintain neutrality." This was, of course, direct intervention in Spain's internal affairs at the highest level as Churchill had hinted in that personal minute to Halifax when speaking about "other favours", besides the trading ones, Britain was offering Spain. Churchill approved the operation and Hillgarth regularly reported to him on how it was proceeding. As we shall see, Churchill later intervened with the Americans to ensure the Spanish generals had untrammelled access to their money. The British public funds made available for them in 1940 totalled $10 million. Today that amount might seem trivial but, at the then prevailing rate of exchange of $4 to the £, the figure for Spain's total exports to the UK during that year under the WTA was the exact equivalent. It was no mean sum therefore.

The second privileged figure bound up with Churchill's conduct towards Franco Spain was the Duke of Alba, Spain's premier nobleman, who served as Franco's ambassador to London throughout the Second World War. Jacobo María del Pilar Carlos Manuel Fitzjames Stuart y Falcó, the 17th duke and 10th Duke of Berwick, as descendant of an illegitimate son of King James II by Arabella Churchill, had come to London in 1937 to be the Nationalist side's unofficial representative for the duration of the Civil War. The English dukedom and an education at Beaumont School ensured Alba a high place in British society as well as in his native Spain. Big landowner and on the board of many leading companies, Alba had been a minister in the last government of King Alfonso XIII. Churchill's faiblesse *for "Jimmy" Alba will be seen in the many "re-assurances" on Britain's intentions towards Franco Spain which Churchill gave his "kinsman" without consulting anyone else, and often to the Foreign Office's complete ignorance. Alba was the more calculating and had initially mistrusted Churchill, preferring Chamberlain's sympathy for the Nationalists' cause and recognition of their victory in 1939. Churchill and Eden (soon to become Foreign Secretary again, replacing Halifax) both owed their wartime positions to being previously firm opponents of Europe's dictators: would they not when in power be against Franco?*

But at a lunch in December 1940, the first of many between the two during the war, Churchill satisfied Alba that he now desired "the best and most friendly relations with Spain." A warm political friendship grew up between them, especially when the pro-Axis Ramón Serrano Súñer, Franco's brother-in-law and both Interior and Foreign Minister, was in the aggressive ascendant in Madrid. Subsequently Churchill's pursuit of a personal policy towards Franco Spain met up with Alba's efforts to moderate the anti-Allied propaganda of the regime and influence Franco himself. Alba conveyed any sweet words he could pick up from the British Prime Minister to his political master in Madrid. Both Churchill and Alba as aristocrats were professing monarchists. But in reality while Alba preferred to serve Franco, instead of the Spanish Pretender, Churchill initially was for a British policy favouring a restoration of the monarchy. As Don Juan de Borbón was to prove incapable of mustering an alternative to the Caudillo, Churchill lost interest in him.

On 14 June – the day the Germans occupied Paris, and four days after Fascist Italy had entered the war – Spain sent her troops into the Tangiers International Zone in North Africa heightening British worries about Gibraltar. Franco's intentions had to be read as menacing for Britain's strategic interests. Churchill turned to devising a line of defence if the Spanish dictator should now follow Musssolini into the Axis camp, either going to war against Britain for Gibraltar or throw in his lot with the Germans if they invaded the Iberian peninsula. On 17 June the Prime Minister got on to the Service Chiefs and ordered the Admiralty to make preparations for the seizure of Spain's Canary Islands. "With the Canaries in British hands," Churchill boldly contended, it would "not be necessary to quit the eastern Mediterranean even with Gibraltar gone." This was the first of a series of military operations, envisaging at times some 50,000 men and the ships to transport them, readied on Churchill's orders if war against Franco Spain or in Spain against the Germans or both proved to be necessary. They were kept up to date until 1942.

The deeper significance of all these strategic initiatives coming direct from Churchill, and endorsed by the British Chiefs of Staff, lies in the proof they give of the extent of the Prime Minister's doubts about Franco's real intentions or how they might evolve. Just as the economic measures Churchill approved were to have the ultimate effect of building up the Franco regime, the Prime Minister's preparations against an outright conflict with Franco Spain in 1940–41 came to colour all his subsequent personal expressions of "gratitude" towards the dictator, notwithstanding the flaws in such thinking.

With France on the brink of collapse, the geostrategic balance altered radically and Spain, astride both the Mediterranean and the Atlantic, became a major factor in the war to secure Britain's survival. The man to play Britain's daunting hand with the third of Europe's dictators, General Francisco Franco, in the hectic days of 1940 had to be found first, policy would follow.

The blunt truth is that Samuel Hoare, former Foreign Secretary, was sent to Madrid as "ambassador on special mission" to get rid of him. The Labour party's condition for entering a wartime coalition government under Churchill, rejecting two principal figures in Chamberlain's outgoing Cabinet, brought things Spanish momentarily into a personal focus for the new Prime Minister. Churchill "parked" Sir John Simon as Lord Chancellor, England's chief law officer. With Hoare personal animosity was compounded by wide-ranging political differences. The Prime Minister might have struck harder had not Halifax, still Foreign Secretary, helped with considerable tact. Halifax had indeed been both the Conservative party's, and the King's preference, to succeed Chamberlain. Hoare, however, commanded little support in the country.

"I have just been seeing Sam about Spain," Halifax minuted the Prime Minister on 15 May,[3] pressing Churchill, five days into the new government, to see Hoare that day and so settle the matter. "I should personally have favoured his selection," Halifax went on, evidently anxious not to arouse Churchill, "indeed I cannot readily think of anybody else who would have anything like the many-sided equipment that the post [Madrid] demands." Hoare had, however, told Halifax of his keen desire to become Viceroy of India, and the Foreign Secretary in the same minute told Churchill that this wish "does affect his judgment both as to doing a special mission in Spain and also as to doing the embassy for, say, six months." Churchill ignored Hoare's desire to go to India and a second plea as Chamberlain's outgoing Secretary of Air that he should assist Beaverbrook, Churchill wanted a complete break for Hoare and the Madrid posting was settled.

The day after Churchill became Prime Minister Hoare had written to congratulate him. The letter[4] is ambiguous, evidently, as to motivation: was he seeking to placate an old political foe now become all-powerful with protestations of admiration for Churchill's "energy and brilliance" which would now have full scope in conditions of war? The letter also contains, however, a remarkable piece of self-criticism. "During these months I have often felt that my dull, drab qualities were better suited for other conditions," Hoare confessed, referring to the period from September '39 to May '40.

Thus Hoare was sent abroad and embarked upon what he called "the most difficult task of my whole career." In his memoirs, written post-war, Hoare carefully puts the emphasis on the strategic significance of the posting, and he quotes as the advice which led him to accept the job the words of the Deputy Chief of the Naval Staff: "It is essential that the Atlantic ports and the Spanish peninsula should not fall into enemy hands." The Madrid mission, Hoare wrote, was thus "not a mere diplomatic post. It was real war-work of great strategic urgency in which the Chiefs of Staff and the fighting services were vitally concerned."[5]

In the London of 1940 others saw things very differently, notably the Permanent Head of the Foreign Office, who had, too, initially preferred "Old Neville" [Chamberlain] to his new master Churchill. His wartime diary entries reveal Alexander Cadogan as bitterly suspicious of Britain's new ambassador to Madrid. "Dirty little dog has got the wind up and wants to get out of this country," he wrote on 19 May.[6] "They all agreed to send him out . . . As long as I see the last of Sam I don't care what happens." The next day when talking to Halifax about the appointment the vituperation continued: "I said there was one bright spot – there were lots of Germans and Italians in Madrid and therefore a good chance of S.H. being murdered."[7] But Cadogan, who had favoured up until 1939 a compromise settlement with Germany, painted an even more brutal scenario for Hoare: "He'll be the Quisling of England when Germany conquers us and I am dead!" When the Spanish government's *agrément* was received Cadogan wrote in his diary "Thank heaven. Good riddance to v. bad rubbish."[8]

Trade and Bribes

"What the hell can he do anyway in Spain?" Cadogan had mused of Hoare's mission just before Dunkirk.[9] It fell to a subordinate to offer Britain's new Prime Minister more level-headed Foreign Office analysis of the possibilities remaining to the British government. "It is hoped the appointment of Sir Samuel Hoare will greatly contribute to the realisation of our objective in Spain," Roger Makins' memorandum, "done for the Prime Minister" and dated 21 May, had begun.[10] Britain's goal was "to keep Spain neutral, to support and strengthen the elements in Spain desiring to maintain neutrality, to counter and reduce German and Italian influence and to obtain greater facilities for our own propaganda." But Makins had to admit that Britain had "little concrete inducement" to offer General Franco as counterweight to Axis predominance but through trade.

Here was the exception, something which became, as we shall see, the

Allies' decisive tool against the Axis' influence in Spain. Efforts must be concentrated on expanding a War Trade Agreement (WTA), signed by Britain with the Franco regime in March 1940, Makins emphasized. Spain had been suffering from severe economic distress since the outbreak of the Civil War. Much of Hoare's preparations in London before arriving in Madrid were taken up in examining with the Treasury the possibilities. Cereals, petrol, cotton and coal were identified as essential Spanish needs offering Britain leverage, and they were to remain so throughout the war. The Board of Trade eventually listed among items the British Empire, as part of the sterling area, might supply Spain – cotton from Egypt, rubber from Malaysia, asbestos from South Africa, jute from India and asphalt from Trinidad. Wheat for Spain might additionally be diverted from supplies to European countries now occupied by Germany. But the dangers were no less clear: the Treasury held out the prospect of 100,000 tons of wheat for Spain, with the first 25,000 tons to be shipped by June. When he got to Madrid Hoare had immediately to recommend going slow on that "sweetener": Germany's military successes made it "more likely" than before that Spain would "be forced to abandon its neutrality", as Britain's new man in Madrid diplomatically put it.

Economics as a weapon of policy was not familiar territory to Britain's professional diplomats of the era. But Makins, who had no professional experience of the Iberian peninsula, had built up a relationship with a British businessman, David Eccles, who was recruited into public service as the war approached. He later became a prominent Conservative politician. The Spanish Civil War had ended with the Nationalist side resentful of the British government's ambiguous stand, and the Foreign Office cast around desperately for anyone with an insider's contacts to the new regime. Eccles fitted the bill: he had been chairman of the London-based company which ran the Santander-Mediterraneo Railway used by Franco to move men and materials to the battle front and with company headquarters in Burgos, the Nationalists' base camp. Eccles even spoke the language. In November he was dispatched to Madrid as "ideas man" to reinforce the slow-moving British embassy. He participated eagerly in the negotiations for the War Trade Agreement. Always pushing, he had established personal relations with Spain's Foreign Minister, Col. Juan Beigbeder, and, more importantly with Dr Antonio Salazar, the Portuguese dictator. In London Eccles always had Makins' ear and well disposed to take his advice on how to handle the awkward Spaniards. Eccles' wartime letters to his wife, *By Safe Hand* published in 1983, brashly reveal the outsider's input aimed at cultivating the Franco regime. "The Spaniards are up for sale and it is our job to see that the auctioneer knocks them down to our bid, " he wrote to his wife in England in November 1940. Eccles' ideas were not in fact original and, at least from when Hoare reached Madrid, he enjoyed every backing.

Eccles' success ingratiating himself with Salazar and the widening of the WTA to include Portugal as trading partner in a triangular arrangement supplying raw materials from its empire to Spain owed much to his enthusiastic efforts. Eccles' contact with Portugal's strongman naturally impressed London. Perhaps most influential at that juncture was Salazar's opinion that the Germans' sway over the Madrid regime would not be strong enough to threaten Franco's own position, something Makins had expressed fears about in his memorandum to Churchill. The dismissal by Franco in the last week of June of the Falangist and pro-Nazi Air Minister, General Juan Yagüe, for being involved in a German-backed coup attempt against the Caudillo, was to prove Salazar right.

Spain's exports to Britain under the WTA were to total in 1940 £2.5 million but in September a £4 million loan on easy terms was also agreed. This was to help Spain to import from Portugal and its colonies. First steps, if the Spaniards fulfilled their part of the bargain, were being taken by the British government in building up the Franco regime against its internal opponents.

With trade in hand by government departments and backed up by the Navy's blockade with well-dosed exceptions, Churchill seized on the most delicate issue – Makins' recommendation to "strengthen elements in Spain desiring to maintain neutrality." If there was to be economic bribery through Anglo-Spanish trade why not go directly for the chiefs of Spain's one year-old military regime and bribe them too? Brother officers of Franco might be found who would argue that Spain's economic state after the devastation of the Civil War, and the war weariness prevailing and in places downright hunger, made going to war on Hitler's side too dangerous, whatever the spoils up for grabs in French North Africa. A sum of $10 million was secretly arranged for selected Spanish generals from British public funds.

The official who, with the help of the Spanish banker, Juan March, fixed up this bribery operation was Captain Alan Hillgarth, the Naval Attaché in Madrid who also supervised British intelligence and counter-intelligence activities in Spain and Portugal. Churchill spoke at length with Hillgarth while he was in London at the end of May. Churchill's biographer Martin Gilbert writes of Hillgarth's chargé: "He returned [to Madrid] with a mission of considerable importance and delicacy – to use his many contacts in Spain in order to try and keep Spain out of the war at least for six months."[11] Hillgarth had made his first personal contacts with the future Director of Naval Intelligence from 1939 to 1942, Admiral John Godfrey, during the Spanish Civil War when Godfrey commanded a battle cruiser serving in the Mediterranean in 1938. The naval intelligence chief had been visited by the banker March at the beginning of the world war who insisted that it was in Spain's interest to be on good terms with the British and offered his services. "We kept in touch throughout the war," Godfrey opaquely noted in his post-war reminiscences.[12] Hillgarth thus had all the contacts he needed for placing the secret funds at the Spanish generals' disposal.

But the scheming also involved Hoare, and Cadogan, as the FO's head, had too to give his approval. Cadogan took a refreshingly unstuffy view of intelligence as "the missing dimension of most diplomatic history."[13] As an old intelligence hand, Hoare – who was in military intelligence in Italy during the First World War – had participated in what was planned for the Spanish generals. While preparing in London he had discussed this with Brendan Bracken, Churchill's political handyman. "I have put a very secret proposal to Halifax on the lines of the talk you and I had", Hoare wrote to Bracken a few days after arriving in Madrid, "and I have asked him if, as I suspect, he is doubtful about it that he would talk it over with Winston." In pen, Hoare added at the bottom of the typed letter: "I hear that my project has been approved."[14] Two days later, Hoare sent a signal to London, which was seen by Cadogan, by the Chancellor of the Exchequer and Admiral Godfrey, reporting that "a safe means of approach is available to Spanish Minister [Beigbeder is evidently meant] and for this purpose the sum of £500,000 is needed."[15] The full text of the signal was removed by the Foreign Office "weeders", who regularly go through all the documents to categorize the duration of secrecy for them from public knowledge, for 30, 50 years or even indefinitely, so that only a bare summary is available in the PRO file. Even that summary is surprising. The sum required is roughly what Hoare learned later the Germans had advanced General Yagüe amidst preparations for his coup attempt against Franco.

Hoare gave the Prime Minister his first assessment of the Spanish situation under the impact of Italy's entry into the war on 10 June. "When I arrived – on 1 June – I found the whole of Madrid in a state of nervous excitement. It was evident that the Italians and Germans were making a frantic effort to push Spain into the war simultaneously with Italy," he wrote.[16] Now Italy had entered, the battle for Spain's participation had taken on even greater force. His presence as Britain's spokesman in a hostile Madrid had however "provided a diversion behind which the anti-war forces had counter-attacked and momentarily hold the position", Hoare told the Prime Minister. "I shall have to make many more requests. Some of them may be of a surprising character," Hoare went on, plunging unblushingly into the bribery operation. "If so, and it looks as if Whitehall is getting shocked, I will confidently write a line to you or Brendan with a view to getting things quickly straightened out." To Halifax Hoare had already written: "With Italy's entry into the war the real pull seems to me to have come and if we are to prevent Franco being dragged over in this uneven tug of war we must put all the weight we can at the other end of the rope . . . This is the justification of our economic policy and it is also the justification of the other steps, as you know, I am taking."[17]

On 12 June Spain had switched to "non-belligerence" in the war, thus replacing the neutrality officially declared on 4 September, 1939, as the conflict between Hitler's Germany and Britain began. It was undeniably to get closer to the triumphant Axis powers. Franco despatched General Juan Vigón, his most intimate military adviser, to Berlin with the regime's terms for armed entry into the conflict. Hoare, in a postscript the same day, told Halifax his best estimate was that "Franco has put himself into a strategic position from which he can enter the war if things go irrevocably badly for the French". The Germans entered Paris on 14 June. The French sought an armistice three days later.

Hoare launched himself into a series of interviews with top-level figures of the regime, seeing General José-Enrique Varela, the Army Minister, Yagüe, the Air Minister (soon to be dismissed by Franco), Ramón Serrano Súñer, the Interior Minister and Franco's then highly influential brother-in-law, Beigbeder, the Foreign Minister, plus a group of leading Spanish businessmen. Only Beigbeder really listened to Hoare or thought Britain stood any chance against the might of Germany. The Foreign Office wheeze of authorizing Hoare to indicate Britain might discuss Gibraltar with Spain at the end of the war aroused no interest in Madrid. Serrano told the British envoy Germany anyway would soon be "omnipotent in Europe".[18] When Hoare got to have his first full length interview with Franco he had to listen to the dictator, like his brother-in-law, expressing the conviction that Britain would never win a decisive victory over Germany. Franco offered to help the two belligerents to come to terms, Hoare reported. He got nowhere and only captured Franco's outward appearance "I never saw anyone so unlike a dictator, nor have I ever heard anyone talk less like a dictator, " he told Halifax.[19] Franco appeared more like "a staff officer who had read a good deal, but who is not sure of himself in the world of politics".

Into this whirlpool of war intrigue there came the Duke and Duchess of Windsor, arriving in Madrid on 27 June from defeated France via the Spanish frontier. Shielding the defeatist-minded royal couple from the press, particularly the American, and from some hare-brained German agents believing they had Nazi authority to kidnap them, could only be an additional burden on Hoare. The significance of the Windsor episode, which lasted until they were got safely onto a trans-Atlantic liner in Lisbon on 1 August, lies for this study solely in how Hoare collaborated completely with Churchill. It proved indeed a kind of refiner's fire for Hoare suspected, as we have seen, by Cadogan of a propensity to be England's Quisling if a deal had been struck, as the Duke favoured, with Hitler's Germany. The telegrams show Hoare not only entertaining the Windsors endlessly, to keep them out of harm's way, but backing up the Prime Minister's insistence the Duke must accept the governor general's post in the Bahamas. The Spanish press, then under Interior Minister Serrano's complete control, reported that the Duke had come to Madrid to make a separate British peace "behind your back," as Hoare told Churchill on 27 June. Hoare recommended giving the Duke a naval command of some kind. "If the chance is lost," Hoare warned the Prime Minister, "there will be a prince over the water who will be a nuisance and possibly an embarrassment."[20]

After almost a month in Spain, Hoare felt able to tell the Prime Minister how he sized up the Spanish situation. The German "machine" was everywhere to be felt, in the military government, key ministries and the press. "I still think however that it is worth trying to keep some influence here. Supposing we can keep Spain out of the war even for a comparatively short time it is worth the attempt."[21] Then came Hoare's crucial point, reaching out to the country beyond the capital, for Churchill's consideration: "I should not say this if it were not for the fact that nine out of 10 people in the country do not wish to be involved in the war. This means that there are strong anti-war forces beneath the surface if we could tap them. This is the message that I have sent back by [Commander] Furse: it is the key to the position." Furse was Hillgarth's deputy, who, as the naval attaché had put it to Churchill in a telegram a few days before, "understands the position absolutely." He would explain to the Prime Minister "what the ambassador could not telegraph," Hillgarth's signal to Churchill went on, referring to the bribery operation of selected Spanish generals. "As the idea was originally mine, I feel you would want me to tell you myself that it is practical and is already showing results."[22]

The extent of the brief on Spain which Hillgarth enjoyed with Churchill, and the confidence underlying the relationship, can be gauged from the signal the attaché sent the Prime Minister in July. "Things are going quite well here really. There is far more strength in the anti-German element than there was . . . . Our new ambassador has done wonders. I am not a professional diplomat so I can, perhaps, be allowed to say that at this moment Sam Hoare is doing better than any diplomat I know could do."[23] Clearly, Hillgarth was speaking of a politician's input. The attaché further commented on the attitude towards Spain in the British press. Editors in London, he suggested to the Prime Minister, should be urged to understand how "middle opinion" (as he dubbed it) inside Spain, comprising leaders in industry, the Army and Navy, the Catholic church and "most of the Spanish people" should be seen as working against the powerful influence of the Falange which eagerly obeyed German orders. These people were Britain's potential friends. Churchill accordingly minuted the Minister of Information: "Please see what you can do with the editors and proprietors. If necessary, I will help."[24]

When the Prime Minister took up the matter with Halifax of the policy to be pursued towards Franco Spain late September he began by recognizing Hoare's initial success in Madrid as Hillgarth had told him. "I think Sam is doing well and has established most valuable contacts." He was to stay in Madrid as ambassador and not to come home "until and unless he is forced to do so"[25] – a proviso which showed Churchill's uncertainty at that time whether Franco would join the Axis in the war.

Starving Spain

Unfortunately for Hoare, and Britain, the friendly Beigbeder was replaced on 18 October as Foreign Minister by the pro-German and Falangist Interior Minister Ramón Serrano Súñer, who assumed the two portfolios as expression of growing influence. The new minister's first official task was to accompany his brother-in-law, to the ominous meeting with Hitler just over the Franco-Spanish border at Hendaye on 23 October. All Hoare had as forewarning was a tip-off from Beigbeder just before he was sacked. A signal went rapidly from the Madrid embassy to Churchill who as promptly informed President Roosevelt. The Prime Minister telegraphed Hoare: "I felt Beigbeder's fate would distress you, but relations you had with him played a valuable part. Now try to get Serrano Súñer."[26] That crude assessment revealed Churchill's lack of the most elementary knowledge about Spain's rulers. Perhaps he felt the ongoing bribery operation might suborn Serrano too. The famous Hendaye meeting between the two dictators represents a good example of the importance of the Wedgwood quotation opening this study. Its very *inconclusiveness* left highly-interested onlookers like Hoare with nothing definite to report to London at the time.

Hitler nonetheless ordered his generals to prepare for an invasion of the peninsula, Operation Felix, for January 1941. The British government had then no detailed knowledge either of Serrano's previous meetings with the

Nazi leaders in Berlin that September, prior to his taking over the Foreign Ministry. But they had been a clear advertisement to everyone in Madrid that he was Germany's man, his star rising with every fresh German victory. As Interior Minister, Serrano in October received Heinrich Himmler, the Gestapo police chief, accompanying him around Spain and taking instruction on how to make the Spanish repression even more efficient. The execution of Lluís Companys, who had been President of the Generalitat, the Catalan regional government under the Second Republic, at the Montjuich fort, Barcelona, on 15 October, a few days before the Himmler visit, had already starkly underlined the brutality of the regime. Companys, who had taken refuge in France, was arrested by the Gestapo and handed over to Spain after the intervention of José Félix Lequerica, Spain's ambassador to Vichy, who later in the war we shall meet as Franco's Foreign Minister.

What was hidden from the British was how shocked Serrano had been in Berlin by the demands made by Ribbentrop, such as occupation of one of the Spanish Canary Islands by the Germans or, ultimately even more important, Hitler's maturing decision to prefer to placate the defeated French before considering Franco's demands in North Africa. Everything continued to look ominous for Britain's interests in the Mediterranean, and Gibraltar quite as threatened by the Spaniards and Germans as before. When Hoare had made his first visit to Gibraltar in August in the face of a press campaign orchestrated by Serrano he pronounced himself "horrified"[27] at the almost total lack of defence preparedness on the Rock. A peacetime sense of security prevailed, he noted caustically. Gibraltar's defences were strengthened, but the threat of a push by the Germans through Spain to take the Rock remained a major preoccupation of Britain's strategic planners well into 1941.

On 14 June, the day the Germans occupied Paris, Spain had sent troops into the Tangiers International Zone, obviously heightening the vulnerability of Gibraltar. The move meant the *de facto* annexation of the Zone. By August Spain had some 26,000 troops in place in Spanish North Africa, British intelligence estimated.

After the Tangiers warning the Prime Minister got on to the Service Chiefs, ordering the Admiralty to make preparations for the seizure of the Canary Islands which he held would be a suitable reply if Spain did slip into outright war and Gibraltar was lost. The Prime Minister told Halifax that a British naval operation on the Canaries should not be shunned for fear of provoking the Germans to invade Spain. Britain would acquire an alternative base to the always vulnerable Gibraltar. "How much do we care whether the [Iberian] peninsula is overrun or not?" he insisted, provocatively. The

Chiefs of Staff endorsed the idea of seizing the Canaries; troops were to be set aside "for any destination".

The Foreign Secretary and Hoare were unanimous in resisting the Prime Minister's gung-ho approach so long as neither Franco nor Hitler actually moved against Gibraltar. They saw a strategic advantage however in airing invasion threats against the Canaries. Franco might be further restrained by the prospect of losing these Spanish islands, and risking blame by his brother generals if he threw in his lot with the Axis. Franco had to show gains, and not losses, by siding with the Germans. There was also Portugal to be considered in striking the best balance, Hoare and the FO pointed out. A treaty of friendship and non-aggression, to last for 10 years, had been signed by Salazar with Franco as the Spanish Civil War ended which was intended precisely to underline that neither country would invoke, or accept, outside intervention in the peninsula, risking engulfing both regimes. A protocol designed to reinforce this stand was added in July '40.

All the difficulties for Britain in terms of military resources responding to an eventual German invasion of Spain were illustrated when the joint planners of the Chiefs of Staff presented a fresh approach in November to a call upon them by Churchill. This foresaw Allied forces occupying a strip of southern Spain along a line from Cadiz to Málaga as a shield for Gibraltar. Churchill had responded to Hoare's conveying a proposal from Beigbeder on eventual Spanish resistance to a German push through Spain. But the "Plan for Operations in Spain"[28] was daunting. It required large forces to be landed and the planners confessed they could neither guarantee to get things fully operational before the Germans could be stopped, nor were they sure of the extent of Spanish resistance. Their intelligence, they said, was a good less optimistic than Beigbeder. Franco would, they thought, have to be shown the plan if and when he received a German demand for passage to the Straits. Churchill contented himself by ordering a less ambitious plan; Hoare was told to take further soundings on the Spaniards' will to resist.

The day after Churchill signalled to Hoare to "try now to get Serrano" the Prime Minister also wrote him a personal letter which dashed the last hopes the politician had of being made Viceroy of India. For a moment Hoare had thought the antagonism which prevailed between Serrano and Beigbeder was so intense, and his relationship with the latter been so close, that the appointment by Franco of so well-known a foe of Britain as new Foreign Minister, might enhance his chance to exchange drab and hostile Madrid for the imperial splendours of Delhi. Churchill's letter used flattery, but did not really hide their old antagonism over India. Churchill preferred to extend Lord Linlithgow's term as viceroy for the sake, he said, of "continuity". Hoare always held the unimaginative Linlithgow largely to blame for the failure to implement key aspects of his Government of India Act of 1935. This was a major piece of constitutional reform for its time, giving Indians self government at the provincial level, put through by Hoare against unremitting and bitterly personal opposition from Churchill. Hoare's approach was anathema to Churchill and his reactionary friends. The dispute over India in the 1930s put Churchill into the political wilderness for years. The Prime Minister bluntly asserted his power over appointments: "I must in no wise be considered as committed to any particular solution of the personal and political issues involved in the selection of a new viceroy." Hoare did not stand any chance of getting that job, nor ever would, while Churchill was at the helm. Then came the flattery. "We should be very sorry if you wished to abandon your mission to Spain", Churchill observed. "The work you have done already has given great satisfaction to the Cabinet. I hope therefore that you will persevere in your difficult task, standing as you do in one of the key posts of imperial defence."[29] Churchill's mission statement could hardly convey more clearly how he regarded Spain from the standpoint of Britain's national interest.

The blow of Serrano's adding the Foreign Ministry to his controlling the Spanish police state as Interior Minister brought for Hoare, however, one benefit utterly unexpected at the time. Serrano had insisted the Falange boss of the Barcelona area replace the army general who was utterly at sea trying to run the Commerce and Industry Ministry. Demetrio Carceller was to become the most important figure in all economic matters for the wartime survival of the Franco regime. He was a remarkably able man and, as Hoare was to discover, a shrewd businessman behind the trappings of a Falangist blue uniform. He had joined the movement to protect his extensive business interests. The bright son of a factory hand had been noticed as a boy and sent by his father's employer to study. Carceller became first an engineer in the Catalan textile industry and then launched himself, as Spain began its own petrol refinery business in the 1920s, into a career as a top oil executive. Participating financially alongside the banks, he soon became one of Spain's richest self-made men. As Franco's economics supremo his corruption became legendary, exploiting all the opportunities offered by Allied and Axis rivalries in Spain. But Carceller was emphatically not one of the autarchists of the regime determined to make Spain self-sufficient: his selection as Commerce Minister probably had to do with his business contacts with the US oil majors. At first surprised, Hoare rapidly found for Britain's wartime needs he could begin a serious relationship with this rough diamond. As he observed in his memoirs: "Carceller was certainly the most picturesque, perhaps I should say picaresque, of the Spanish ministers

. . . His opportunities for amassing wealth expanded with every day of his ministerial life."[30] It is surprising no full-scale biography exists in Spanish. Carceller will figure prominently in this book.

Taking over as Foreign Minister, Serrano staged a full-blown Falangist parade inside the ministry and harangued the assembled diplomats with the demands to be made upon them by "our revolution". Hoare could only advise London to stake everything on Britain's economic weapon. With Serrano in the ascendant, Hoare said, he would not prophesy which way the Franco regime would go – into war against Britain on the Axis side or continue for the present its ambiguous course of non-belligerence. "But," he went on with a sense of drama, "we have in our hand one very high card. The economic position of Spain is desperate. Without our foods and raw materials, without in particular the wheat from the US and our Navi-certs [navigation certificates] for such necessities as phosphates, there will be famine and revolution in the next few months."[31] This meant that the new Foreign Minister, and his nominee the new Commerce and Industry Minister, "will have to make up their minds definitely and quickly. I will do my best to bring them up against these realities." Hoare added chillingly: "The Spanish government may be ready to starve Spain as Stalin starved Russia, they may see that we alone can save the country from this fate."

"The Spaniard is better at starving than most people," a British consul at Valencia mordantly observed on touring his part of Spain in the aftermath of the Civil War.[32] Hillgarth, new to his post in Madrid, had estimated in 1939 that a quarter of the Spanish population was more or less in that condition as a result of the disruption caused by that war.[33] Things had not improved by the summer of '40 when a particularly bad harvest underlined Spain's dire straits. Apart from bad weather, the poor harvest was blamed on the lack of fertilizers and land still out of cultivation. The Franco regime's returning the big estates to their old owners had only increased the sullenness of the day labourers.

The economic regime imposed by the Falange, in pursuit of autarchy, proved both inefficient and corrupt, only making things even worse. Under the Servicio Nacional del Trigo, set up by the Agriculture Ministry, all farmers were obliged to hand over their harvests at fixed low prices: the inevitable result was land left uncultivated, aggravating the hunger threat in the cities.[34] The Abastos, the food stores officially set up to feed the population, became for ordinary Spaniards one of the most hated institutions of the new regime. In October 1940 special courts had to be established to combat a rash of economic crimes due to the growing scarcities and abuse of the system by the regime's own functionaries. Food rationing in that context produced hoarding and black marketeering. When these special tribunals failed the remit of the courts-martial was simply extended. The licensing by the authorities of officially-designated importers and exporters, in the name of autarchy, led to favouritism amongst those newly-privileged by the regime and gross profiteering. The *"estraperlistas"*, the black marketeers, even managed to obtain for themselves protection in official quarters, and often flaunted their wealth with highly-expensive, imported American cars.[35] Existing business interests, if they had not been selected for the bandwagon, began to doubt the worth of the Nationalists' victory. Petrol quotas had been introduced from September. In Catalonia there were fears of serious labour unrest as cotton mills could work only two to three days a week on less than half the raw cotton supplies needed. Large numbers of beggars appeared on Barcelona streets. Writing on those first years of the Franco regime after the advent of democracy, a group of Spanish economists argue powerfully that Britain was fortunate that the period of Franco's greatest temptation to join the triumphant Axis coincided with the regime's direst economic crisis.[36] In other words, it was then that British, and subsequently American, government policy could exercise great influence since the Franco regime's ability to manoeuvre was minimal, at times non existent. Survival was the regime's fundamental objective.

But British official circles in London at the time were thrashing around in a debate whether Franco's economic plight was not so acute that he would be driven into Axis arms – or whether he might still be sufficiently bribed by trade to stay, at least nominally, neutral. The British naval blockade and the system of "navi[gation] certs[ificates]" required by the British authorities at all sizable ports in Spain of the officially licensed importers and exporters, plus the contraband controls of shipping passing the Straits of Gibraltar, represented a formidable degree of control by one country over another. Such was the incorrigible degree of corruption prevailing in the regime that a lively trade by "intermediaries" in navi-certs to sell to desperate importers and exporters developed on the black market. Spain was then a country highly dependent on sea traffic. British control over Spain's external economy was enhanced by the requirement of trading through a specially set up UK Commercial Corporation, a state trading organization, which concentrated on key supplies to Spain and Portugal from abroad. A carefully dosed arrangement to supply Spain with an estimated minimum amount of petrol had been agreed by the British that September. But, typically, it became the source of acute suspicion and scrutiny whether the Franco regime was not drawing from it secretly to supply the Axis.

The cries that Spain was starving redoubled that autumn of 1940 and those of Eccles, now chief economic adviser in the Madrid embassy, were among the most dramatic. There was nervous tension at the Madrid ministries, he reported, for they knew that "another bread-less period will see the end of this regime with one sure result, a short period of chaos followed by an Axis occupation [of Spain]".[37] The choice confronting Britain was put by John Lomax, the more sober economics counsellor in the embassy, when writing to the Board of Trade: "The UK will either have to lend her [Spain] money or starvation will ensue."[38] The Germans, in overall control of the regime's propaganda apparatus, already had it put abroad that the British blockade was to blame for Spain's dire straits, Lomax warned. Negotiations were in fact underway for an extension of the WTA and by mid November the Board of Trade accepted that Spain had effectively run out of funds under the March agreement. It asked pointedly whether Spain was "to be left permanently bankrupt?"[39] Alba, Franco's envoy in London, was kept busy on an unending, and humiliating, round of errands via the Foreign Office for items such as more British coal, for Spain, or more grapes, for export to Britain. The ambassador did not forget also to ask for extra clothing coupons in wartime Britain for his London-tailored suits.

Hoare was in the thick of the debate and for increasing economic assistance as Britain's only real weapon. In September he had already suggested to Churchill that the United States aid in food and other necessities should be sought. But he got only the vaguest reassurances that Spain wanted more trade with Britain when he saw Franco on 16 October. The dictator was adopting his customary stance above the fray and gave no sign he perceived a threat to his regime from a starving population. Spain's armed forces, as British consuls reported, were kept well fed and well enough armed to maintain the victors' law and order. The shooting of Companys and other prominent Republicans was a grim example to all.

The British ambassador had to face a tempestuous Serrano when he met the new Foreign Minister on 22 October as Spain's economic crisis worsened. The Foreign Office was still deeply uncertain how to attempt to keep Franco out of the war. A memorandum approved by Halifax and sent to Hoare for his views, posed the dilemma: should the British government first "insist on assurances [of neutrality] in return for help or should we 'Cast our bread upon the waters'"; Makins, its author, was quoting from *Ecclesiastes,* in the hope as the *Bible* puts it, to 'find it after many days'.[40] Spain's food situation was now "so dire" Britain could not 'go slow' and see what happened, Hoare advised. "We must face the big issue at once of wheat and credits."[41] The former Foreign Secretary suggested: "We should try the effect of promising substantial Anglo-American help" to countries outside

Hitler's Continental bloc and advised pressing the US to send wheat shipments immediately to Spain. London and Washington must keep "walking
closely in step," he emphasized.

Serrano, who unlike the autumn of 1939, had avoided this time visiting
Barcelona to gauge for himself the popular discontent, joined in at a second
stormy, two hour-long meeting with Hoare on 28 November, declaring that
the British government was, as he put it, "starving Spain to death." The
Foreign Minister instanced a consignment of wheat from Argentina for
Spain held up, he said, by a navi-cert refusal. At one point he threatened
Spain would go to war if Britain continued with its "restrictions," Hoare
reported.[42] Spanish high officials were at last realizing what foreign experts
had been telling them for months – Spain did not have enough wheat to
last until the next crop. The most Serrano could do was to tell Hoare that
Spain "had not finally chosen her friends and enemies". The Foreign
Minister gave the impression of "a desperate man who has failed to get
wheat from Germany," Hoare told London. But it was Serrano who had
given a bad jolt to Britain early that month by ordering the incorporation
of the Tangiers International Zone into Spanish territory.

In reality, Hoare's attitude towards Spain had been more affected by the
interview he had had with the Commerce and Industry Minister, Carceller.
That meeting was undoubtedly the most significant of all Hoare's contacts
with Spain's leaders during 1940. It gave the envoy the confidence to bring
the hesitant FO to his view, a chance must be taken with the Spaniards.
Hoare correctly sensed that Carceller was a practical businessman
confronted by a national economic crisis and desperately wanted Britain's
trade. Spain was determined to keep its economic independence and its
national sovereignty were the telling re-assurances Carceller gave Hoare in
that first of many interviews.[43] Wheat and more credits were his "obsessions", the envoy reported. Spain now had a frontier with Germany on the
Pyrenees, but it did not want wheat to come over it, Carceller said pointedly enough. That did not, of course, prevent him from writing in the
German press about Spain's place in Hitler's New European Order after the
victory of "the totalitarian powers".

The Commerce Minister promised Hoare he "would do what he could"
to get publicity in Spain for any provisioning by Britain under further trade
arrangements and to put a stop to the campaign against Britain for "starving
Spain" as Hoare had demanded. The March 1940 WTA had never appeared
in Spain's official Gazette and the British embassy had to distribute copies
in Spanish in an effort to make the agreement known. "Do what he could",
for Serrano as Interior Minister had complete control of the regime's press
and propaganda.

As the situation regarding supplies to the factories and of food worsened even more in his home base of Catalonia by mid November, Carceller joined the starvation chorus. Spain "must get wheat from somewhere, starving men could not sit still and do nothing," he told Hoare's deputy, Arthur Yencken.[44] Spain, Carceller repeated, had no wish to join what he called the Moscow–Berlin bloc, a reference to the Ribbentrop–Molotov pact ill viewed by Spain's anti-Communist regime. The British Consul-General in Barcelona, Francis Patron, a Gibraltarian with his ear close to the ground, was then reporting on disaffection with the regime for the lack of recon-struction 18 months after the Civil War's end among industrialists and the middle class.

Appeal to America

Churchill made dramatic use of the economic weapon wielded over Franco Spain by appealing directly to President Roosevelt on 23 November. Gibraltar was behind his appeal for food. The FO was inclining to the view that Spain's economic plight was so acute the regime would bow to German pressure. "An offer by you to dole out food, month by month as they keep out of the war, might be decisive," the "Former Naval Person" declared.[45] How grimly Churchill judged the German threat to Spain, and how doubtful he was of Franco, the secret telegram made clear: "The occupation by Germany of both sides of the Straits [of Gibraltar] would be a grievous addition to our naval strain, already severe. With a major campaign devel-oping in the eastern Mediterranean and the need to supply our armies there all round the Cape we could not contemplate any military action on the mainland [of Spain] or near the Straits. The Rock will stand a long siege but what is the good of that if we cannot use the harbour or pass the Straits? We must gain as much time as possible." Hillgarth, who had just written to Churchill, giving his view of the Spanish situation, was to be told of the telegram to Roosevelt, the Prime Minister added, when the FO informed Hoare. Churchill had behind him the advice of the British Chiefs of Staff, who had renewed their demand that "everything should be done to prevent Spain entering the war against us".[46]

Churchill's invitation to the US to join in helping the Franco regime on strategic grounds had major long-term consequences. But the US was far from ready yet to think of them. The home-spun Cordell Hull, with 12 years behind him as Secretary of State, personally symbolized many of the pre world-power American values. That first appeal by Churchill regarding Spain in the Second World War also brought the first disagreement between the two governments as to how to deal with the Franco regime. If the British Prime Minister's eye was always on Gibraltar, the American administration, backed by a freer press and a liberal-minded public opinion, viewed Franco as a European dictator, who had emerged from a bitter civil war thanks largely to help from the Axis powers.

After Serrano's inveighing against Britain's "starving Spain" the Foreign Office gave orders that navi-certs for 200,000 tons of wheat and maize from Argentina should be issued for consignments in November and December. An extension to the WTA, signed by London and Madrid on 2 December, provided a technically bankrupt Spain with an additional £2 million on top of the original £4m. In a secret protocol, the Franco regime agreed to supply monthly reports of all import and export movements to the embassy. This led to a constant practice of falsification by the regime. Britain also tried turning in such a crisis to Canada for wheat for Spain with a request for 100,000 tons. But the Ottawa government demurred: it did not want a direct deal with Franco Spain, suggesting Britain should instead make some wheat available from its extensive stocks in Canada. "This is about as much pressure as the Canadian government will stand," Makins minuted.[47] The *Globe-Mail*, a leading Canadian daily, showed no enthusiasm for helping Franco Spain, commenting that "appeasement has never done Britain any good."

But just as Britain agreed to make 25,000 tons of wheat available from those stocks, in addition to the cereals from Argentina, and the Spaniards were informed accordingly, Serrano went further – replacing with Spaniards all the British and international officials of the former Tangiers International Zone. Hoare had egg on his face. The envoy was instructed by London to demand of Serrano that the British officials receive compensation – without such a move all the wheat supplies would be held up. Carceller piled on the pressure, telling Eccles late December the rapid rise in food prices over the past month was due to "starvation conditions existing in many areas" of the country.[48] Unless foreign wheat arrived soon the minister said he saw no chance of holding Spain's internal position.

Before Churchill's appeal to Roosevelt the Spanish regime had already asked Washington directly that autumn for a line of credit of $100 million to buy US wheat, cotton and petrol, and received a brush-off. Alexander Weddell, Hoare's opposite number, had been instructed he must first obtain a pledge from Franco that Spain would stay genuinely neutral in the European conflict. On hearing of the Hendaye meeting between Franco and the Führer, and with the pro-German Serrano's appointment as Foreign Minister, the US government withheld any help and adopted an attitude of wait and see.[49] On 31 October Serrano actually told Weddell he foresaw "a closer rapprochement between Spain and the Axis". Unlike the British government, the American administration was wary of public sentiment, and had good reason to be. On Thanksgiving Day Falangist students had demonstrated before the US embassy in Madrid, thrown stones at the building and even attempted to oblige Weddell to join the singing of "*Cara al Sol*". Of course, Serrano, as Interior Minister and Falangist boss, knew all about the demonstration. The *New York Times* had run a story on the Spanish request for the $100 million[50] and Hull felt obliged to declare publicly that such a proposal had already been refused. Instead, a food aid programme on a smaller scale was agreed, put under the aegis of the American Red Cross expressly as a humanitarian programme for starving Spaniards. Hull failed to get satisfaction from Franco on the pledge of neutrality. It was Carceller, with his American contacts, who conveyed the message that Spain simply could not allow itself such a public pledge with the Germans on the Pyrenees. The Commerce Minister was, of course, not willing either to deprive himself of the opportunity to play off economically the Axis and Allied powers.

As Churchill was making his appeal to the US President, Cadogan had penned a classic statement on what was to be Britain's dilemma throughout the Second World War. As an "old school" English diplomat – when a junior in the Vienna embassy he had actually sent off the telegram giving London the first news of the assassination of the Archduke Franz Ferdinand, the signal for the start of the First World War – he was critical of American "neophytes". But Britain now simply could not do without the Americans' resources, as he was forced to admit. The basic problem, as he saw it, lay in the idea of demanding a Wilsonian-style public pledge of policy from Spain. That was "somewhat unreasonable" and he went on: "We should do our utmost to persuade the Americans to take a different line, emphasizing the strategic danger of the loss of the Iberian peninsula . . . If we fail to move them it is doubtful whether we ought to part company on this point (a) owing to the political inadvisability of diverging from them and (b) owing to the doubt whether without American participation we can outbid Germany."[51]

Hull did not succumb to British arguments, nor did Roosevelt do more than approve the Red Cross subterfuge. So the British at that juncture went ahead alone, casting their bread upon the waters in Makins' phrase, and helped Franco. The Treasury, however, disagreed with the Foreign Office and one of its mandarins nicely marshalled a French expression – for being duped – when giving a few days later Britain's diplomats a warning: "We must not look *poires*, above all in Spain . . . I am frightened that we may seem to convince Spain that we are beaten and ready to play any card because we have no trumps – so any conditions are better than none." [52] It may well be that the Treasury had got it right. After a tour of Spain, which lasted several weeks, Cmdr Furze, Hillgarth's deputy, was reporting to the FO that opinion in Spain – which could, of course, not manifest itself publicly – was "moving more and more in Britain's favour". The Madrid embassy, he pronounced, was "painting too dark a picture" of prevailing Spanish sentiment outside official circles.[53] A man with a thorough knowledge of things Spanish, Professor Walter Starkie, who had been made that summer head of the British Council centre in Madrid, was also reporting the Spanish mood outside Madrid at that time in very similar terms.[54] "Madrid is our black spot, the rest of the country is better disposed towards us," William Strang minuted after listening to the professor. But the Foreign Office ignored such advice, distrusting, as is often the way with bureaucrats, independent-minded assessments from outsiders.

Churchill had a lunch with the Duke of Alba that December, the first since he took over as Prime Minister. It served to conduct the high-level diplomacy Cadogan preferred, far from the pressures of public opinion. As Spain's ambassador reported it to Madrid, Churchill told him: "We desire the best and most friendly relations with you and if they should change you can be sure that it will not be our fault. We are determined, and I have intervened personally already in this matter, to help so far as we are able in the provisioning of Spain."[55] Alba was disposed to listen closely now with Churchill in office. The Prime Minister's intention was to influence Franco to resist German pressure to join in the war. At this time Churchill was however also urging the British Chiefs to prepare for the Cadiz operation, and worried about intelligence reports on the Germans' Operation Felix. He was sending off signals declaring that Spain was now "trembling on the brink." [56] The next month he observed that "at any time the Germans may by force or favour come down through Spain, rendering unusable the anchorage at Gibraltar and take effective charge of batteries on both sides of the Straits."[57]

With seeming frankness, Churchill attempted over the lunch to explain to Alba his differing attitudes towards Spain since the outbreak of the Civil War in 1936. He wanted to establish the firmest possible basis for a future personal diplomacy through Franco's envoy in London. Clearly, Churchill's explanations reveal his guiding principle regarding Spain – always to pursue Britain's interest, as he saw it, wherever that led. When the Civil War first began, the Prime Minister told Alba "I was one of your [i.e. the Nationalists'] supporters." But with the intervention of Germany and Italy Churchill said, he judged "as a good English patriot" a Nationalist victory would not be in England's interest, and he wrote against the Nationalist side accordingly – a reference to his article in the *Daily Telegraph* of 30 December, 1938. "Later still, I realized that I was wrong and I spoke so in the Commons," Churchill told the ambassador, though regretting his words had not been taken up in Spain. The Prime Minister intended, of course, all these remarks for Franco's eyes. But in his Second World War memoirs Churchill gives yet another version of his attitude, saying that initially he was for recognition of the belligerents of both sides in Civil War. "In this quarrel I was neutral. Naturally, I was not in favour of the Communists. How could I be," he goes on, "when if I had been a Spaniard they would have murdered me and my family and friends?" The Spanish government was then "in the hands of the most extreme revolutionaries" he writes, revealing an extraordinarily personal focus on things Spanish, and far removed from the political facts in Madrid at the beginning of that conflict.[58]

It was Hitler's *not* ordering his armies to move into Spain in the autumn of 1940 which was alone decisive. Neither Britain nor Franco could have resisted Germany in Spain at that juncture, whatever the schemes prepared if such a crisis had opened up. As to the Spain beyond Madrid, and so far from the centres of power in Berlin and London where its fate might have been decided, an eloquent event took place in Málaga that December. As Robert Goldie, the British Consul reported it, a crowd of hungry people had become incensed as they had gathered to watch some 50,000 tons of rice and salted codfish thrown back, on official orders, into the Mediterranean. The rice and fish had gone bad after more than 12 months kept in storage. Though they had gone increasingly hungry, such staples of popular diet in Andalucia had either not been distributed, and gone bad, because of the Franco regime's indifference or because well-connected hoarders had misjudged their speculative opportunity. Shortly afterwards, a British steamer had put into Málaga – the Royal Navy's blockade that winter allowed selected British vessels to enter southern Spanish ports. The crew had been so touched by the condition of poor people on the shore, Goldie recounted,[59] that they began to distribute bread from the ship's bakery. So large was the crowd of hungry people who came to the ship's side that the police were called in to disperse them. It was perhaps the Spaniards' being "better at starving than most people", as another consul had put it, which was to save the Franco regime.

2

Spain, a Balancing Country
1941

Much of 1941 was marked by British fears that Hitler would invade Spain and a searing awareness if that occurred Churchill's government could little to oppose it. Even after the German dictator sent his armies to attack the Soviet Union – the event for Europe that fundamentally divides the year – those fears hardly abated. So great was the impression made by Germany's military prowess it was held that Hitler might seek an easy victory driving through Spain to Gibraltar. Churchill was frequently sending off signals to Roosevelt that spring describing Spain as a "balancing country"; it would, the Prime Minister held, go either way depending upon the fortunes of world war. Even the assurances of his naval trusty Hillgarth about a growing Spanish mood of resistance if the Germans came in had little effect on Churchill's thinking.

In Parliament Churchill was justifying Anglo-Spanish trade to a "starving people" and he welcomed measures, however slight, such as the American Red Cross sending in US-packaged foods. Churchill wanted to encourage a Spanish resistance should the Germans invade the peninsula in the spring, speaking of "crashing in food before the Pyrenean snow melts". That opened up possibilities for opposition elements in Spain to the Franco regime, and thus for the potentially most influential among them, the Monarchists and for Don Juan de Borbón , the Pretender, if he were minded to unfurl his banner after the death of Alfonso XIII, his father. The ex king's passing stirred a notable popular sympathy in Spain. An embryonic "Free Spain" movement began to be cautiously encouraged by London.

Franco's hostility continued unabated despite Britain's economic aid and in July the dictator publicly pronounced that the Allies had "lost the war". A Spanish "Blue Division" was mobilized to fight alongside Hitler's troops against Communist Russia, Britain's new-found ally. The Spanish generals, Franco's rivals, continued to be watched closely by London. The signals on their manoeuvrings were ambiguous. Serrano lost control of the Interior Ministry when Franco moved to satisfy the anti-Falangist generals. But Serrano remained a high profile and noisy pro-Axis Foreign Minister. Churchill intervened energetically to ensure the funds selected generals had secretly received were fully protected as the United States, moving nearer to outright war, had imposed financial controls on foreigners' assets.

The Prime Minister hastened to meet President Roosevelt when in December 1941 Japan struck against America, the second decisive event in 1941. Churchill now reckoned upon better access to America's resources to reinforce Britain's economic weapon and so, hopefully, still keep Franco Spain out of the war.

In a secret session of Parliament Churchill once spoke of the "fallibility of human foresight in the fog of war." One of the characteristics of Britain's handling of the hostile Franco regime that year was to be misjudgments as the dictator manoeuvred against crises at home and abroad. In the nature of things, Britain's representatives had most contact with those better disposed and the true balance of forces in such a personal regime was often hidden from them. There was much "fog of war" with Franco's uneasy peace.

When Spain's ex King Alfonso XIII died in exile in Rome on 28 February, 1941, Churchill was moved to a declaration of his monarchist sympathies. The Spanish king had been included among the personalities in *Great Contemporaries* he published in 1935. "Being a strong monarchist, I am in principle in favour of constitutional monarchies as a barrier against dictatorships and for many other reasons. It would be a mistake for Great Britain to try and force her system on other countries and that would only create prejudice and opposition," he wrote in a personal minute. Then came the Prime Minister's general instructions but with Spain in mind. "The main policy of the Foreign Office should however be to view with a benevolent eye natural movements among the populations of different countries towards monarchies. Certainly we should not hinder them, if we cannot help them."[1] His sympathy for Don Juan's cause in March '41 was clear. The Foreign Office, however, persistently defied Churchill's instruction in the name of *Realpolitik*, because, in other words, Franco was seen to be in effective control of his country and that fact alone was judged to matter to British interests. As we shall see, Alfonso's son was not to prove to be the man to make adequate use of the opening Churchill's words might have offered him. Churchill's minute has a longer-term significance worth noting here: Hoare, who shared the Prime Minister's monarchist views, was to be constantly suspected by the Foreign Office of defying their instructions on how to handle the monarchists in Franco Spain. Whatever Hoare was doing, he was not defying the Prime Minister.

Churchill was responding to a report by Hoare on the Spanish reactions to Alfonso XIII's death. In the light of the "enthusiasm" and the nostalgia for the late king's reign, Hoare believed that a restoration would give Spaniards the chance of believing they were starting upon a new chapter for their country. A generous amnesty for the defeated Republicans was one of the benefits widely anticipated as this was traditional in Spain for an incoming reign. Without an amnesty "half Spain will continue to be at war with the other half for years to come", Hoare emphasized prophetically. "Naturally I do not suggest any premature intervention, you can rely upon my discretion here. We should be wise, however, to show a warm and sympathetic interest in the [monarchist] movement," sentiments to which the Prime Minister had responded. "Don Juan is an excellent young man . . . If I were in his place I would force the pace," Hoare concluded.[2]

The extent of popular feeling at Alfonso's death was undeniable. Essentially it was a lament for the much happier, and economically better, times when he was on the throne compared to the harsh and bitter repression and economic misery experienced by all but the well-to-do, and the well-placed, during the first years of the Franco regime. "The death of Alfonso not only gave Don Juan an undisputed claim to the throne, uniting moderates and Carlists, but provided the opportunity for an informal plebiscite on the Fascist regime," Thomas Hamilton, the *New York Times* man in Madrid, observed in an eye-witness account of reactions. The line of monarchist sympathizers calling to sign the condolence book in a leading Madrid hotel stretched for two days out onto the pavement. "Far more important," the American journalist wrote, "were the home-made banners which were displayed by the working people of Madrid and other cities throughout Spain. Even the poor hung out the national flag or a sheet with Alfonso's portrait pinned to it if they had nothing else to show their feelings." Spain's poor were still Republicans at heart. "But they saw that unless they received help from outside, the monarchy was the only hope of ridding Spain of the Falange and regaining some limited form of free government", Hamilton explained.[3] When Franco was informed that the ex king had, one month before dying, abdicated in favour of Don Juan, and accompanied this by a testimony highlighting the prosperous times Spain had enjoyed during his reign, the dictator observed angrily; "Whoever asked him for this?" To the censors the dictator gave orders the ex king's testimony should not appear in the press.[4] Hamilton, however, was surprised how many ordinary people, like shopkeepers and taxi-drivers, did know of Alfonso's words. Underground Republicans were evidently in contact with royalists. Hundreds of Spanish monarchists managed to attend Alfonso's funeral in Rome despite the Interior Minister's stopping the boat about to sail from Valencia. Serrano's excuse was that Italian-laid mines in the Mediterranean might endanger their lives. A monarchist leader joked that if the Italians had indeed laid so many mines this would be the Falangist Minister's surest way to get rid of many of his enemies.[5]

The funeral in Rome represented Don Juan's first opportunity to be his own man, but he did not take it. So far from Hoare's "forcing the pace" the

Pretender contented himself with reading the acceptance statement, prepared by his advisers, which he had addressed to his father when he stepped down. When the hour arrived to become king, Don Juan declared, his "irrevocable goal" was to restore a Traditionalist, i.e., authoritarian monarchy. He praised moreover the political and social values of "the Crusade", the Nationalists' term for the Civil War. [6] The Pretender's statement notably abjured the parliamentary system of government Spain had enjoyed under Alfonso until the ex king submitted to the dictatorship of General Miguel Primo de Rivera from 1925. The Pretender had not evolved from the anti-parliamentary position he took at the beginning of the Civil War when he had observed: "A new state has been born in Spain. It rectifies the false liberal and democratic ideas which have poisoned the nation's soul."

Don Juan bowed to pressure from those monarchist leaders who had come to Rome from Spain that nothing must be said which might offend Franco. There was nothing in the Pretender's remarks of building bridges to the defeated Republicans or to ordinary citizens. "The great mass of Spaniards" were vaguely promised they could look forward to a monarch "working for a more just and better society". The Pretender had sided with the temporizers among the monarchists, often aristocrats and the well-to-do, who felt gratitude to Franco for obvious reasons, and against some younger monarchists, such as the middle class, right-wing intellectual Eugenio Vegas, who believed strongly that the dictator had betrayed the monarchist cause at the end of the Civil War. Neither groups were democrats. In addition, Don Juan's supporters were divided over the world war; General Juan Vigón, who had served as Alfonso's aide-de-camp and Don Juan's tutor and was now Franco's most influential adviser among the professing monarchists, was sure of a German victory over the Allies. Only a minority of monarchists was then pro-Allied.

The British government watched the procession of monarchists to Alfonso's funeral for possible signs of any latent pro-Allied feeling and were disappointed. One month after the funeral, Don Juan's next move was, to London's surprise, to make soundings with the German side about assistance for a restoration. Such was the "weight" of Germany, the impression left by Hitler's *Blitzkrieg*, that almost all elements of the upper reaches of Spanish society sought German help to advance their cause in Franco's fragile regime, pulled hither and thither by the fortunes of the European war. The Falangists inside the regime were constantly seeking the aid of the Nazi party and its influential henchmen in Spain. Pedro Sainz Rodríguez, one of the leading monarchists, who from Spain offered advice, had written to Don Juan in Rome suggesting that the tactic must be to seek support for a restoration from both sides in the war. [7]

Who represented Don Juan in Berlin that April is not known, but the existence of such soundings is clear from the files of the war-time German Foreign Ministry. The relevant papers were scrutinized by British officials after capture at the end of the war; these reports only speak of a representative sent by Don Juan to the Wilhelmstrasse.[8] Hoare does not seem to have got wind of Don Juan's parleyings with the Germans, nor, perhaps understandably, did any of his contacts in Madrid enlighten him. But in July, when he had got the full picture and was understandably alarmed, he advised Eden to put "counter-pressure on the Pretender".[9]

A journalist from Ribbentrop's private office reported the Pretender's emissary had urged Germany to play a bigger part in a restoration of the monarchy. The German Foreign Ministry outwardly opposed plotting against Franco, but a high official ruled that policy on Don Juan must be to "make sure he's available for Germany (*für Deutschland sicherzustellen*)". The reports reveal clearly the Germans' desire not to allow Britain a possible trump card – Don Juan was half English on his mother's side – if Franco's brother generals did decide to launch a putsch against his unpopular regime. The fluidity of the situation prevailing at that time is further illustrated by the secret contacts that the politically-astute General Antonio Aranda, and an opponent of Franco, was having in April both with the British embassy and with the Nazi party's *Auslandsorgansation* boss in Spain, Hans Thomsen. Aranda, it seems, was basically seeking to find out if Serrano did fall in a putsch, and the generals set up a junta, the Germans would respond by intervening militarily in Spain. All this uncertainty helped, if paradoxically, Franco to stay in power.

"The Germans are making determined efforts to persuade Don Juan to visit Germany and negotiate a German-inspired restoration," Hoare told Eden in July when recommending counter-pressure on the Pretender via the Berne Legation. "He has so far withstood pressure, but I am anxious lest, in his anxiety to return and his ignorance of great affairs, he may eventually succumb," Hoare explained, giving by now a more sober appreciation of Don Juan's qualities than on Alfonso's death. The Pretender should be warned of the "suicidal nature of a German restoration and the advantage of keeping in with us [for] making any new regime popular in Spain," he contended. Don Juan, however, remained in Rome after his father's death, enjoying the capital's social life, and was not to resettle permanently in Lausanne until the next year.

Don Juan did not find in the end support from the Germans to gain the throne. Ribbentrop, the Foreign Minister, who had initially kept the German embassy in Madrid in the dark, decided to inform Serrano of the Pretender's démarche to avoid damaging Spanish–German relations. Don

Juan was uncovered. Both the belligerents were seeking to use a possible restoration of the monarchy with Don Juan – if they came to see it suited their war ends.

"We Three Men"

This brings us back to the fundamental issue in early 1941 – would Hitler invade Spain and so push Britain to promote some kind of alternative regime possibly built around the monarchists? Hitler in the autumn of 1940 had set 10 January '41 for launching "Operation Felix"[10] – the plan for a drive by the Wehrmacht through Spain to attack Gibraltar and so cut Britain off from the Mediterranean. By the incorporation of the Tangiers International Zone Franco controlled both shores and had permitted a considerable German presence on both sides. Admiral Wilhelm Canaris, chief of the Abwehr , had been dispatched by Hitler to Madrid to put pressure on Franco to collaborate in Felix. Hitler's ploy was that the German action would forestall a British seizure of the Canaries. Hitler promised that as soon as the German troops' march into Spain commenced German economic cooperation, notably a supply of cereals, would begin. Canaris' visits caused Hoare much unease – the influential German counter intelligence chief had been close to Franco since the days of the Civil War. It was only after the world war that Hoare could learn from US-captured German documents what had transpired at the dictator's talk with Canaris early in December 1940. The details are in a memorandum by General Vigón, who was present, with a copy sent afterwards by Madrid to the German Foreign Ministry.[11] Franco made excuses, pleading that Spain was neither economically nor militarily ready to join the Axis in the war. He told Canaris of his fears Britain would respond to any attack on Gibraltar by seizing the Canaries. What the dictator called restrictions on Spain's foreign trade were preventing any quick improvement in Spain's preparedness. As always with Franco, his words have to be seen through the prism of his interest in his survival, but here was testimony from the dictator himself both on the effectiveness of the British Navy's blockade measures and the system of navi-certs as a hold over Spain's economy and of the deterrent value of British defence planning to seize outlying Spanish islands. Canaris failed when he pressed Franco to give a later date for joining the Axis in the war. The Spanish dictator's mood was beginning to waver; he still believed Germany's might was invincible, but he now also perceived the war would not be a lightning one allowing Spain to join in for the spoils. The effect of that Canaris visit to Madrid was, in fact, to reinforce the views of those generals who had resisted Spain's joining the Axis all along.

Hitler however kept up the pressure. On 6 February 1941, the Führer wrote personally to Franco, including a promise of 100,000 tons of grain for Spain as soon as Franco set a date for entering the war. Hitler pointedly complained of the time lost since 10 January: "Gibraltar would now be ours, Caudillo. I believe that we three men, the Duce, you and I, are bound by the most vigorous compulsion of history."[12] To this rhetoric Franco, when he did reply on 26 February, only repeated Spain's unpreparedness. But the reply is notable for Franco's complete personal identification, as the Führer had suggested, with the three dictators' indissoluble destinies – a pledge Franco was to break with both.

Days before the attack on the Soviet Union in June Hitler set the Wehrmacht the task of planning to secure the Iberian peninsula's entire Atlantic coastline. This was as the Battle of the Atlantic intensified, Hitler's attempt, as Churchill put it, "to strangle our food supplies and our connections with the US". At a secret session of Parliament the Prime Minister admitted to "heavy and effective" U-boat attacks on British shipping off the African coast and named Spain among what he dubbed "the balancing countries"[13] undecided whether to join in the war – in Franco's case obviously on the Axis side – or to stay out. The background to Churchill's many signals to Roosevelt was always his uncertainty not only as to Hitler's intentions but also the Spanish people's mood. To what extent might they resist if the Germans invaded their land? "We shall have to make up our minds upon the degree of assistance which could be afforded to a friendly Spain," the Prime Minister was telling the chief of the British General Staff on 24 January.[14] How far could Britain go if Hitler sent troops into Spain? At the planning stage, quite far was the answer if an invasion appeared imminent to British intelligence. Yet the Prime Minister had to be reined in again, as in 1940, because Britain's armies were already over-extended elsewhere.

"My hope is that the Germans will not go through Spain by favour ever, nor by force until at least the spring," the Prime Minister had told Hoare in January[15] after having what he described as "long and excellent talks" with Captain Hillgarth in London. Thanks to his relations with Churchill, the naval attaché attended a meeting of the Cabinet defence committee when Spain was discussed. Hillgarth expressed his doubts that the Germans could obtain a passage through Spain "by favour" and suggested an opening of "contacts with Spanish resistance forces" and the sending of a British support group in the event of a German invasion. This approach was agreed.[16]

This was not, however, a full go-ahead. In an analysis in January of many of the war fronts to the General Staff chief, the Prime Minister crucially ruled: "We must now be most careful not to precipitate matters in Spain, or to set the Spanish government against us more than it is already or provoke Herr Hitler to a violent course towards Spain."[17] Military operations could not be contemplated unless and until Spain offered passage to German troops or Germany began to force one. Churchill further cautioned the General Staff chief: "All these matters are highly speculative." It was "a reasonable working assumption that any German adventure in Spain will at least wait for the spring". "Brisk" was the code name of plans for a military operation to seize the Portuguese Azores to provide an air and naval base against U-boats attacks on British shipping. The Prime Minister drew a grim picture of winter conditions in Spain and pointed to General Wavell's victories in Libya and the collapse of the Italian Empire as hopefully influencing informed opinion in Spain about the fighting ability of Britain's armies.

Churchill took up again the food "weapon." In a February directive to the FO he wrote trenchantly: "Assuming Hoare and Hillgarth [are] about right . . . and Spain refuses to give Hitler passage or join the Axis immediately, it becomes of the utmost importance to crash in food, i.e. wheat as much as we can and persuade the President of the USA to act similarly. The more food we can bring in the better before the Pyrenean snow melts. This will give the best chance of a favourable reaction when the German invasion comes on Spain. Don't boggle but feed!"[18] Churchill also went before the Commons to declare: "I certainly consider that the starving condition of the people of Spain fully justifies assistance being given by Great Britain."[19]

But the difficulties of supplying food aid to such an obstreperous regime were well illustrated when the Americans supplied Spain with $1.5 million worth of flour, dried and condensed milk and medicines, all approved by Congress and distributed in Spain directly by the American Red Cross. The *New York Times* man Hamilton, who watched shipments landed at Cadiz, denounced the chicanery, and downright corruption, of Spanish officials who took over the distribution of the supplies. When the flour sacks were loaded on to Spanish army lorries they were stacked so that the inscriptions (in Spanish) "Gift from the American people to the people of Spain" could not be seen.[20]

In mid February Eden – recently made by Churchill Foreign Secretary, with Halifax dispatched as ambassador to Washington – met in Gibraltar with Hoare and the Governor to take the planning of a military response to a German invasion of Spain a stage further. The so-called "Plan B" emerged for a British expeditionary force to be landed on Spanish territory.[21] Any preparations, it was argued, when signs became visible on the Rock (where thousands of Spaniards came daily to work), would strengthen the hand of those in the Spanish Army "telling Hitler not to come in". Hoare was again on to the Prime Minister early March, eager, in a reversal of former roles, to persuade Churchill to encourage eventual Spanish resistance, and not an appeaser at all. Spaniards, Hoare insisted, could only be induced "to fight on our side," should the Germans invade, "if we are prepared to give them at least the help contemplated in 'Plan B' as discussed at Gibraltar." Even if Spanish resistance collapsed swiftly before a German onslaught, and a British Expeditionary Force had to be withdrawn, Britain would have obtained, Hoare underlined to Churchill, the right of entry into the Canary Islands and Spanish Morocco and stirred up guerrilla warfare on the Germans' lines of communication.[22]

The Prime Minister sought the Chiefs' view, but they reported negatively. "We have reluctantly come to the conclusion that we cannot for the time being contemplate operations even on a limited scale in Spain or in Spanish Morocco", they said.[23] Any schemes for sending British troops into Spain required RAF fighter units and anti-aircraft guns at Gibraltar. But "Operation Lustre", the ferrying of British troops from Egypt to Greece going on against a German invasion soon to come, simply meant there were no resources in either aircraft or shipping for commitments elsewhere. Hoare, the Chiefs bluntly recommended, should be told that Britain was not in a position to give the Spaniards the help contemplated under "Plan B". Churchill, however, did not agree with them and, taking up Hoare's contention, riposted: "It is not certain that we must exclude some kind of Spanish stimulant because of Lustre. It will be very important to get the Spaniards to resist because that enables us to take their islands as allies and perhaps to get a footing on the African shore . . . I suggest without making positive promises [we] allow hope to grow for what it is worth in the springtime."[24] Churchill wanted an advance party to go to Gibraltar for a smaller-scale operation coded named "Ballast", but the Chiefs again rejected that, pointing out to the Prime Minister it would mean 32 fewer Hurricanes for the Middle East theatre of operations. So Churchill had lamely to advise Hoare: "We fully agree with you as to what we should like to do, if we could, to encourage Spanish resistance. For the moment we have a pretty heavy overdraft and it is difficult to draw further on our capital."[25]

With regular military operations in the Iberian peninsula ruled out, the Chiefs turned to the Governor of Gibraltar, and C. in C there, General Noel Mason Macfarlane, one of the most politically-aware senior officers then in the British Army, to take charge of planning any help to come in response to a German invasion. "If Spain resists, guerrillas and demolition operations are to be undertaken," he was instructed, collaborating with Peter Quennell, chief operations executive in Gibraltar of the Special Operations Executive (SOE), who was to remain in position with his staff at the ready.[26] An SOE station had been established at Gibraltar, but kept strictly on leash by Hoare and Hillgarth. Only if Spain came under the Wehrmacht's heel were agents of the secret organization, set up in 1940 as part of the Ministry of Economic Warfare, to indulge in Spain in operations of the kind deployed against Hitler's occupied Europe. Macfarlane was also instructed to plan to liaise with the Spanish High Command, or with those elements minded to resist the Germans, via Hillgarth. The attaché had since January been given supervision of all British agents, including SOE men, in Spain. Hugh Dalton, the Minister of Economic Warfare, wrote to Churchill at the time signalling a polite end to the turf war with SOE and MI6: Hoare had insisted on stamping out any "dirty tricks" in Spain so long as the Germans had not come in.[27] Prodded by Churchill anxious not to discourage Hoare and Hillgarth, the Chiefs agreed the officers and men in Gibraltar envisaged to help liaison with the Spanish military if the Germans invaded, plus "sleeping" SOE agents inside Spain, should all stay on. Plans should be updated and ready to receive an eventual BEF if the troops could be found.[28] But, once again, Hitler's non-intervention in Spain was the deciding factor – and Britain, anyway, did not have enough fighting units for a Spanish adventure.

Germany's military might was, however, much in evidence elsewhere for Spain's leaders to watch, with the twin attacks on Yugoslavia and Greece. General Erwin Rommel's armies, after he arrived in North Africa in February, had driven the British back from their Libyan conquests to the Egyptian frontier. The Spanish reaction to these feats by Germany was well conveyed to the British Foreign Secretary by the Duke of Alba who told Eden early May that Spain would only be able to resist a German wish to send troops through Spain, and finally get to Gibraltar closing the Mediterranean, as long as England held the Suez Canal.[29] In Madrid German propaganda had already been boasting that Rommel's armies would reach Suez by 1 May.

Amidst all that gloom for the British cause in Madrid there was, however, some relief when Franco in May cut down to size his brother-in-law. Serrano was increasingly threatening the Caudillo's predominance, occupying as he did the posts of both Interior and Foreign Minister as well as head of the political committee (junta) of the Falange. Many people thought Serrano was the all-powerful figure of the regime, something Franco obviously could not stand. The British were delighted and, led by Hillgarth, over-reacted. In a move which took Madrid completely by surprise, Franco showed his masterly abilities over men, replacing Serrano at the Interior Ministry with General Valentín Galarza, one of the most astute conspirators in the 1936 uprising.[30] The Spanish military were also delighted for Serrano's truculent deployment of "his" Falange was one of the generals' main complaints. Serrano was kept on as Foreign Minister by Franco so as not to annoy the Germans. When the Falange manifested their anger the Caudillo proceeded to reshuffle the top leadership there as well, naming Falangists he was better able to control.

"Better" Cadogan noted, with surprising swiftness, in his diary when he heard of Galarza's nomination.[31] But Hillgarth ventured a good deal further when he reported to Naval Intelligence – adding a "Please pass to the Prime Minister." Britain's bribery operation among the generals, he concluded, had worked one of its most important successes. "Galarza asks most eagerly," Hillgarth told London,[32] "that the British press and broadcasting should not make any comment on internal events as it would give a British aspect to what he wishes to appear purely national movement."

Hillgarth and Cadogan, with his reading of intelligence, had been aware for some time of the background of mounting restiveness among the Spanish generals towards Serrano, his lust for power and his flagrant steering of a pro-Axis course. Obeying the British Chiefs of Staff directives on Spain, Brigadier Wyndham Torr, the Military Attaché in Madrid, though he enjoyed less prestige than his naval colleague with his Churchill connection, maintained close contacts with the Spanish Army generals. He was now frequently seeing General Aranda, identifying him as the probable head of an eventual junta replacing Franco.

Now head of the Escuela Superior del Ejército (ESE), the Spanish Army's general staff college, Aranda possessed the best political brain amongst the generals dissatisfied with Franco's leadership. Events led Aranda towards supporting Don Juan's cause. He was not a monarchist of the first hour and had served the Second Republic, notably putting down the 1934 left-wing rebellion in the Asturias. He had first been identified to British intelligence as a possible sympathizer by the London correspondent of *La Vanguardia*, the Barcelona daily, throughout the Second World War, Felipe Armesto. Aranda's opposition to Franco continued after 1945; his efforts were finally to be honoured with the advent of democracy.

The Spanish Army was "strongly for neutrality" and opposed to Germany's entering Spain, Aranda told the British attaché in one of their meetings in April, after taking soundings among the generals. Aranda reckoned the army's staff college might serve as planning centre for a "palace revolution", to correct an increasingly pro-Axis regime abroad and an increasingly corrupt and inefficient Falangist takeover of the state at home.[33] For this he blamed the hated Serrano. Franco's fate would depend on what attitude he took. The immediate bone of contention with Franco for the generals, Aranda explained, was Serrano's proposal, under Italian pressure, that Spain should sign the Tripartite Pact of the Axis powers. It had been Serbia's signing of that pact which provoked a British-backed army revolt in Belgrade and Hitler's answer of invading Yugoslavia that month. When Aranda had seen Franco three days before, Torr was told by Aranda, the dictator had been given a clear message not to sign. Franco now knew he would be removed if he did not carry out the army's wishes, Aranda claimed.

In London Hillgarth reinforced the tenor of Aranda's message when he was seen by the Foreign Secretary. But Eden was deeply, and indeed abidingly, sceptical about the Spanish generals, some of whom he knew, of course, had taken bribes from secret British funds. "Cmdr Hillgarth told me today that if Franco and Serrano signed the Tripartite Pact there would be an immediate *coup d'état* and they would be thrown out. I hope he is right, but I often have qualms that our embassy are being fooled," Eden minuted.[34] Illustrating the British foreign policy-makers' uncertainty, the Foreign Secretary confessed: "I find it increasingly difficult to form a just assessment of the present position in Spain." Cadogan immediately drafted instructions warning Hoare in Madrid that the British government could not "associate exclusively with one party," adding that "little material assistance" would be possible anyway if a palace coup were attempted.[35] Not for the first time the permanent head of the FO was making policy and helping Franco.

The dictator, with his obsessions, was suspicious of Aranda as a Freemason, and thus of pro-Allied sympathies, anyway. He had Aranda under the closest surveillance and his informers inside the ESE. But most importantly for Franco was the fact that Aranda's post had no direct command of troops on the ground. The Germans were now bringing all their influence to bear against Aranda; General Carlos Asensio, the Army Chief of Staff, was thoroughly pro-German – he had previously been in charge of the Spanish units which trained for assaulting Gibraltar – and was duly impressed by all Germany's victories that spring. Asensio was a mediocre figure and Franco was to make him the Army Minister in 1942 as reward for his reliability. But the Caudillo did not sign the Tripartite Pact and Galarza replaced Serrano. Thus Franco circumnavigated army discontent and outsmarted Aranda, isolating him from the other, more cautious, generals. Aranda lost credibility with the British, especially in London.

A War Lost

Serrano seized the opportunity of Hitler's attack on Russia on 22 June for a great upsurge of Falangist agitation, in solidarity now with the Axis powers against "God-less Communism". Spain raised immediately the Blue Division to fight alongside the Germans against the Soviet Union. The 18,000 volunteers, overwhelmingly Falangists and commanded by General Agustin Muñoz Grandes, a Falangist and pro-German, were however, at the Spanish Army's insistence, to have regular officers and NCOs. This was to avoid the risk of the Falange obtaining even greater sway within the regime. The Blue Division was to stay on Germany's eastern front for much of the world war.

Amidst a deafening pro-Axis press, Serrano himself launched the recruiting campaign after Hitler's onslaught. "Russia is to blame and must be exterminated," Spain's Foreign Minister declared. The inflamed crowd of Falangists present, mostly university students, marched afterwards on the British Embassy, chanting "Gibraltar for Spain: British assassins". They threw stones, breaking the windows and bringing down the Union Jack. Serrano, though he had lost the Interior Ministry, was evidently showing his strength. Hoare, with his full staff, called at Serrano's official residence, demanding an immediate apology for "the carefully organized riot".[36] The Falange had spent the previous night organizing that "spontaneous" demonstration, according to the US Associated Press man in Madrid, Charles Foltz, and assembling the supply of stones.[37] Hoare got nowhere when he also protested directly to Franco.

"The war has been badly planned and the Allies have lost it," the Caudillo declared when he addressed the Falange's National Council on 17 July, the eve of the anniversary of the 1936 uprising. The dictator stoked the fires, highlighting his responsibility for the Blue Division and expressing solidarity with the Axis. He praised the German armies "leading the battle for which," as he put it, "Europe and Christianity have longed for so many years." Franco looked forward to the young Spanish volunteers' blood "mingling with that of our comrades of the Axis".[38] Present at Franco's harangue, Hamilton noted how he paused frequently to see whether the US ambassador was "getting the full effect".

But the most important passage in the speech for Britain and the US came when Franco, after sneering at the "plutocratic democracies", spoke of Spain's justified resentment against those nations which had attempted to take advantage of her distress to infringe her sovereignty. This was an open attack on Britain's, and increasingly America's, supplies of petrol and food aimed precisely to keep Franco Spain from joining the Axis' war. Franco's language was so gross that Eden had to answer a question in Parliament. "If economic arrangements are to succeed there must be good-will on both sides," the Foreign Secretary observed, and then gave a warning to Franco: "His statement makes it appear that he does not desire further assistance for his country. If that is so, the government will be unable to proceed with their plans and their future policy will depend on the actions and attitude of the Spanish government."[39] The sharpest comment on the dictator's speech came from Francesc Cambó, the veteran Catalan politician and big financier living in self-imposed exile in the Americas. "It is curious the case of this man," he wrote in his memoirs, "in action always so cautious and prudent, but in words he is of an inconceivable levity. In this speech he surpassed himself . . . saying in foreign policy, where he should not have strayed, everything possible to offend Britain and the US, who have in their hands the provisioning of Spain."[40] We shall have future occasions to quote this shrewd observer from afar.

Many among Spain's most prominent generals did think that Franco had thereby tied Spain's future to an Axis victory; even Vigón took that view. So here, it appeared, was an opportunity for the dissenting generals to get rid of the hated Serrano once and for all. They naturally blamed the Foreign Minister for such an irresponsible speech but Serrano, though on a propaganda "high" for Germany at the time, was not involved. Franco, for whom words never had any intrinsic worth, simply read, it seems, an address drafted by the Falange secretary-general.

Hillgarth was in the thick of all the reactions provoked by Franco's anti-Allied speech. "Franco's absurd speech has cost him his last scrap of prestige," the naval attaché wrote to Churchill on 12 August, "he has openly identified himself with a German victory – he thought the Russian war would be over in two weeks, and our friends believe their chance has come."[41] Hillgarth had already signalled to the Admiralty mentioning a junta of generals who now thought Franco "had gone too far" and that they "must get rid of him or [be] compromised by him".

"Now we can take the next step and prepare for an open if gradual change of attitude on the part of the Spanish government. Money couldn't do that," Hillgarth told the Prime Minister. Serrano's removal as Foreign Minister, he forecast, "will not be much more than three weeks [away] as a first step." There was agreement among the leading generals, and others, to nominate a junta with full powers. Hillgarth even named Generals Aranda and Luis Orgaz, the High Commissioner in Spanish Morocco, among its members, together with Sainz Rodríguez and José María Gil Robles, the leader of the right-wing CEDA grouping in the Second Republic – the first time these two civilian politicians are mentioned for such postings. The junta would constitute an alternative national government in the event of a German invasion "or obstinacy by Franco", going to the Canaries or Morocco. Only the Falange and the extreme left would not be represented, Hillgarth asserted. The leading item in the alternative Spanish government's programme would be reaching "an understanding with Britain", Hillgarth informed Churchill, adding: "But don't help the Germans by seizing the Canaries! It is still the case of the longer a [German] invasion is put off the better, but we shall now be able to have a *coup d'état* if necessary without much risk of interference" Hillgarth had blundered, we now of course know, in his advice to the Prime Minister. He, and Torr, had listened too closely to one side, principally to Aranda, in the power struggle going on that summer between Franco and rival generals. The dictator's subtle tacking was unknown to the British attachés.

Relying on Hillgarth and Torr, Hoare reported to the FO that Orgaz, a long-standing opponent of the Falange when Captain-General in Barcelona, had an audience with Franco on 1 August and demanded Serrano's removal; Spain must follow a course of strict neutrality. In light of the 17 July speech, Orgaz said, the Caudillo should in future make important pronouncements on foreign policy only after fully consulting the top generals.[42] Aranda had reinforced that message, repeating the Foreign Minister must go, when he in turn saw the dictator.[43]

But Franco reacted to these two démarches by a display of carefully assumed supreme self-confidence. He left, as every summer, for his cool retreat in Galicia, but knowing that he could trust the troops in Madrid, the Captain-General there, and to Asensio, the Army Chief of Staff, against his opponents. With Orgaz, to whom in May Franco had already given the High Commissioner's post, one of the most lucrative of the regime, the dictator indulged in characteristic temporizing: he acknowledged the necessity of what the generals requested, but asked for time so as not to provoke a crisis for the regime. Orgaz, with declared monarchist sympathies, was that summer in contact with Gil Robles, urging him to use his influence to align all former CEDA followers with the monarchist movement. Orgaz, though he often did the Germans favours, feared a German takeover of Spanish Morocco in the event of an invasion of Spain.

Franco told Aranda that the military part of his 17 July speech – that the Allies "had lost the war" – was based upon German General Staff appreciation, particularly of operations in Russia, which had subsequently not gone according to plan.[44] Nothing could illustrate better than Franco's remarks how German military prowess impressed him, or the degree of subjugation to Germany of that closed regime at its higher spheres. Hoare subsequently made efforts to get London to provide him with estimates of British military strengths to counter-balance the German influence prevailing on Franco and Vigón.

Because we know "the end", in Wedgwood's observation, of Hitler's disastrous gamble – the defeat of the Germans by Stalin's armies and later advance of the Red Army into eastern Europe – it is difficult to recapture the mood prevailing in 1941 in what then seemed almost a satellite of the Axis. Could the Soviet Union hold that summer, would Rommel reach the Suez Canal, and how would Franco then react those in the Spanish regime asked themselves? Talking to Aranda after the lesson German troops had given the world in Yugoslavia, Franco had observed that it would be "impossible" for Spain to resist, Aranda recounted to Torr.[45] The ups and downs of the world were crucial for Spain's military crisis that summer. The dissident generals knew that they were watched by their British paymasters, but they, in turn, also watched British fortunes in the war. Serrano, both parties assumed correctly, was only waiting for a resounding British defeat, such as the loss of Suez, to join the Axis at the last hour to obtain a share of the victors' spoils. Franco's defiant leaving Madrid as usual for August can only be explained by his assessment that the internal military crisis must await the outcome of events on the bigger stage. The very danger of a possible invasion of Spain by Germany paradoxically strengthened the Caudillo's position, hence his appeal to Orgaz to do nothing to provoke instability.

Perhaps influenced by Eden, Churchill reacted to all the effervescence in top military circles in Madrid by ignoring, completely, the signals from his trusted aide on Spain. To Hillgarth's pronouncement that Franco's 17 July speech was "absurd", the Prime Minister countered: "I do not think it would be a sound deduction that Franco had given himself over to the Axis."[46] Churchill ruled out resorting to any kind of armed action against Spain "in the absence of further developments." The British Cabinet had in July approved plans for eventual military operations in Spain, with a force of 20,000 men at the ready.

Here is one of the first of those "strategic moments" in Churchill's personal handling of the Franco regime during the war. Despite the carefully-directed public insults over Britain's economic programme of supplying Spain with essential raw materials as Franco endorsed Hitler's attack on Russia, the Prime Minister was still prepared to deal leniently with the regime – because of Britain's immediate national interests. Readying plans to seize the Canaries was for Churchill also a means of signalling obliquely to the Spanish dictator the limits of Britain's self-interested tolerance of the regime. But Churchill was completely overlooking

Franco's sending the Blue Division to fight Britain's new ally and was to forget his own words broadcasting on the night of Hitler's attack on Russia: "Any man or state who fights Nazidom will have our aid. Any man or state who marches with Hitler is our foe."[47] The Blue Division certainly marched with Hitler, increasing the Russians' sufferings in the war.

Hoare was still, disastrously for him, reporting to London on the Spanish generals' schemings. On 13 August he said that a military junta was "determined to get rid of Serrano by the end of the summer. If Franco yields there will be no need of a military coup. If he does not, a coup will get rid of both him and the Foreign Minister."[48] That was from "our best source", Hoare added, meaning Aranda. Over the generals' getting rid of Serrano Eden's anger erupted: "They have been for months and months!" he commented to his officials. Of the junta Aranda talked about, Eden observed: "I fear I shall only believe all this when it materialises."[49]

The long-term consequences of the Madrid Embassy's misreading of the military crisis within the regime of 1941 can hardly be over-estimated for British policy-making towards Franco. Hillgarth had proved himself in Cadogan's harsh phrase in his diary "rather a charlatan."[50] Worse, he had got things wrong in Spain. Eden's intense suspicion of Hoare, compounded by his erroneous trusting in the plotters, was to develop considerably when it came to the envoy's handling of the Spanish monarchists in 1943. But, above all, Aranda's reputation was damaged in British eyes. This was to have serious consequences, as we shall see, when the general appealed directly to the British Prime Minister in 1944. Roberts, now becoming increasingly important in the Foreign Office over the handling of Spain, had commented before Eden had exploded that it was a mistake to trust the pronouncements of such "unreliable and illogical people as General Aranda."[51] (It is easy to speculate that such an extraordinary outburst by such a balanced diplomat as Roberts was left in the files at the PRO with no longer embargo than the customary 30 years by the "weeders" because Aranda had been the loser in the battle of wills with Franco during the world war.)

The impact of Hitler's war on the Soviet Union dominated the strategic thinking in Madrid all that summer and autumn, whichever way it might go – a Russian collapse proving Hitler's troops irresistible everywhere, or the Soviets fighting back, making a German attack on the "soft" target, Spain, highly attractive to a frustrated Führer. There was even a third possibility – if the Russians held down a sufficient number of German troops in the east they might not be able to intervene in Spain. While some strategists held Hitler's attack on Russia relieved the pressure on Spain – as with hindsight we now know to have been the case – others judged the attack only increased the risks and uncertainties for Spain. Hoare, amidst all this speculation, told Eden at the end of August that if the Germans were not on the Pyrenees "the Spanish Army would have taken control months ago".[52]

Hoare was in regular contact with Pedro Sainz Rodríguez, the right-wing politician of the Second Republic and former Cabinet Minister of Franco, now meeting generals like Aranda. Sainz in his account of these contacts, in memoirs published after the dictator's death, claims it was he who first got Hoare to see a restoration of the monarchy as the way forward for Spain.[53] The Spanish politician regarded Hillgarth, whom he also often saw, as "almost an ambassador" in view of Britain's history as a sea power. "Spent several hours yesterday with the principal civilian leader of the anti-Serrano and Franco movement," Hoare told London mid September. Sainz and the generals were determined to remove the two but, Hoare added, "the timing depends on the Russian front".[54] If the Germans did take the "soft" option and invade, an alternative government would be established by the plotters, he said, in Morocco or the Canaries. It would make a confidential approach to the British government seeking immediate recognition. Hoare's talks with Sainz had included his offer to the Allies of bases on the Canaries, something the Spanish politician's memoirs carefully omit. Central to opposition to the course set by Franco and his Foreign Minister was "the strong monarchist feeling now shown in every walk of Spanish life," Hoare maintained. "It is this strength of feeling . . . that has convinced me of the wisdom of an early monarchist restoration." Arthur Yencken, No. 2 at the embassy and a professional diplomat, was no less impressed by the generals' schemes for a putsch when he reported to London. Eden replied, surprisingly in view of his habitual antipathy towards the generals, in a conciliatory tone this time: "We have no wish to stand in the way of an early restoration if the monarchists think they can make an early move without endangering their liberty of action in the future," he informed Hoare.[55] Eden, characteristically, gave no clear lead, but didn't discourage the ambassador either.

At this delicate juncture in Spain the whole bribery operation concerning Spanish generals was threatened when the US government froze foreign accounts held in banks on American soil, including millions of dollars in secret British funds for the generals, at the Swiss Bank Corporation in New York. "'Malta' becoming most urgent. I trust it can be arranged quickly, if necessary giving President Roosevelt a hint as to the position," Hoare signalled to Eden on 13 September, using the code name. The matter was indeed urgent, with the fear "our Spanish friends", as Hoare put it, would suspect Britain was conniving, if London did not now intervene with the Americans, at baulking paying the generals their promised reward.[56] Hillgarth was dispatched by Hoare to London to get the Prime Minister to intervene, which he promptly did. A slim file at the PRO entitled "Spanish dollars blocked in the USA"[57] contains the details of Churchill's mobilizing the Chancellor of the Exchequer, Roosevelt and the US Secretary of the Treasury to obtain secret exemption for the Spanish generals from the provisions for foreign-held accounts.

In a note to the Prime Minister hand-written on Chequers stationery, Hillgarth recommended: "The American government should tell the Swiss bank merely that $10 m. are unblocked, without stating what 10 million or why. If the President has power to order unblocking without explanation it would be far quicker – and speed is important." "Can't you give them something on account?" Churchill asked the Chancellor, Kingsley Wood, on 23 September, observing of the generals: "We must not lose them now after all we have spent – and gained. Vital strategic issues depend on Spain's keeping out or resisting. Hillgarth is pretty good." When Wood demurred, saying he was "most reluctant to explain the full circumstances to the US government" Churchill insisted that a request to the US Treasury Secretary, Henry Morgenthau, be regarded "as personal" from him. Halifax, Britain's ambassador in Washington, subsequently ascertained "unofficially" that the US treasury would approve the exception, and was instructed by the Prime Minister to tell Morgenthau that he was "most grateful"; the need had been to fulfil "an outstanding obligation." "Good" Churchill jotted on a minute from the Chancellor of the Exchequer on 5 November that the matter had been "satisfactorily adjusted." The generals could continue receiving their pay-offs. What is most remarkable in this whole operation is the high value Churchill continued to place upon it, a measure of his continuing doubts late in 1941 where Franco's cunning opportunism might take him.

Lunch with Alba

So when Churchill had another of his lunches with Alba early October his unease was deep; Britain still held the Suez Canal, but Franco had publicly spurned Britain's provisioning of Spain. The Prime Minister took Eden and Hoare, who was enjoying his first home visit since May 1940, along with him to the Spanish Embassy but even together they could only muster the old familiar argument, trade. As Churchill rephrased it, Britain was offering its assistance in rebuilding Spain's prosperity. "We are determined to aid Spain in all: only we ask of her that she will not allow the Germans to cross her territory," the Spanish ambassador reported Churchill saying.[58] Expressing himself frankly at this time, Churchill told Oliver Lyttelton,

Minister of State in the Middle East, what while it would be a very dangerous step for Hitler to add Spain to the list of occupied countries of Europe, Britain had "scarcely any military credit" in Spain.

While on leave Hoare's most important engagement was with Churchill, staying at Ditchley, in Oxfordshire. "Malta", then unsettled, was doubtless discussed but between the two politicians the main theme was high strategy, the advantages of a successful Allied campaign in North Africa for its effect on wavering Spain. Hoare had been early amongst those envisaging American involvement via North Africa, offering as he put it "the nearest and easiest way for entering the battle zone".[59] In July he had written to Churchill: "If we are to deny the Germans the Atlantic seaboard and the control of the Straits [of Gibraltar] a great military effort will be needed that in actual practice will mean an Anglo-American occupation of French North Africa . . . What I do believe is the USA should undertake [it] the moment they decide to come into the war."[60] An Allied occupation would strengthen the Spaniards' will to resist, or neutralize a German occupation of the peninsula if that were attempted. Hoare had seen General Mason Macfarlane, Gibraltar's Governor, when he visited the Rock on his way to London that autumn. "He made the military case for an African landing . . . His conclusions gave me confidence for the London visit," Hoare later recollected.[61] By October this foreshadowing of Operation Torch, the Allied invasion of November 1942, became the common talk of the British military planners.

"Go back to Spain, the peninsula is of great strategic importance. The war may sweep over North Africa, and one of these days you may have to go down to Africa from Madrid," Hoare reported Churchill had told him, flatteringly, as they parted after their Ditchley weekend talks.[62] The Germans put about rumours in Madrid that the British ambassador had come back with an ultimatum for Spain as Hoare returned from his leave. When he reported to London, Hoare had to admit the generals had not moved, not even against the hated Foreign Minister. "As to Serrano's position I cannot make any prophecy," he had to tell Eden, consoling himself with the thought that while the Germans' influence was keeping him in power the opprobrium helped Britain.[63] Eden had already circulated a pretty negative paper to the War Cabinet. "I am sceptical of the likelihood of a *coup d'état* by the Spanish generals in the near future, and I am doubtful whether a less unpopular regime would be to our advantage until German influence lessens and a new regime [comes] able to carry out a more truly independent policy," the Foreign Secretary declared.[64] The Foreign Office paper was essentially based on a talk the British assistant military attaché in Madrid had late October with Beigbeder, the former Foreign Minister, when he depicted the generals' personal rivalries, including competition for the regime's most lucrative posts. Beigbeder argued that Aranda did not enjoy the full confidence of the monarchist generals among the dissidents because of his pre-1936 Republican past. Eden's Cabinet paper maintained that the Wehrmacht's fighting in Russia did not alter the strategic fact that Germany was "still in a position at relatively short notice to dispose of any Spanish resistance" to an invasion. The Germans were then at the gates of Moscow and Leningrad, though Hitler had stopped the offensive because of winter. Any Spanish government in these circumstances, he contended, would still be vulnerable to the Germans.

The monarchist generals' discontent with the overbearing influence of Serrano and the Falange remained unresolved, however, and at a meeting the Spanish Army's Supreme Council in the Pardo on 15 December, with Franco present, General Alfredo Kindelán, Captain-General of the Barcelona region, presented a full list of the dissidents' complaints. Kindelán emphasized the widespread popular discontent and disillusionment, corruption and abuse of power by the Falange at home and a foreign policy which endangered, he said, the most vehement wish of all Spaniards to live in peace. Worse perhaps for Franco was to be told – by one of the generals who had actually made him the Nationalist side's supreme leader shortly after the outbreak of the Civil War – that he had now personally lost the prestige of that victory, and the Army as well because of its involvement in what should be civilian tasks. Kindelán instanced the courts martial for economic offences and the death penalty for black marketeers introduced that October. Officers were occupying top posts in the regime's economic bodies, such as the distribution of foodstuffs and raw materials. "It is above all necessary that you come to see that you have followed the wrong road and that the time has come for a decisive rectification of things," Kindelán told Franco.[65] The armed forces should, the general recommended, withdraw from all non-military tasks and there must be changes amongst Franco's collaborators "to save us from the World War". This was as far as Kindelán's otherwise very open speech came to demanding Serrano's sacking. Kindelán's account of the generals' gathering is based on the notes he made shortly afterwards.

Franco, in his reply, brushed aside Kindelán's suggestion to nominate a chief of government while remaining chief of state, and insisted Spain's armed forces must play a full role in the state. The Caudillo did make a very rare reference, for him, to popular discontent. He had anticipated during the Civil War, he said, that the first two years of peace would be difficult; with the outbreak so swiftly of the world war everything had worsened, the dictator admitted. Reporting to Don Juan in Rome about the meeting,

Eugenio Vegas, the monarchist intellectual who was in close contact with Kindelán, commented shrewdly that General Franco must be content for he "had circumnavigated the storm" without conceding anything of the substance of his power.[66] The generals, on the other hand, could feel they had done what their consciences demanded conveying to the dictator "the feelings of a broad section of national opinion."

On 7 December Japan launched the attack on Pearl Harbour, bringing the United States into the war. Following Japan, Hitler declared war on America on 11 December. To plan their joint response, Roosevelt and Churchill started in Washington their lengthy Arcadia conference, the first of the Allied wartime policy-making meetings between the two. For Spain, the most important conclusion from Arcadia was the President's acceptance in principle of a proposal from the Prime Minister for an Anglo-Amercan landing in North Africa. In spite of the severity of the Japanese onslaught in the Pacific, Roosevelt ruled that US troops must be engaged against Germany as early as possible in 1942 and North Africa was the best way to go about Germany's defeat, which would entrain that of Italy and Japan.

Underpinning this was the setting up of the Combined Chiefs of Staff, formed from the joint chiefs of staff, army, navy and air force, of the two nations for the duration of the war. There would accordingly be the joint exploitation of all military and economic resources – though, obviously, the US was to become, in Roosevelt's phrase, "the great arsenal of democracy" – under the supervision of the US President and the British Prime Minister.

Britain had dire need of America's help. That November and December proved one of the darkest periods of the whole war. There were two resounding defeats for Britain as a sea power by Japan, and Hong Kong was soon to be lost too. The *Ark Royal*, Britain's first aircraft carrier, was sunk on 14 November and, only three days after Pearl Harbour, Japanese planes added the battleships *Prince of Wales* and *Repulse*, which had been dispatched to Singapore to discourage the war party in Tokyo. Churchill later, in a secret session to Parliament, disclosed that a further strategic disaster occurred in December 1941 nearer to Spanish shores – there were no longer any British battle squadrons in the Mediterranean owing to successful Italian limpet bomb attacks. On Serrano's instructions, the Spanish Foreign Ministry congratulated Japan on the Pearl Harbour attack. "The enemy propagandists," Hoare recollected, "had been given a story that seemed unanswerable. Was not the British Empire, that depended on the Navy, breaking up? These were the questions that re-echoed throughout Spain."[67] Washington was told by Britain of its fears that Germany might now be tempted "to clean up the position in the Mediterranean in her favour"[68] by pushing through the Iberian peninsula. If Spanish bases on the mainland

and in North Africa were to fall to the enemy, and Gibraltar was no longer available as naval base and staging post, this would have the severest consequences for Britain's fighting efforts in the Middle East and even the Far East.

On Christmas Day – the day Hong Kong fell to the Japanese – a senior Foreign Office man went in to pen a memorandum facing up to the situation as it affected Spain. "A German move in the Iberian peninsula must be regarded as more likely today than it has been at any time previously," he began. Britain's objective must now be "to ensure some form of resistance to a German occupation. This would enable us to recognise whatever entity resisted as a true government of Spain. I think we should definitely decide to try and organise some form of Free Spanish government or movement," he proposed. This FO file, entitled "Free Spain Movement in 1941",[69] only became publicly available after 50 years. Approved on 26 December by Cadogan's deputy, a second position paper suggested, however, that Spain's army leaders might, in the last resort, choose "to throw in their lot with Germany" rather than oppose it with a useless resistance. This vivid revelation of how deeply uncertain London was about the Spanish generals at the end of 1941, despite the previous bribery operation, went with British intelligence noting a growing cooperation by subordinates of the Spanish High Commissioner in Morocco, with German agents.

The Foreign Office position paper concluded somewhat lamely that, if anything effective was to be achieved, it would be necessary "to find suitable leaders from Spain itself round whom such a [Free Spain] movement could be built." Surveying the potential leading figures for it was not a promising exercise. Apart from the politician Sainz and General Aranda, with whom Hoare, Hillgarth and Torr were already in contact, the other potential opponents of the Franco regime were pronounced mutually antagonistic. "The only unifying factor among the various Socialists, Republicans, Basques and Catalans," the FO man acidly observed, was "the detestation" of Dr Juan Negrín, last Prime Minister of the Second Republic, who spent the war years in closely watched exile in London. As to the Pretender Don Juan, the Foreign Office was suspicious: the Germans were well aware how unpopular the Franco regime was in Spain and might seek a change of regime utilizing him by engineering a restoration. The Special Operations Executive had plans, from the previous spring, for stimulating Spanish resistance if a German invasion came. These were to supply automatic weapons and ammunition for anti-Franco groups in Navarre, the bastion of the Traditionalists, with whom Don Juan had flirted, and who felt cheated by Franco after making a major contribution to the Nationalists' victory in the Civil War. Selected ex Republicans were to be trained by the

S.O.E. for demolition and sabotage activities against German invaders.

All this was still only at the preliminary stage. What is striking is that while the British government did not trust Franco at the end of 1941, and had no reasons for doing so, it remained hesitant about the advantages of promoting any opposition to the regime – until the German armies launched an outright invasion. But if there had been a Blitzkrieg over the Pyrenees it is doubtful if Britain would then have the means, or sufficient time, to respond. In spite of Hitler's war against the Soviet Union, all the uncertainties about Spain remained in 1941.

It had been a bitter year for Britain in Spain, and for Hoare, whose hopes had been deceived of a somewhat friendlier regime emerging, purchased by trade and other favours. So when Hoare reported his conviction to London that Spain in November was "nearer a *coup d'état* than at any previous moment in the year,"[70] and Eccles, the expert on Spain's economic affairs who prided himself on his direct access to top sources in Madrid, was confiding to his diary a conviction that "Franco and Serrano are done",[71] Eden amused the department at their expense, mocking "our ever hopeful and ever mistaken embassy in Madrid". By the year's end Kindelán had come out criticizing Franco to his face, but Hoare had to learn that the Spanish general might honourably inform Franco of the army's discontents, but never take action behind his back.

In power in Madrid there remained a regime *malevolently* disposed towards Britain. It wanted the world war lost by Britain and its Allies, as the dictator had publicly proclaimed, for the sake of his own survival.

3

Ambiguous Assurances
1942

For a statesman of Churchill's cast of mind and sense of strategy the overriding event of 1942 was the execution of the American and British invasion of French North Africa, code-named Torch. In Churchill's war memoirs there are almost glowing tributes to General Franco's services at that time: "Spain held the key to all British enterprises in the Mediterranean and never in the darkest hours did she turn the lock against us."[1] That was Churchill writing in retrospect after the war, and keeping, defiantly, to his version of Franco's "services" to Britain. The role of Britain's economic weapon and the risks he felt acutely at the time about Franco's moves were forgotten, or at least omitted, by the memorialist.

Yet 1942 opened with great uncertainty about Spain. This was not only because of Franco's studied attitude of non-belligerency, gainsaid in reality with Spain's Blue Division fighting alongside Hitler's armies in Russia, but because of the impact on one of the "balancing countries", as the Prime Minister himself had called Spain, of the Allies' continuing string of defeats in the world war. The resounding blows to Britain's prestige at the end of 1941 were followed by the Fall of Singapore in February 1942 and Rommel's taking Tobruk from the Eighth Army in July, opening the road to Egypt. The nightmare scenario came nearer of a German and Japanese link-up, the one pushing from the east, the other from the west, which could break the British Empire in two. Many informed Spaniards who followed the war thought Britain would lose the Suez Canal and its Mediterranean base of Malta, then under siege, during the summer of 1942. Not till October–November and the victory of El Alamein did Britain convincingly secure Suez, the imperial life-line.

Britain's war in the Atlantic against Hitler's U-boats was watched closely from Spain. In February Admiral Donitz changed the secret codes and so Bletchley, "Station X", could no longer read the German signals to locate the U-boat threat. It was to take the code-breakers 10 months to solve the problem. Only in 1943 was Radar able effectively to oppose the U-boat menace to vital sea-borne supplies to Britain. The losses in March 1942 were the worst monthly toll in the war so far. Churchill had to withstand two "no confidence" motions in Parliament during '42, each triggered by serious reverses for British arms. But without increasing supplies of war equipment and materials and food supplies Britain could not sustain fighting efforts in the various theatres of the war. "On no account let any word be spoken in disparagement of the war effort and war impulses of the United States. Our lives depend upon the growing application of their power," Churchill told MPs bluntly in a secret session speech in April to Parliament. There were however serious differences between the two governments that year. Churchill had to make an effort to overcome his natural instincts: an American general, Dwight Eisenhower, was put in charge of Torch and, symbolically, British troops taking part in the landings wore American uniforms to soften the resistance of the Vichy defenders of French North Africa.

It can only be called a stroke of luck for Britain that Franco dismissed his brother-in-law, Serrano, from the Foreign Ministry in September, replacing the pro-Axis firebrand by the more cautious General Francisco Gómez Jordana, and a monar-chist, just as the invasion plans went into top gear. It was after withstanding another year almost as terrible for Britain as 1940, but ending with the initial success of the Torch landings and victory at El Alamein, that the Prime Minister could make his famous speech at London's Mansion House when he celebrated "the end of the beginning" of the war.

Discord over Petrol

As the United States entered the war Spain swiftly revealed the differences of approach between the two allies, anticipating deeper difficulties to come in the decisive period for Franco's survival, 1944–45. The supply of petrol was the key element of diplomatic suasion. Churchill signalled to Roosevelt[2] in the first days of January: "Please will you very kindly consider giving a few rationed carrots to the Dons to help stave off trouble at Gibraltar? Every day we have the use of the harbour is a gain, especially in view of some other ideas we discussed." This was a reference to their talks at the Arcadia Conference in December and, in London's eyes, the Americans' need to see the Bay of Algeciras, facing the Rock, as a vital facility for the eventual build-up of an invasion fleet. Churchill wanted British views and interests to prevail.

By the middle of the month Halifax was however reporting from Washington to the Foreign Office "serious differences" with the Roosevelt Administration over Spain. "In fact, the United States government are not prepared to follow us wholeheartedly in our Spanish policy – any more than we are prepared to agree in every respect with their conception of the way to handle Vichy [France]," he observed tactfully. [3] The Americans were to continue pursuing the lenient policy towards the Pétain regime they had adopted when still a neutral in an effort of penetration aimed to soften even-tual French resistance. They kept this up until Torch.

An essential difference lay in the British conviction about the strategic usefulness of trading, above all in petrol, with Spain to deter her from giving in to Axis pressure and join in the war. In the United States public opinion remained antagonistic to the very idea of trading with the victors of Spain's Civil War and thus strengthening Franco's pro-Axis regime. The American press was still untrammelled by the dictates of war, still doing what a press in a western democracy was conventionally supposed to do, and the State Department under Cordell Hull took close heed of it. As one Administration insider put it, Hull's nightmare, after Pearl Harbour, was that if the Germans marched through Spain Spanish tankers would be found in all the harbours full of oil from Texas.[4] Hoare had told London of his fears that in the spring Spain would be facing "a very dangerous period of German threats, blackmail and even possibly occupation".[5] The envoy brought Churchill in, referring to their talks at Ditchley and emphasizing how important the Iberian peninsula had become with America's entry into the war. Hoare complained of a "rigid" US stance towards Spain's economic needs; it might "drift into German hands," he warned.

In November 1941 the Americans had, for the first time, temporarily suspended petrol shipments in Spanish tankers to Spain and Alexander Weddell, the envoy in Madrid, was recalled to Washington after repeated clashes with Serrano. With secret inspections on the spot, the Americans had proved to their satisfaction the Spanish authorities were systematically deceiving the British as to the real petrol situation. The Franco regime had been stocking up on supplies by inflating the figures of their monthly minimum needs. Carceller, the oil-man, was suspected of double-dealing, promising the Germans they would benefit too if American supplies could be upped, while seeking to blackmail the Americans by maintaining he could obtain petrol from the Germans if the US policy of cut backs continued. A couple of months of fruitless negotiations ended when Hull lost his temper and gave Madrid's envoy a dressing down. "Your government's course has been one of aggravated discourtesy and contempt in the very face of our offers of aid," the US Secretary of State declared, protesting over the "coarse and extremely offensive methods and conduct" of the Spanish Foreign Minister "and in some instances of General Franco."[6] Just before Pearl Harbour a secret understanding had been reached whereby, in return for a regular supply of petrol, Madrid would allow the setting up of US oil attachés and the making of systematic checks on Spain's petroleum needs and with no supplies smuggled out to the Axis war machine.

The United States' toughened approach had the effect of showing up British appeasement. The Americans pointed to Franco's frequent services to the Germans in the Battle of the Atlantic. German U-boats were permitted to re-victual at northern Spanish ports and elsewhere; in one flagrant case two Spanish supply ships were anchored in the Canaries to service the German submarines. Britain protested, but so did the Germans referring to a secret promise made by Franco that Spain would give them such aid. Hillgarth, who kept such practices under surveillance, managed in January to sneak himself aboard a German submarine in a Spanish port and noted how the crew carried Spanish-made matches among their provisions. Acting on Hoare's warnings, Churchill drafted one of his "Former Naval Person" messages to Roosevelt: "We are becoming increasingly anxious about Spain," it began.[7] There was a significant change in the Prime Minister's attitude however probably under the influence of Hillgarth. Churchill showed himself as now convinced that Franco and the Spaniards in general "did not want to be forced into war". Of oil shipments the Prime Minister observed: "We ought to look upon them as part of the rent for Gibraltar Bay and cheap at that." Roosevelt was urged by Churchill to give "some directives for action in the sense I desire." That signal did not actually get sent. Washington had already agreed to allow three Spanish tankers to proceed with oil supplies to Spain.

The US was asserting its control over a vital aspect of Spain's domestic economy, and consequently over America's freedom of manoeuvre in policy-making with its ally. Carceller, Hoare reported, recognized the force of these facts. Franco's economic supremo even volunteered the calculation that British and American purchases of minerals from Spain "would be sufficient to cover [the cost of Spain's] oil imports".[8] The Commerce Minister mentioned wolfram among Spain's minerals for export: here were the beginnings of the "wolfram war" so important for the Franco regime's economic survival.

A shift in Britain's priorities for trading with Franco occurred that February when Hugh Dalton, a Labourite, was replaced as Minister of Economic Warfare by the Conservative Lord Selborne. Explaining things to Hoare, Churchill telegraphed: "Government changes will I hope relieve special difficulties under which you suffer."[9] The Prime Minister viewed Dalton as anti-Franco. The no-nonsense Selborne, an old friend of the Prime Minister, promptly instituted a series of personnel changes, and the trade aspect, such as raw materials for Britain, counted for more and more.

A "Patriotic Group"

In a memorandum early spring Hoare tackled how Spanish resistance might be stimulated if Franco, already on record that the Allies had "lost the war", were pushed into joining the Axis. In view of its importance the paper was immediately put before the Prime Minister. Hoare was blunt. The loss of Singapore and the failure of the Eighth Army's Libya offensive had, he wrote,[10] "made even our best friends doubtful of the efficiency of our fighting machine." If Suez were lost, the envoy judged, "the totalitarian tendencies of General Franco and Serrano are likely to show themselves, possibly facilitating an attack on Gibraltar." Britain "ought now to be ready with our Free Spain movement," Hoare went on, referring to his contacts, on London's instructions, with Sainz Rodríguez and Generals Aranda and Kindelán since 1941. Hoare went to the nub of the problem: "the patriotic group," as he called it, would, he believed, "be ready to show greater activity if I could be somewhat more precise than hitherto in the undertakings I have given them." Sainz and Aranda had already accepted that a Free Spain government must be fully representative, including ex Republicans, the Basques and Catalans. They agreed to restoring the monarchy under Don Juan and a wide-ranging amnesty "at the first possible moment". Hoare wanted London to allow him to assure them "that we will give all possible assistance within our own war limitations, economic and military, and . . . do our best to facilitate their flight from Spain if it proved necessary". As a punch line for Churchill and his military advisers in London Hoare added: "Keep in mind the fact it is only by means of careful preparations with this group that we are likely to succeed in getting the Canary Islands without having to fight for them." It was to these Spanish islands that the "patriotic group" would be taken if they had to leave the mainland and where a government of Free Spain would be set up.

Churchill ordered Hoare's memorandum to be forwarded to Britain's military chiefs, but he included no observations of his own. He was, it seems, sticking to Hillgarth's line on Franco and did not wish to give encouragement to an alternative regime before the Germans struck. Hoare obtained from the Foreign Office the assurances he sought for the anti-Franco group we now know from a file titled "Free Spain Movement – 1942", embargoed under the 75-year rule until 2017 but obtained by the author under the Freedom of Information Act. The commitment to Sainz Rodríguez, Aranda and others, above all to take them to the Canaries from mainland Spain to set up a rival government, were sufficiently documented pledges for British diplomats to judge they needed hiding away from the Franco regime which survived intact the war.

London's diplomats appear reluctant conspirators. Alone Hoare, on the ground, perceived the weaknesses, speaking of "a regime so tyrannical and incompetent" if faced by an internal challenge.

The file allows us to follow the doubts in British government circles about the Free Spain group and its chances of success if the Germans had invaded. "The nucleus of a Free Spain must be found inside Spain rather than outside," the FO ruled when instructing Hoare to concentrate on the anti-German and anti-Falangist elements in the armed forces, the Catholic Church and among moderate Republicans. Economic "and other assistance" was promised, together with provisional recognition.

"The sympathies of a majority of the Spanish people are now with us but only as against the Germans" was the highly cautious view taken by London even in the context of an invasion; Spain's armed forces would turn immediately against Free Spain mid-1942, it was judged, if left-wing leaders got involved.

The files reveal a distaste for Spain's leaders, many of them in exile in London. "A motley collection of Spanish Republican refugees quarrelling amongst themselves" was Roberts' relatively polite view; Juan Negrín, the last Prime Minister of the Republic, was described as "both a crook and a Communist". Eden stopped Attlee, deputy Premier in the coalition government, from meeting Negrín. MI5 even investigated an anti-Communist association of Spanish exiles living in London after Alba had lobbied both Eden and Churchill.

The FO held, the documents show, that no regime based on political parties could re-establish Spain's national unity: a restored monarchy must therefore be supported as Hoare wanted, though Eden disagreed, judging a monarchy would not last long in Spain.

With all these caveats and ambiguous assurances, it can be no surprise that the British government summed up its position in secret with the words: "We are careful not to develop these contacts to a degree likely to endanger relations with the present Spanish government."

Franco tolerated Sainz's efforts at plotting only until June '42 when the former Franco minister received a tip-off of what was in store for him – arrest and confinement to the Canaries – and fled to Portugal without a passport. Eugenio Vegas, the monarchist intellectual at whose Madrid house several of the plotters' meetings had been held, escaped via Vichy France to Switzerland, where he joined Don Juan's staff.

The Pretender was still in Rome and that April accepted an invitation from Count Ciano, Italy's Foreign Minister, to go hunting with him in Fascist-conquered Albania. That put Don Juan's sympathies in the Allies' eyes in grave doubt. Was he still looking to the Axis powers to put him back on the Spanish throne? In the year since Alfonso XIII's death in Rome his son had done precious little to show himself as Spain's best hope for an alternative regime to Franco. The many months Don Juan tarried in Mussolini's Rome after Alfonso XIII's death in February '41 were to be passed over by the Pretender in his reminiscences published after Franco's death.[12]

In January Franco paid a carefully-staged visit to Barcelona, where Kindelán was Captain-General. It was Franco's bid to show that he was in control and curb any conspiring after the showdown with the generals the previous December. The Caudillo denounced the liberal monarchy of Alfonso XIII, blaming it for most of Spain's woes. "We say we will never agree to re-establish the Spain which brought us the Republic," Franco declared in a speech,[13] blaming the late king's reign for Spain's colonial defeats in Africa. Franco was signalling to Don Juan unambiguously that until a regime had been firmly established on what he, paradoxically, called a popular base there could be no thought of instituting a monarchy. "No one should be so mad as to attempt to build on sand," the dictator observed contemptuously. Alfonso's widow, ex Queen Victoria Eugenia, a daughter of Queen Victoria's youngest daughter who had married a Battenberg, had been expelled from Rome by Ciano that January, allegedly for being "a British spy". She went and set up her home in Lausanne.[14] Don Juan made an ambiguous speech when he addressed Spanish monarchists assembled in Rome to mark the first anniversary of the king's death. As representative of a past institution he appealed, he said, to the youth of "our National Movement to build a new Spain at whose head, full of enthusiasm, I put myself".[15] The speech went down badly with the more convinced monarchists for its clumsy expression of sympathy with the Falange.

Feeling for a restoration of the monarchy was, undoubtedly increasing despite Franco's visit, the British Consul-General in Barcelona, Harold Farquhar, reported in March.[16] Farquhar gave a survey of his impressions after talks with Kindelán, several local businessmen and Julio López Oliván, the Spanish diplomat, and former high official of the International Court at The Hague, who would soon join Don Juan as his most liberal-minded adviser. He was passing through Barcelona. But the consul sketched a picture of caution, typical Catalan caution. Politically-minded Spaniards judged, Farquhar said, that it was for the present unwise to seek to change their government for a less Germanophile one so long as Spain was in no position to prevent a German invasion. Would the British or the Americans, they were asking, be able to stop the Germans or ensure adequate food supplies for Spain? There existed little chance of a political change until the Allies looked like winning the war, Farquhar concluded.

Yet Franco was worried by the monarchists and in a letter dated 12 May 1942,[17] conveyed to the Pretender before he finally left Rome, the dictator invited Don Juan to join the Falange and endorse its principles. Franco offered the prince the mirage of (eventually) leading the whole enterprise.

The letter was also a virulent attack on political parties and parliaments, all pronounced incompatible with the regime's "revolutionary ideals". The letter was the first in a secret correspondence between the two men going throughout much of the world war.

When Aranda heard about Franco's letter he wrote to Don Juan[18] calling upon him to give a clear and public definition of a monarchist government's programme. Among the regime's wrongs Aranda instanced an "outrageous abuse of personal power", "blind and unending repression" and barring men of ability from public office "with obedience as the sole qualification required." Hoare, on learning of the letter, was moved to one of his most outspoken critiques of the Franco regime. It went down badly in London. "Never was a government more justifiably unpopular . . . without judicial base, without political experience, the ready victim of foreign dictation, the treasure trove of gunmen and adventurers, it has made life intolerable for practically every Spaniard except the Falangist profiteers and German hirelings. If Spain had not been so completely exhausted and demoralized by the Civil War and if there were not still a German Army upon the Pyrenees, this detestable regime would long ago have been swept away," Hoare wrote.[19] The ambassador told the Foreign Secretary that he had taken "careful note" of the disadvantages of forcing a change of regime in the near future, yet prophesied nonetheless: "One of these days, probably when we least expect it, the change will come."

As the heat of the Madrid summer had grown, Hoare was increasingly taken up by the restoration idea. In May he had been shown by Sainz the draft of a letter Don Juan was proposing to send to all the Spanish generals that summer.[20] The Pretender was portrayed as declining to play an active part in the regime. In an optimistic tone, Hoare repeated his request to London to help the "patriotic group", but he had to admit their plans to set up a provisional government outside mainland Spain were dependent on Axis and Allied fortunes in the war.

Eden and the Foreign Office were disturbed by what the Foreign Secretary dubbed Hoare's "pet monarchist project".[21] Churchill, busy elsewhere with the war effort, took no interest, though the juncture was clearly important. Eden felt he lacked control of the politician-ambassador in Madrid. His suspicions of Hoare had been heightened by the interview the ambassador had with Count Fontanar, a young monarchist just returned from three months in Rome as equerry to the Pretender. Don Juan's duck-shooting trip with Ciano in Albania, Fontanar told Hoare, was part of an Italian drive to recruit him for the Axis. The Pretender had been treated "almost as if he had been the King of Italy", banqueted everywhere and given a sword of honour. But only the generals could act against General

Franco, the young monarchist observed. When the dictator visited Barcelona in January Kindelán had repeated his criticisms of the regime's unpopularity but Franco had riposted that the crowds in the streets there had cheered him. General Vigón, who was still counted as a monarchist, was pressing the Pretender to wait until the war's end before he moved. Hoare remarked to Fontanar that the Pretender seemed embarrassed by "a multiplicity of counsel". "If I were the King," the envoy-politician went on and, worse, reported to the Foreign Office, "I would take my courage in both hands and declare that it is my bounden duty to return . . . and fulfil this divine mission at the earliest possible opportunity." Hoare rebuked Don Juan for his Albanian escapade and for spending his time "playing so constantly with Roman society". Fontanar was told by Hoare that he "could not understand why the generals did not go to Franco and tell him that the time had arrived for the first steps, at least, to be taken towards a restoration".

This outburst of monarchist enthusiasm, though tempered by criticism of Don Juan's personal conduct, led Eden to administer lengthy instructions[22] to Hoare on the British government's line towards Franco Spain. Hillgarth, on one of his visits to London, was involved in the preliminary FO discussions on this policy paper. It was an important statement leaving open the possibility, when key conditions the Foreign Secretary mentioned in the 1942 paper had been achieved, for a change of policy towards Franco and his regime. It was to be Churchill who, as we shall see, in 1944 opted against change.

"We have decided if Germany invades Spain, or Franco threw in his lot with the enemy, it will be in our interest that a Free Spain movement should be formed, capable and willing to carry on the fight from overseas," Eden declared, adding that "a movement aimed at restoring a king would at present seem likely to obtain a wide measure of support". The British government would give what support it could, subject to its own war needs, "to any new [Spanish] government willing and able to pursue an independent neutral policy".

Then came Eden's two key conditions: Britain had hitherto not felt it necessarily in her interest "to bring about an early overthrow of the existing Spanish government and replace it by a monarchical regime since (a) if such a change were brought about before the Germans had been so weakened that they could not intervene in Spain or (b) before the United Nations had built up such overwhelming strength to deal effectively with any German intervention, there was a risk the new [Spanish] government could be rapidly overthrown by the Germans." The Franco regime, the Foreign Secretary judged, "although it is by no means ideal", had maintained a sufficiently independent policy where Britain's major interests in the war were concerned. An input by Churchill's trusted naval attaché is perceptible here. Eden did endorse, however, Hoare's claim that the mood in Spain was evolving against the regime and in Britain's favour. The Foreign Secretary said he was anxious not to upset "the process of internal crumbling which seems to have begun". This option fundamentally ignored, of course, the repressive powers of the police and army and, even more, the counter-effect of British and American economic aid which bolstered the regime. Eden informed Hoare that the Berne Legation would be trying to convey through ex Queen Ena in Switzerland how disturbed Britain was by Don Juan's establishing "close contacts with the Italians". These would prejudice public opinion against him in Britain if they became known.

Hoare had been told the time was not ripe for the monarchists, at any rate not yet. But the professionals at the FO pressed Eden for more. "Sir S. Hoare has repeatedly declined to listen to our warnings about forcing the monarchist pace," they maintained. The conversations with Sainz and Fontanar were against the established Spanish government and if they became known might lead to serious consequences. Eden compromised: "Perhaps I am being unduly cautious in wondering whether your remarks to Fontanar may not have been taken as encouragement for an early monarchist uprising," he wrote. This was the reverse of Churchill's instructions to the FO on how to look upon the monarchists' cause he had penned in March '41.

At Hoare's last meeting with Sainz on Spanish soil before he fled the politician sought a written assurance of Allied recognition of a Free Spain government if Germany invaded and facilities to leave in the event of invasion. Hoare was now non-committal but, reporting to London, suggested Halifax should seek a full discussion with Roosevelt "on the future of Spain".[23]

When Clifford Norton, British Minister in Berne, following Eden's instructions, met Don Juan and his mother for long, separate conversations in Lausanne,[24] the Pretender told him that he believed Hitler had "washed his hands of Spain and did not care if there was a restoration or not". Don Juan sought to assure the British diplomat that his hands were, as he put it, now "entirely free". In other words, there was no "German option" for his regaining the throne. The ex Queen, however, revealed she was urging Don Juan to seize an opportunity which might not come again. The Foreign Office was aghast and got Lord Carisbrooke, a Mountbatten and a relative to warn her privately how disastrous a premature restoration might prove for her son. In a letter to William Strang, head of the FO's central department, Norton described the Pretender as unsure of his advisers and uncertain what to do. The British diplomat repeated Eden's line to Don Juan about waiting until Britain and the Americans were strong enough in the war and could afford to display benevolence, as he put it, towards a new regime. Norton was playing it strictly to London's instructions at that time, but Hoare, as Eden put it in a minute,[25] was "listening to monarchist gossip – I hope he is not being fooled or trapped by it". The FO was convinced the envoy-politician had laid himself open to charges of interference in Spain's internal affairs. Towards Ena, Eden indulged his short temper, describing her in another minute as "a very stupid woman " for urging her son's early restoration.[26]

Vegas, new on the Pretender's staff and pointedly calling himself a "non-collaborationist monarchist", addressed a memorandum to Don Juan in August[27] urging him to stop drifting and adopt a more activist stance. "You must order all these things to be done – unmasking the present regime by pamphlets, handbills, prepare political programmes and people," he wrote. He advised Don Juan to give clear indications to the pro-monarchist generals – Kindelán was particularly in Vegas' eye – who were, he held, "able to put the Armed Forces at the service of our cause. It is necessary those generals who acted in 1936 should receive your support, encouraging them with your enthusiasm". Vegas confessed he had thought it had been agreed by the Pretender that he (Vegas) should come to Switzerland "to be ready for imminent events". It was to be the beginning of a slow, but sure, disenchantment with Don Juan for the right-wing intellectual.

Norton's words to the Pretender, apparently approved by the Foreign Office, were potentially highly important: advice to postpone an attempt to recover the Spanish throne left the implication that the Allies might indeed assist him later. Of course, this advice to postpone was exercising an influence over Spain's internal affairs by a representative of the British government. But the Foreign Office's half-open door, advising Don Juan to wait upon the war's further outcome, theoretically allowed him time to prepare, but also to Franco for more time for his defences for when the Allies were nearer to victory over the dictators.

Operation Torch Approaches

Nothing of all this reached Churchill, in spite of his professed favour for monarchical solutions to bring political and social stability to Europe. Where Spain did excite him was as the military preparations for Operation Torch entered the final planning stages. After the success of the Torch landings the Prime Minister sent Hoare a signal: "Thank you so much for your important help."[28] But when Churchill came to write his war memoirs the ambassador politician's input was simply ignored. In the spring of 1942 a démarche by Hoare with Franco brought immediate rewards and, with benefit of hindsight, can be seen as suggesting future Spanish attitudes when Torch was unleashed as well. Insisting on seeing Franco personally, Hoare had protested against the substantial improvements the Germans had just completed to their ship-watching facilities astride the Straits of Gibraltar under Operation Bodden.[29] These were already extensive: some 20 messages a day were going to the German Admiralty reporting on Allied ship movements from Algeciras, the principal of nine stations which stretched along the Andalucian coast and Spain's North African littoral. Spanish participation, including the manning of some of the observation posts, was proven by Allied intelligence. Now special night telescopes had been added. The British Joint Chiefs had decided against an armed attack to put the stations out of action, and trying diplomatic pressure was preferred. Franco promised Hoare a personal inquiry after the ambassador had suggested Allied-supplied petrol had been used in building the facility – a clear hint of economic pressure. The dictator saw Admiral Canaris, who naturally valued Bodden, telling him the posts must be closed down. After Torch the Germans were told by Spain all such activities must cease to avoid giving the Allies a pretext to attack Spain. Franco being Franco that was not quite the end of the matter: the Germans obeyed him, but quietly began to rebuild new stations in lieu of those closed. But the whole episode did suggest pressure on Franco might work.

Giving his "thoughts" to Roosevelt on 26 August,[30] Churchill had decided it reasonable to assume that Franco would not go to war with Britain and the US because of Torch. It would, moreover, take "at least two months before the Germans can force their way through Spain or procure some accommodation from her," he now held. Hoare, who had that August come to London, was more cautious. In a memorandum, "The Political Implications of Torch" [in Spain][31] – barred from public knowledge by the FO under the 50-year rule till 1993 – Hoare emphasized the Allied landings must be of such strength as to ensure swift success against all resistance by the Vichy French. "Any initial failure or fumbling would be almost certainly fatal so far as the Spaniards are concerned," he warned. He worried above all about Gibraltar, soon to be the lynchpin for the Allied forces assembly and back-up, but vulnerable, he said, to Spanish artillery or German bombing from southern Spanish airfields. So a striking force, air, sea and land, should be got ready, Hoare recommended, "to make immediate retaliation against Spanish territory for any hostile Spanish action". He observed bluntly: "Our military stock is already so low on the Continent that only outward and visible evidence of success will enable the anti-war majority in Spain to make their influence felt on Franco and Serrano." From the Spanish point of view it was most important, Hoare said, that the US government should take the lead in the invasion. Roosevelt should send a personal message to General Franco assuring him of the Allies' "respect for the integrity of Spanish territory, metropolitan and overseas". The ambassador's analysis proved sound when the Cabinet met in Madrid under Franco to decide Spain's reaction. Britain and the US, Hoare urged, must step up their trade to Spain, above all petrol. "The Allies must accumulate the maximum Spanish goodwill in the next few weeks," he contended.

Serrano goes

To the Allies' complete surprise Franco dismissed his brother-in-law Serrano as Foreign Minister on 1 September and in a Cabinet reshuffle brought back the general Count Jordana for the job. It was one of the dictator's masterly timed manoeuvres which mingled luck, self-aggrandizement and tactical skill. It brought subtle consequences for Spain's foreign policy and the regime's future. Hoare was in Norfolk resting at his country home when the startling news came through. "Providence had certainly intervened in our favour," he was to write in his memoirs.[32] "How glad I am to have lasted him out!" was Hoare's reaction of sheer relief to Eden at the time.[33] The crisis resolved by Serrano's departure had everything to do with the unabating tension between Spain's armed forces and the unpopular, corrupt and inefficient Falange ensconced in the state apparatus at all levels. Luck was on Franco's side for the timing of the Foreign Minister's departure before Torch allowed Franco to claim that he had anticipated events, and thereby closed Spain's aggressively pro-German phase.

Events certainly conspired against Serrano. Just as an inflamatory article he had written for the Nazi publication *Macht und Wille* appeared there was fighting in the streets between the Falangists and the staunchly monarchical Carlists at Begoña, a Catholic sanctuary outside Bilbao. The monarchists, particularly the right-wing Traditionalists, had assembled to pay their respects for the Requetés who had fallen in the Civil War. Unlike the Falangists, the monarchists had received little reward for the victory they had conspicuously helped to achieve. Two bombs were thrown as General Enrique Varela, the Army Minister and a leading Carlist, was emerging from the church and fighting started. The general escaped, but some 70 people were injured. The Falangists had been angered by the monarchists' shouts at the ceremony of "Viva España! Viva el Rey!" After protesting vehemently to Franco that he had been the Blue Shirts' target, Varela obtained from the dictator the firing squad for one of the Falangists' local leaders. Franco imposed a Solomonic judgment: Galarza was dismissed as Interior Minister for not having foreseen Carlists and Falangists in close proximity might come to blows and Varela replaced by the pliant General Carlos Asensio as Army Minister. It was to compensate for this obvious assertion of personal authority that Franco, on the advice of Luis Carrero Blanco, also dismissed Serrano. This was the first significant policy advice by Admiral Carrero, who was ultimately to become Franco's Prime Minister two years before the dictator's death. "If after the [Begoña] incident Serrano doesn't leave the government Spaniards will say he is the ruler in this country, not you," the adviser reportedly told Franco.[34] Here was an essential ground for animosity between the brothers-in-law: the dictator was no longer in a mood to tolerate the Foreign Minister's outbursts. The two Polo sisters, the respective wives, had moreover united against Serrano for his public display of yet another new mistress. Ciano, the Italian Foreign Minister who had never liked Serrano, made a prescient comment on his replacement by General Jordana. "This will not be favourable," he wrote in his diary,[35] "Jordana has always been a sympathiser with France and England . . . Many events lately show that the Iberian peninsula is beginning to entertain doubts as to the future."

Churchill did not apparently grasp the significance for the Torch preparations of the pro-German Spanish Foreign Minister's departure, nor have anyone explain it to him. Indeed his message to the British Service Chiefs revealed, mid September, more anxiety on the lines expressed by Hoare before Serrano's departure. "We have to watch very carefully Spanish reactions to preparations for Torch which will become evident at Gibraltar," he wrote.[36] The Spaniards might "turn against us" or the Germans help the Vichy French to resist. The crux of the problem would, he thought, be the arrival of large numbers of aircraft: he wanted a timetable and assembly figures of all war material. "What will happen if a fortnight before Torch the Germans put pressure on Spain for an explanation of these preparations and demand either that the neutral ground [the Gibraltar isthmus] is cleared or that they are allowed to install their own aircraft on the Valencia airfields? What Spanish reactions are likely to such pressure? We might be faced with a showdown with Franco at an awkward moment. I think we should have plans prepared," the Prime Minister told the chiefs.

The final decisions on Torch were to be taken on 22 September for landings in early November. British intelligence closely covered the western Mediterranean those weeks in the run-up to the Torch landings, including photographic reconnaissance from Gibraltar. They did not spot any German movements suggesting a counter offensive. The Joint Intelligence Committee stuck to its analysis that the Spaniards would not move against Gibraltar and that Germans could only deploy forces if they made withdrawals from the Eastern Front.[37] Hoare was kept uninformed about the SOE units, trained in Britain, which were ready to stir up guerrilla operations in Spain under Operation Skiddaw if the Germans made to seize the Seville airfields.[38] If German planes were spotted assembling on Spanish airfields, as Torch began, Allied plans included attacks on them by US strategic bombers.

Back in the peninsula, Hoare conducted a two-pronged operation. He continued cultivating Sainz in Lisbon. Sainz was now joined by José María Gil Robles, another Second Republic politician turned opponent of Franco who had decided to become pro-monarchist. The former leader of the right-wing CEDA party was later to call his cautious involvement "playing the English card".[39] What that arch egotist really meant was that the British might be preparing to play him against Franco. Hoare, before arriving in London, had reached agreement[40] in Lisbon with the two Spanish politicians that they would be evacuated from Portugal in the event of German invasion under the plan to set up a Free Spain government in the Canaries. The Home Office granted them visas in September so that they could both eventually come to Britain.[41] Cadogan approved the evacuation plans for Sainz and Gil Robles, to be superintended by Hillgarth.[42] Nothing of Torch was communicated to the two Spaniards. When Hoare had asked them what they and Don Juan would do if the Germans made a demand for Spanish airfields for a drive on Gibraltar, and Franco acquiesced, neither could find a reply.[43] Seen by Hillgarth the next day, Sainz and Gil Robles promised they would be warning the Pretender to be ready for such a contingency. A Foreign Office man minuted caustically: "Sir S. Hoare does his best to educate the Spanish monarchists."

The FO explained its thoughts about fostering an eventual Free Spain government to Washington without much circumlocution. Only if there was a German invasion would Spanish leaders find the will and the power to pursue a firmly pro-Allied and anti-Axis policy, Ronald Campbell, No. 2 man at the Washington embassy, told Sumner Welles, Hull's deputy.[44] Britain wanted to be sure if there was Spanish resistance it could help Spanish politicians hostile to the Franco regime to form a government outside Spain. "Our policy is therefore confined to maintaining discreet contacts and giving them general assurances of support . . . We are careful not to develop these contacts to a degree likely to endanger relations with the present government [of Spain]," Campbell said. Welles however feared that any disturbance of the regime might provoke a German occupation, something worse than the existing situation. Eden, apt always to succumb to firmer opinions than his own, minuted on Campbell's despatch: "I agree entirely with Mr Welles' views." He was completely forgetting the Foreign Office's "half-open door" policy to the monarchists of only weeks before. Hoare, when he saw the despatch disagreed flatly – the serious and growing unpopularity of the Franco regime made a restoration of the monarchy "very probable", and he marshalled Churchill's favourite, a strategic argument, that a more sympathetic regime, such as a constitutional monarchy, would help safeguard the sea routes "upon which our existence depends".

Eden bowed to Welles, but Hayes, since June the new US ambassador in Madrid, did not. The prevailing mood he summed up thus: "No longer is it a prime question whether Spain will intervene in the war . . . The prime question is what will happen inside Spain within the next few months?" Among the conceivable answers, he told the State Department, was the restoration of the monarchy through a military coup or under Franco's patronage. "The restored monarchy would almost certainly be more liberal and more friendly to our cause," Hayes judged. "The British ambassador is actively encouraging the monarchists," he observed.[45] Hoare, as the man on the spot, was cultivating the monarchists as the element around which an alternative regime might assemble, and getting involved at the personal level. The British government was preparing an alternative, going so far as London judged it was in Britain's wartime interest. It was Hoare's misfortune to see his hopes for a restoration in Britain's, and he believed Spain's, best interests suffer disillusionment.

Guarantees for Torch

The second thrust by Hoare was with Franco himself. Seeing the dictator on 19 October, the envoy heavily stressed Spain's dependence on Anglo-Saxon resources. A programme of imports – petrol, cereals, rubber and cotton, all vital to Spain – was presently under consideration and if it was to go through it would be essential for Spain "to avoid serious incidents with us".[46] Though not, of course, communicated to Franco, Hoare meant the Allied build-up around Gibraltar for Torch must be allowed to proceed unhindered. Jordana, Spain's new Foreign Minister, accepted that warning, Hoare believed. This was the beginning of an intense personal cultivation of Jordana by the ambassador, with wives included.

Essential for Franco were the guarantees he received from the Allies about respecting Spain's territorial integrity – which he naturally broadened out to include himself – when they launched the major offensive against the Axis. The Spaniards did not know where that would be, but proximity to mainland Spain and its African possessions was an obvious possibility. Hoare had received authorization to give such guarantees and at the 19 October interview Franco acknowledged them.[47] The equivalent for America was Roosevelt's personal message to Franco – and unctuous in tone in accord with the need of the hour. "Dear Generalísimo Franco," it began and declared: "Spain has nothing to fear from the United Nations", i.e. Spain's integrity would be fully respected as would the Spanish people's wish to maintain neutrality. The President ended: "I am, my dear general, your sincere friend." He justified the American action claiming it was to forestall an Axis occupation of French North Africa. General Dwight Eisenhower, commander of the invasion, was one of those who had reservations about the letter. "Ike growled to me that military necessity requires dealing with Franco," his military aide noted in his diary. Eisenhower "thoroughly disliked", the aide went on, the despotism he stood for.[48] The US President claimed to speak for the United Nations, but Churchill had to accept Roosevelt's refusal to make any reference to British forces' participation in Torch until Vichy's defeat in North Africa was secure. There should be no publication of Britain's assurances to Franco, the Prime Minister ruled. He merely urged upon Roosevelt that the Spanish and Portuguese governments should be informed confidentially about the objective of British forces concentrating at Gibraltar "to remove any suspicion about the objective".[49] By a nice irony, the President's message to Franco was transmitted by a British secret code for Hoare to hand over for delivery by Hayes since the US embassy was not regarded as safe.

While British intelligence found no suspicious enemy activity building up in mainland Spain, there was concern about the situation in Spanish Morocco. Would the Franco regime not seize the opportunity of the confusion of war, which Torch could afford, to shift the frontier line and so obtain territory and assets in richer French Morocco? The US warned the Spanish against any such move; Britain temporized, adopting the old diplomatic ruse in that area – the matter was entirely one between the Spanish and French governments. A close eye was, however, kept on Orgaz, Spanish Morocco's High Commissioner, until it was established Spain's 100,000-strong forces there lacked the petrol supplies to sustain any attack. The Allies' policy curbs on petrol for Spain worked.

Hoare kept Churchill well informed how Jordana, a monarchist, was responding to his offensive. But Spain's new Foreign Minister adopted a tougher approach with the US envoy, denouncing the idea of Americans "waging war at Spain's door." Three days before Torch the pro-German Army Minister, Asensio, got seriously alarmed and poured out his heart to the British military attaché. He confessed that he had not slept for two nights "wondering where your hammer is going to strike its blow".[50] Torr, alone with Hoare and Hillgarth in the know in Madrid about Torch set for 8 November, could only refer to Hoare's broad assurances to Franco.

Hayes woke up the sleeping Jordana at one a.m. that night as the landings were about to be made on the Casablanca and Oran coasts and gave him the news and the contents of Roosevelt's message for Franco. "Ah, so Spain is not involved," was Jordana's relieved response in the night, Hayes reported [51] – indicating the Spanish Foreign Minister's real suspicions and worries about the Allies' intentions towards the regime. Hoare delivered a British note to Jordana later that day.[52] After repeating the "solemn assurances" about Spanish territorial integrity, the note pointedly hoped the trading exchanges between the countries would improve as a consequence of Torch – in fact, Spain experienced a serious loss of phosphate imports from French North Africa. The note ended with the British government's wish for Spain "to take her due place in the reconstruction of the Europe of the future". The Spanish Foreign Ministry, in reply, maintained it took Britain's assurances covered the entire duration of the war. But Jordana's frank admission goes with all the others genuinely surprised by the actual target for the Allied onslaught. Alba in London got word that the Allies would be opening a front in North Africa. Though correct, this was hardly sufficient – Spain's military needed to know where and whether the Allies planners had really excluded Spanish territory. Don Juan passed to Madrid a hint carefully given him by Allen Dulles, then in Geneva for the newly-established US Office of Strategic Services. But the Pretender received only trouble for his pains. The German ambassador in Madrid, Erich von Stohrer, got the location spectacularly wrong and was to be punished by dismissal by Ribbentrop. Only the Italians came near to being right. Ciano wrote in his diary the day before the Torch landings: "What will the various convoys do that have left Gibraltar? According to our General Staff, they are for the occupation of French bases in North Africa . . . [The Duce] believes the landings will be accomplished by the Americans, who will meet almost no resistance from the French. I share the Duce's opinion: All this is of exceptional gravity for us." [53]

Grave it certainly was for the American-led landings were swiftly successful as Hoare had insisted they must be to win acceptance from Franco. But in Cabinet the pro-Axis Ministers were only grudgingly subdued. There was now confirmation of the superiority of Allied arms, something long seen as an essential element in influencing Spain's military rulers. So Spain did not move, neither over Gibraltar, the Bay of Algeciras nor in Morocco. The German response, after the initial surprise, was to put troops into Tunisia and occupy all of France. The victory of El Alamein, with Rommel's Afrika Korps in retreat, 3–5 November, was a vastly important win for Britain, not least with Spanish doubters.

Yet under the immediate impact of the Torch landings Asensio urged that Spain should declare war, throwing in its lot with the Axis. Franco adjourned that meeting, letting wiser counsels prevail. The dictator did not have to face up to German demands for passage through Spain to the Straits of Gibraltar and soon, in a striking policy reversal, the Germans were seeking in Madrid assurances that Spain would resist any Allied landings on Spanish soil. By 10 November Hoare was giving Churchill his "most admiring congratulations"[54] and reporting: "We have held the position. No signs of any Spanish reaction to our detriment." Hoare was careful to praise his two service attachés, Hillgarth and Torr, and to suggest the Prime Minister recommend a CMG for his naval friend. Eden praised the Madrid embassy's skilful diplomatic contribution to the Allies' military success. But to his officials he spoke of administering "the congratulations syrup".[55] Cadogan was no less personal: "Sir S. Hoare has done very well and is, of course, not the last to say so."

"Anything for the battle. Politics will have to be sorted out later," Churchill telegraphed Eisenhower as the handling of the Vichy regime in French North Africa troubled the Allied armies. "That's all right, but will they be?" Cadogan, always the realist, commented in his diary.[56] Among the accommodations for the sake of "the battle" were the meetings the American general George Patton had with General Orgaz. On the spot understandings between the soldiers meant that the Allied military infrastructure would be utilized solely to secure French North Africa and in no way against Spanish Morocco or Tangiers, despite the influential German presence there. Franco sent a personal emissary, José Antonio Sangróniz (whom he had known since the start of the Civil War), to the French provisional government set up in Algiers under Allied aegis. The "battle" had also required the assassination of Admiral Darlan.

Churchill Celebrates Torch

Churchill seized the opportunity for friendly remarks towards Spain when speaking at the Guildhall on 10 November. Britain, he said, looked forward to Spain taking "its rightful place in the community of European nations" after the war. Neutrality, even benevolence towards the Allies now, would be the price, he implied, for that "place".

But the Prime Minister had, more importantly, already pursued his personal diplomacy before Torch was launched with the Duke of Alba at one of their lunches. Churchill's key assurance, as reported by the envoy to Madrid,[57] was that the British government had no intention to affect Spain's sovereignty or influence Spain's internal regime. Britain's desire was that Spain should return to its rightful position in Europe, Alba in the despatch assured Jordana. He was convinced, the envoy added, of the sincerity of Churchill's words.

The tense situation for Franco Spain provoked by the Allies' landing in North Africa galvanized the duke into an intense round of contacts in London at the highest level, seeing Conservative ministers in the Cabinet and even British generals involved in Torch planning, besides the Prime Minister. This all produced one of Alba's most famous telegrammes which, though apparently late – it was dated 26 November[58] – summed up the situation highly satisfactorily for the regime. It went, of course, up to Franco. The Premier's words were judged so favourable that a version of them quickly appeared in the regime-controlled press.[59] "Churchill is full of optimism, and more sure of victory than ever, repeating to me that his only desire is to have a strong, prosperous and contented Spain. In his judgment, as a result of the war, Italy and France will remain weakened," Alba reported, "and that will lead to Spain's occupying a position such as it had not held for centuries." Among the observations Alba picked up was Churchill on the Atlantic Charter – promoted by him only the year before. It was not to be applied literally, that would result "in anarchy and disorder" in the post-war world.

Jordana quickly pressed Hoare on Churchill's views as conveyed by Alba. The intention was to wrest from the Allies, as their war fortunes took a decisive turn towards victory, guarantees for Franco's survival. The United States was pressed to make President Roosevelt's message into something more than an effusive temporary pledge by the supreme tactician of American politics. Spain's ordering a full mobilization of its armed forces on 14 November was taken by the Allies as a signal of heightened German pressure on Madrid. Welles accordingly told the Spanish envoy in Washington that Roosevelt's assurances applied to "the entire duration of the war which now involves the US"[60] Cadogan likewise told Alba that the assurances given by Britain represented government policy "not only for the period of operations now in progress, but for the duration of the war".[61]

Franco nonetheless decided upon an ostentatious gesture towards the Germans, or against the Allies: he sent a message to Hitler expressing his wishes for "the triumph of German arms in the East". No matter that the disaster of von Paulus' surrender to the Red Army at Stalingrad was only two months away, Franco was indulging in his "two wars" theory, with

Christian Spain fighting Bolshevism in the East. The episode is significant for the extraordinary remarks it brought from Churchill. Eden faced a question in the Commons about Franco's step, but his answers to a Labour MP did not satisfy the Prime Minister. They earned indeed the Foreign Secretary a rebuke – in Franco's favour. "I must say these answers might well make a evil effect in Spain . . . I should have thought you might have said General Franco is the Head of State of a powerful state with whom we are in friendly relations. Neutrals [are] within their rights sending messages to belligerents," Churchill minuted him. [62]

The Allies might now be beginning to win, but 1942 was to end wretchedly for Don Juan – the possible beneficiary, if he played his cards well, of their victories. A front-page interview with the Spanish Pretender appeared in the *Journal de Genève* on 11 November, three days after Torch began. It represented Don Juan's first public intervention since the death of Alfonso XIII in February '41. It was in response to many calls that he should set out the policy he would pursue in a restored monarchy. The interview was Don Juan's answer to Franco's insistence that a future monarchy in Spain must respect the principles of the National Movement. Spain under a restored monarchy would have "a scrupulous and impartial neutrality" in the world war, Don Juan proclaimed,[63] in clear opposition to the Franco regime's pro-Axis sympathies. Amidst the fears of an eventual German invasion, heightened by Torch, the Pretender warned that if Spain's territorial integrity were not respected the Spanish people would fight the invader, with himself at their head. "I am sure that the monarchy will be restored when the interests of Spain require and not a day later," Don Juan asserted. Yet when he claimed that only the monarchy could reconcile Spaniards he still thought only of the authoritarian Traditionalist version. The Pretender omitted any reference to an amnesty for Franco's many political prisoners which earlier drafts had included. Gil Robles, whose suggestions for the text had not been used, commented: "It seems Don Juan prefers to limit himself to a vague declaration of principles."[64] But for many monarchists in Spain, especially those in regime jobs, he had gone too far. The monarchist generals considered his remarks premature. The Traditionalist monarchists, however, were delighted by Don Juan's stance, and had clandestinely-printed handbills with excerpts of his remarks circulated by hand in Madrid and Barcelona.

What Don Juan really thought was shown when he wrote a letter asking to discuss "important matters" with Norton at the British Legation.[65] The Pretender wanted to ascertain the British government's attitude, he said, to a restoration if the Pretender should go back at the invitation of the Spanish government. If Germany should intervene against a restored monarchy "would the British government be prepared to give active help, or place of refuge and recognition as in the case of other occupied countries?" Such a naïve démarche by the Pretender received the inevitable response, only setting back Don Juan's claims.

"Let us keep out of this," Eden minuted tersely on Norton's despatch, setting the FO's line. "If Norton goes too deeply into this question [of assurances] we may get some embarrassment . . . We clearly do not wish at this stage to encourage the monarchists, at the same time we should not discourage them by appearing to go back on anything we have previously said to them," Strang observed, revealing the Foreign Office's awareness of its own ambiguities. "It is in my view most unwise and unfortunate that Don Juan should at this moment ask for such assurances from the British government," Hoare agreed, going on to emphasize that the strength of the Pretender's position must be based on his freedom from commitments to foreign governments. Otherwise, Don Juan was wide open to the charge "that he is half an Englishman, returning under English control. He and López Oliván ought to have realized this elementary truth . . . He has put us in an awkward dilemma." Eden pencilled in the margin again: "Surely we had better keep out of this." With Torch still under way, Hoare suggested to London going to Jordana to emphasize "in a very confidential talk" that Britain was not seeking to interfere in Spain's internal affairs – by so much had Don Juan damaged his own cause.[66]

In contrast to Franco's brilliant sense of timing in politics, Don Juan had fired off his remarks in the Geneva daily just as the Allies, because of Torch, felt maximum need to play along with Franco Spain. Perhaps it was a typical case of exiles out of touch, but German propaganda had been dunning into Spaniards that the British were interfering in Spain's internal affairs; first it had been to restore a republic with "the Reds", such as Dr Juan Negrín in reserve in London, now it was under a "puppet" and half-English Pretender. Cadogan instructed Hoare to tell Jordana that the restoration was "a purely Spanish question". Britain was "not intriguing with either the monarchists or the Left". Again, the permanent head of the Foreign Office was assisting Franco and effectively telling him so. London also informed Norton that monarchist affairs would be handled by Madrid – another rebuff for Don Juan who, naturally, felt his affairs should enjoy direct contact with British representatives in neutral Switzerland. Norton did point out to the FO that the Pretender had "taken a big step by his newspaper interview and his approach through me".[67] López Oliván told the British Minister Don Juan thought "an emergency" might arise – an evident reference to Hoare's alerting Sainz and Gil Robles to be ready if a German invasion of Spain activated British schemes to set up a "Free Spain" government. The Pretender "wanted to know where he stood with us", Norton fairly reported the Spanish diplomat saying.[68] Norton was instructed to deliver a "cold douche" to Don Juan's adviser the next time he encountered him. Don Juan's move had weakened Hoare's position inside the Foreign Office. "Sam Hoare is working like a beaver for a restoration," Oliver Harvey Eden's closest aide minuted, even to suggest that the time for a restoration of the monarchy was for the Spaniards to decide was "an implicit admission that we favour a restoration." "Who knows what he [Hoare] may be saying which we don't know?" Eden minuted: "I agree."[69]

The dictator gave his reply to Don Juan's newspaper interview when he addressed a reshuffled National Council of the Falange, the first since he had taken over the movement's leadership from Serrano on dismissal as Foreign Minister. Franco spoke almost sneeringly of being willing to consider a possible return of the monarchy if it "respected the Nationalist revolution" Spain had made. He praised the Falange highly – it was in reality an essential element of his personalized regime against the monarchists and his brother generals.

Don Juan had failed to start to mount any challenge to the Franco regime as 1942 ended. By appealing to Britain he had contravened the advice of Kindelán, who held that Spaniards must themselves act to put a monarchy in place before an Allied victory in the war. Kindelán, the Captain-General in Barcelona, who was by now increasingly disposed to see such a possibility, received a personal briefing from the embassy on Torch and on 11 November had gone to see Franco about it in Madrid. During a two hour-long meeting at the Pardo, Franco was all deviousness and Kindelán all frankness, one might say all naïveté. The latter spoke of his contacts with brother generals, naming Jordana, Aranda, Orgaz and Varela among others. Franco offered Kindelán a top post in the government – and was promptly refused. Expressing his belief that Spain's regime was compromised with the Axis, Kindelán urged a speeding up of the restoration of the monarchy. Franco would be proclaimed Regent "for a certain time".[70] The dictator, by way of reply, professed that he did not want to stay in a post which every day was becoming more disagreeable to him. He would "think over" their talk, and ended the conversation expressing pleasure that the two had "coincided in the essentials". Franco only spoke out when he branded Don Juan's interview "inopportune" to which Kindelán responded that it was "very appropriate". Kindelán returned empty-handed to Barcelona where, to a gathering of officers of the Barcelona command, he repeated his criticisms of the regime and belief in Spain's need for strict neutrality under a restored monarchy. On Franco's orders, the Army Minister promptly had him relieved of his post. Kindelán wrote to Don Juan a long letter afterwards about the meeting with Franco, but accepted his dismissal quietly – and none of his monarchist fellow generals made any move against Franco. "I fear the monarchy will not be restored smoothly but influenced by the result of the world war," Kindelán told the Pretender. "If Franco were not purblind he would see this risk: it is in his hands to avoid it."

"Anything for the battle" Churchill had signalled General Eisenhower: Don Juan's disastrous démarche, just as Torch was under way, brought out how far the British government was prepared to go to placate Franco politically and economically to achieve an immediate war aim. Yet the lesson Spaniards in the country and within the regime were beginning to draw as 1942 ended was that Germany, bogged down in Russia and faced by Allied victories in North Africa, was no longer in a position to retaliate in Spain. The menace for Spain of German troops over the Pyrenees began to decline. That gave General Franco additional room to manoeuvre, but might not the Allies now be able to do the same? They had been willing to pay a high price for Spain "looking the other way", in Churchill's phrase, for the sake of Torch, but would they go on pursuing identical policies in the future and so contribute to the build-up of the Franco regime?

4

Franco Toughs It Out
January–October, 1943

We have now arrived at the first of the two cardinal years, 1943 and 1944, for Franco to secure his regime and so put himself in a position to survive beyond the end of the World War. In February 1941 the Caudillo had agreed with the Führer that "the destiny of history" had united them, and the Duce of Italy, in an indissoluble way. But as the United States, the Soviet Union and Britain began in 1943 a series of victories in the war Franco's guiding principle became to avoid going down with them. He schemed and worked to reinforce his regime internally with arms, chiefly from Germany, and economic help, chiefly from the Allies. The extent of the Allies' role in assisting Franco to survive begins to assume its fundamental importance for this study.

For Britain, however, there was still the deadly U-boat offensive in the Atlantic which reached its height in March, the worst month of the whole war in terms of Allied shipping losses. Spain's economics supremo, Carceller, was insisting as late as May that Germany would continue to wield strong influence over Spain until the British overcame the U-boat threat to his country's vital supply lines. In January Hitler ordered the German Army to prepare a plan code-named "Operation Gisela" for the occupation of Northern Spain and all the ports from San Sebastian to Vigo as a German reply to the Allied offensive in North Africa. Allied fears became not of Franco voluntarily joining the Axis war but of his becoming a victim of Hitler's aggression.

Franco in early 1943 did give a signal that he felt his regime threatened by German reverses when he offered both belligerents to mediate in a "peace offensive" for which he feigned to believe both sides would be grateful. Its unspoken purpose was to save his regime. The fall of Mussolini in July was a grave prestige blow for all Europe's dictators. The Caudillo was initially deeply worried for his own fate, yet he also began to sense that he might be able to brazen things out with the Allies. At home he adopted a skilled mix of blandishments, arrogance and repression.

The principal threat to his regime came from the monarchist camp because of the weight and connections this privileged group enjoyed in Spanish society. Learning from the skirmishes of 1941 and '42, Franco opted to challenge his opponents head-on. His "royal progress" through Andalucia in May was a sign of his unease, but his subsequent "Secret Orders" to the Captains-General put Spain's armed forces under his personal command to a unique and absolute degree. Franco was thus ready when a group of monarchist generals urged him in September to make way for a return to the monarchy. A somewhat larger group of monarchist members of the Cortes, who had petitioned him likewise, were that summer dismissed and humiliated by the dictator.

Twice in 1943 Churchill rejected British Service Chiefs' advice that the Allies' victories offered room to manoeuvre with Franco. After the surrender of Hitler's armies in Tunisia in May the Germans, the chiefs pronounced, were no longer in a threatening position for Spain along the Pyrenees. At the Quebec Conference in August the Prime Minister and Eden set aside a second call by the Service Chiefs, backed by their American colleagues, for more pressure to be applied. The chiefs spoke of "a stranglehold" the Allies exercised over Spain's economy – a judgment Germany's Admiral Canaris had already reached. A remarkable symmetry can be seen in some clear thinking by soldierly minds: Franco in seeing his regime menaced by Allied victories and the British chiefs in sensing the time was thereby rendered ripe for what they called "a less anti-Allied government" in Madrid.

But Churchill, after the fall of Mussolini in July, gave "reassurances" via the Duke of Alba and these notably assisted Franco to outsmart eight of his fellow top generals in September when they petitioned him to step down from personal power and make way for a restored monarchy. With sufficient appeasement by Britain's wartime leaders, the goal the Spanish dictator had set himself of survival at all costs might perhaps be accomplished.

While Alba played his part as the Prime Minister's advocate in Madrid, Churchill's other help with Spanish affairs, Hillgarth made a striking defence of Hoare directly to the Premier. The "super attaché" offered a first-hand account of how Britain's ambassador-politician had evolved during his three years at the Madrid station. At Mussolini's fall Hoare pressed London to face up to the dilemma posed about what to do about Franco. Hoare's pre-war reputation was however still being exploited in London and used as a shield against critics rightly accusing the Foreign Office of appeasing Franco even though the Allies' fortunes of war were changing.

How to Handle Spain

Early in January 1943 Churchill received advice on the situation of Spain post Torch from both the British Chiefs of Staff and the Joint Intelligence Committee. The Prime Minister had asked the Chiefs about the possibility the Germans might seek to deal a counter-blow to the Allies' presence in North Africa by seizing the Balearics. The Germans would not be successful, the Chiefs replied. The JIC estimates were even clearer: "The course of the campaign in Russia makes it daily more remote that the Germans could undertake major military operations in the Iberian peninsula," they said.[1] The German armies were finally to surrender at Stalingrad on 2 February after resisting the Red Army encirclement since November. All reports indicated the Spanish government was "determined to preserve their neutrality". Events since Torch had shown Franco had been effectively in control of the situation. The Chiefs and JIC were laying the basis for an input by their political masters. The risk of doing something which might bring on a German invasion of Spain across the Pyrenees could no longer be invoked, they judged, as excuse to go on showing leniency to Franco and his favouritism of the Axis. There was room to debate how to handle Spain.

Hoare had a lengthy talk with Franco himself at the annual Twelfth Night reception where the dictator revealed that the impact of Allied victories in North Africa had not shaken his belief in, and wish for, Germany's ultimate victory in the war.[2] Franco spoke only of the prospect now of a protracted war. The ambassador sensed that Spain's military ruler was still heavily dependent on German intelligence as to the war's course and urged London to give him Allied intelligence showing the Axis powers' diminishing resources for war compared to the massive Anglo-American build up under way. This was conveyed by Hoare to Jordana. The day before his meeting with the envoy Franco had spent two and a half hours with Viscount Mamblas, Spain's Chargé in London, instructing him to launch a peace initiative with Britain's leaders. The dictator cast himself, of course, as honest broker between the Allies and Germany: Russia was the growing menace at whose expense a compromise peace in Europe had to be devised by Germany and Britain. Franco's purpose was the survival of his regime menaced by Allied victories. The clear "no" administered to any such peace feelers at the Casablanca Conference, when President Roosevelt himself, speaking to the press on 24 January, announced Allied policy required "unconditional surrender" from Nazi Germany, went ignored by Franco. With the Blue Division fighting at Hitler's side and the many thousands of ex Republican political prisoners locked up in Spain's gaols Franco might well fear for his personal fate after an Allied victory in which the Soviet Union shared. Admiral Canaris concluded, after a visit to Spain in January and February, that the leading personalities of the regime risked their necks if the Allies won.

Jordana had no less than four talks with Hoare during February, and Mamblas got to see Eden, to press their master's concerns for peace.[3] They were couched in shrill appeals to the anti-Communism Franco sought to stimulate in Churchill and Hoare. The conversations annoyed Eden: "I wonder if the Spanish Foreign Minister is really as simple," he minuted when Hoare retailed Jordana's fears that Germany's defeat would inevitably mean Communism triumphing all over Europe. Hoare had already rebuked Jordana about that, remarking tartly that he "could not understand why, whenever there was a Russian success at the other end of Europe, so many Spaniards lost their nerve and became convinced they were all going to be murdered by Communists the next day".[4] Churchill's "Good European" speech at the Mansion House in March,[5] in which he sketched a post-war future for Europe, provided Jordana however with a new line of attack and he turned to probing the place of the neutral states postwar. The Prime Minister had declared: "To these countries our policy is that they shall be independent, free, prosperous and at peace." Churchill promised that Britain, with America, would do all it could "to enrich the economic life of the Iberian peninsula". Would there be a place, Jordana wanted to find out, for Franco's authoritarian regime in Churchill's vision of Europe? Hoare gave a robust reply when the Foreign Minister returned again to Franco's anti-Communism, showing well how different Hoare's liberal approach was compared to Churchill's emotionalism on that issue. "The Communist threat to Spain was largely due to internal discontents and brought about by bad, ignorant administration," Hoare observed. "If I were a Spanish minister I would remove these discontents and embark upon a generous programme of social reform," he went on, adding, perhaps with a touch of irony, that if Spanish experts wished to study the Beveridge Report the British government would supply the necessary information.[6]

Suddenly at the end of March the Spanish authorities closed the Pyrenean frontier with France to all escaping British and Allied prisoners of war. This "safety valve" had functioned well since the fall of France in 1940, and such "tolerance" by the Franco regime towards the Allies had been one unspoken ground for not putting pressure on Madrid for its blatantly pro-Axis stance. The hand of the Falangists was behind the closure, doing the Germans' bidding. Jordana's excuse to the British was that the influx of refugees had become so large the "safest course" was to close the frontier. The Foreign Minister was engaged in a fight with the Falange over influence on affairs – the closure was an additional way to embarrass and hopefully weaken him. The decision to push back the escaping POWS was taken by Franco with the Falangists; no ministers had been consulted, Pereira, the Portuguese ambassador, learned from General Vigón.[7]

The frontier closure was a rebuff for the policy an already sceptical Eden had nonetheless endeavoured to urge upon the Spanish chargé in February, for a shift to more genuine neutrality. The Foreign Secretary had promised

Britain would reply "on the basis of reciprocity". Churchill had to intervene over the closure, and this proved fruitful after meeting Alba on 7 April. "Marvellous lunch," Cadogan wrote afterwards in his diary, "towards the end Winston did his tricks and held the attention of the table. After, he slipped it to Alba about closing the frontier against refugees and escaped prisoners."[8] The Duke gave a full report to his Foreign Ministry, also referring to the Prime Minister's rejection of any peace feelers by Spain and insisting on unconditional surrender by Germany. "These are truths that it is good they should be heard in Spain," Alba subsequently told a British official, expressing his delight at Churchill's remarks.[9] It was well that Alba gave Madrid an unvarnished account for Churchill after that lunch joked with the Foreign Secretary that he looked forward to seeing Alba's despatch – British intelligence was regularly reading the diplomatic traffic from the Spanish embassy in London.[10] Alba's messages interested, among others, Kim Philby. In *My Silent War* the super-spy praised their "quite exceptional quality – he simply moved with people in the know", Philby observed, "Churchill, Beaverbrook and Bracken and reported what they said."[11] Since the Madrid Foreign Ministry would make them available to the Germans Alba's despatches represented a serious leak, Philby went on, but as the duke was Churchill's friend nothing could be done.

The frontier was re-opened, but other words of Churchill's to Alba gave the Foreign Office much less satisfaction. "We wish Spain well," the British Prime Minister had assured Alba, thereby reiterating his Mansion House gesture to Spain and Portugal, and knowing this assurance would echo at both ends – from Churchill in London to Franco in Madrid. An opportunity for the FO to correct the Prime Minister's stance came when replying to Jordana's pressing Hoare on Spain's place among the neutral nations in a post-war world. Eden's team were especially anxious to counter Alba's constant effort, on Franco's behalf, to get the "assurances" given the regime as Operation Torch was launched widened into promises on the regime's future – if possible after the war's end as well. Churchill's Mansion House words were toned down. "I like this better," Eden minuted to a first draft, "but I still doubt whether it is right to give the Spaniards so full a reply – they have done nothing to deserve it . . . something curter would seem to me more appropriate."[12] Hoare was instructed to warn Spain's Foreign Minister discussion with neutrals about any post-war settlement policy was premature. It would be hard to justify such discussion taking place in the first instance with Spain, "a country whose official policy is still one of non-belligerency in favour of the Axis and which has volunteer forces [the Blue Division] fighting against the USSR".[13] Eden's firm tone to Jordana kept to his line of demanding "true neutrality". He complained Spain was still "indulging in many flagrant breaches of neutrality flouting public opinion throughout the United Nations".

Jordana in Barcelona on 16 April nonetheless offered Spain's good offices "to negotiate peace between the belligerents". Hull, the US Secretary of State, replied insisting the Allies were only interested in Germany's unconditional surrender. Eden gave a no less public "no" a few days later. Between March and May the Foreign Secretary battled to delay supplies of aviation spirit to the Spanish Air Force, whose planes were suspected of flying sorties for the Germans spying on Allied shipping. Eden wanted a quid pro quo in the form of release of Allied POWs then detained in Spain, and complained bitterly about "that stinging jellyfish Spanish goodwill" to his officials.[14] In Madrid's eyes, Churchill was emerging as the friend, personally approachable through Alba to counter Eden's enmity. Franco, who had often sent Hitler congratulatory telegrams on his victories, decided the British Prime Minister deserved similar attention: that February he enquired about Churchill's troublesome health. Alba volunteered to Cadogan it would be "an excellent thing" if the two statesmen could correspond whenever a suitable occasion presented itself.[15]

A Fluid Situation

Under the impact of the Allies successes in North Africa there was undeniably some waning by Spain's opportunistic ruling class in their support of General Franco. The German pressure on the regime in Madrid let up considerably after Ribbentrop's dismissal of von Stohrer, Germany's long-established ambassador, for his failure to learn of the Torch landings in time. The influential German business community in Madrid suffered a blow to their prestige. As one straw in the wind, Hoare reported "a landslide in Madrid society in our direction" of invitations of all kinds.[16] Spanish industrialists were by now disaffected, resenting the constant interference by the Falangist bureaucracy, their arbitrary decisions on trade transactions and their favouritism. Factory owners in Catalonia felt they had only escaped from "the Reds" under the Republic to a similar lack of law and order under the domineering and corrupt Falangist local bosses. A fluid situation regarding the allegiances of such groups marked 1943, which Franco's subsequent long detention of power must not be allowed to overlay. It was the dictator's dogged reluctance to accept an Allied victory coming nearer with the risks for his own survival, which stemmed that trend of social uncertainty. Hoare's unwilling tribute to Franco at the time stands up well. "Though his methods are difficult to follow, he has a technique, and the will, determination and Galician cunning to apply it," the politician told Eden, "and shown himself remarkably well-informed regarding internal developments in Spain and of the views and actions of individuals."[17] With the Falange, the political police, military intelligence, and key informers in those fields which interested him, Franco was indeed kept exceptionally "well informed".

The dictator concentrated his efforts on three elements of his regime which exercised effective power and lent support to his personal leadership: the Armed Forces, above all the Army, their rivals the Falange, which had installed itself throughout the state bureaucracy besides penetrating the economy, and the monarchists who exercised a residual power through the landed aristocracy, financial circles and the old ruling class generally. Franco's suborning, and dividing these last elements was masterly, mingling threats and arrests against a minority of dissidents and favours and reassurances to those, more numerous, who, while parading their monarchical sentiments, were in reality more concerned about preserving their longstanding interests and privileges which had been seriously threatened in the Civil War. Here was one of the abiding difficulties for Don Juan's cause.

All the creaking machinery of the Franco regime went to work when the Caudillo staged an eight-day tour of Andalucia in May, accompanied by the secretary-general of the Falange, José Luis de Arrese. Franco made daily speeches, insisting on the need for Spaniards to rally round him against the dangers of Communism. Andalucian day labourers, the wretched *jornaleros*, were each given a suit and boots by officials of the *sindicato* (the regime's organ to control the labour force in lieu of the abolished trade unions) in order to attend the obligatory parades at which the dictator spoke – and then had the items taken back afterwards. Franco's progress filled the front pages of the regime newspapers every day on orders from the Falange to editors. This nicely excluded stories of Allied victories over the Germans in Tunisia. The dictator stayed in the Alcázar, Seville's former royal palace, but, according to Alba, the local aristocracy resented the Caudillo's persistent unpunctuality and virtually boycotted his levée in the palace. Franco ended up meeting only the regime's numerous local officials.[18] Franco, Alba later told Hoare, was still going around saying that the world war would go on for so long both sides would welcome peace negotiated by him. Alba was in Seville for a vast coming-of-age party for his daughter Cayetana, which coincided with the famous Holy Week. More than 2,000 guests, plus gate-crashers, attended, some of them staying on specially-chartered ships in the river port as the hotels were overflowing. The Duke was content the occasion should also be a monarchist demonstration of strength. Yencken, the

British Minister, who was in Seville for both events, suggested to London that Franco's large retinue and stay at the Alcázar was intended to "bring back the Falange into the limelight".[19] "If Don Juan had driven into the Alcázar in a taxi to turn Franco out and take possession nothing would have happened," one leading Seville citizen told Yencken so high monarchist enthusiasm was running, and the dictator's popularity so low.

Churchill decided to get involved when news of such ostentation in poverty-wracked southern Spain by Spain's ambassador to London reached the ears of the British press. There was an invitation to British naval officers to attend. "We must not put any slight upon the Duke of Alba, who is a good friend to this country and there is no objection to a few officers, not more than say a dozen, attending the ball," the Prime Minister instructed General Mason MacFarlane, the Governor and Commander-in-Chief, Gibraltar.[20] Rarely was the value Churchill placed on the conduit for his personal diplomacy towards Franco Spain so clearly expressed. "On the ground as you infer of 'ill-timed display of luxury' I thought it would be a mistake for you to go," the Prime Minister went on, "and you were quite right to refuse the invitation straight away." Churchill sensed the British commander's presence at such a gathering of monarchists might offend Franco. The Foreign Office disagreed: "In point of fact, Mamblas strongly criticized the ambassador's decision to hold this ball," Roberts minuted on Cayetana's coming-out and British press reactions.[21]

Franco's chief purpose behind the tour was to reassure himself of local army commanders' continuing support. As the visit manifested, the dictator was now relying increasingly on the Falange, but the Armed Forces remained crucial – and the dictator was uneasy. Reporting to Eden on the significance of Franco's tour in the political situation prevailing in Spain, Hoare observed: "His objective was to gain time to dig himself in and, by building up an unassailable position based on the Falange, to swindle the monarchists and his own supporters in the Civil War . . . He is trying to gain another respite in face of the approaching problems of peace."[22]

The Dull Generals

As we are going to be concerned with the Spanish generals all through the summer of 1943 when they played, or failed to play, a major role in the country's politics, we had better study them here more closely. It has to be confessed immediately that, for all their importance so close to the apex of power in a military regime, it is difficult to bring them convincingly to life and convey something of the influence and respect accorded them. For all the power they exercised as regional captains-general and local commanders across the country, few if any of them were "big personalities" in the familiar Spanish way. They were mostly dull men by such standards and only that dullness prevailed, colouring society in those early post Civil War years which coincided with the world war. They were distant figures, yet there was a widespread awareness of their brooding presence, and resentment among the middle class that top military also enjoyed civilian jobs as well.

Even Franco conformed to that dull mould, an uncharismatic figure among contemporary European dictators, and disappointed all those foreigners who had access to him. Franco left to subordinates all the technical matters of government, except military matters and choices for important posts and, arching over everything, security and his regime's survival. Many of the generals in authority had little conception of political affairs, some were regarded even as slow-witted by members of the old ruling class. An honest-minded army general put in charge of Commerce and Industry, a ministry vital for Spain's reconstruction after the Civil War, had to be removed as simply out of his depth, and replaced by the businessman, Carceller, who, as the British Minister in Madrid told London with a rare frankness, was by 1943 "making a fortune in the Ministry".

The most vivid evocation of that Spain is Carmen Laforet's appropriately named novel *Nada* – nothing.[23] All is there, seen through the eyes of a young girl studying in Barcelona in the early 1940s – the solitude, the hunger, the cold (for lack of fuel or money or connections to secure it), physical brutality, denunciations and the businessmen making a killing out of Spain's neutrality in the world war. The heroine finds nothing to satisfy her in that repressed society. Culturally, Spain was indeed a waste land – Franco's vast Valle de los Caídos monument, built by imprisoned ex-Republican labour to honour, alone, the Nationalists' dead in the Civil War, was the biggest single artistic initiative of the Franco regime. It was not until the end of the 1940s that the first post-Civil War movement in the pictorial arts, in which Spain traditionally expresses itself best, began to emerge in Catalonia. Painters like Tàpies, Tharrats, Cuixart and Ponç began, going back first to recover an avant-garde tradition of Surrealism, forbidden since 1939. Repression was an essential theme in the young Tàpies' work.

While the regime propagandists tried to build up the personality of the Caudillo as best they could, Franco strove to prevent any potential rival from attaining a position of military strength from which to challenge him. Though affecting a supreme self-confidence, he remained abidingly suspicious of the generals and had military intelligence watch constantly over them. Only a handful had potentially the calibre to head a military junta to replace Franco – Generals Luis Orgaz, Alfredo Kindelán, Antonio Aranda, and that is really about all. Yet Franco also watched keenly others like General José Enrique Varela, who outshone him in military prowess having twice won the Gran Cruz Laureada de San Fernando, Spain's highest decoration for bravery, the obvious yardstick for such close-minded men imbued with strict hierarchical values. All these generals, often "Africanistas" in Spain's colonial wars, had by fighting in the Civil War been further bonded together, an asset for the Generalísimo but a difficult barrier for his opponents to surmount if they were to depose him. Intense personal rivalries existed nonetheless between them further weakening the opponents. Other generals like Juan Vigón or Jordana were loyal to Franco from nature or conviction. Figures like generals Carlos Asensio, Juan Yagüe and Agustin Muñoz Grandes were either chosen by the dictator as second-raters when replacing Varela as Army Minister or outsmarted by him on the political terrain – Muñoz Grandes overreached himself by heading Spain's Blue Division fighting with the Germans in Russia. General Juan Beigbeder, so useful to the British when Foreign Minister in 1940 and an inveterate womanizer – one of his mistresses had been the wife of a British Army officer – had by 1943 taken himself off to the United States, dedicating himself essentially to a life of pleasure.

Luis Orgaz, in 1943 aged 62, had a truculent personality and been moved by Franco in 1941 to be High Commissioner in the Spanish Protectorate of Morocco, one of the plum postings of the regime both for its strategic importance – and business opportunities. Orgaz enjoyed himself in both aspects. He had been Captain-General in Barcelona since the Civil War's end, a demanding posting but had gone down relatively well in defeated Catalonia because of his marked anti-Falangist attitude. He established good civilian contacts in Barcelona – all motives for Franco to decide to "buy him off" with command of the Spanish Army in Africa. Orgaz's relations with Jordana were bad, and he always reported directly to Franco.

Pro-German in attitude throughout the world war, Orgaz protected their extensive espionage activities based on Tangiers. At the time of the Torch landings, he nonetheless assured the US consul of Spain's "neutrality" and subsequently met General George S. Patton, the American commander, putting relations between their two armies, it was then said, on a friendly if wary footing. All trade in Spanish Morocco, chiefly in phosphate, was under state control. Orgaz had the assistance of a corrupt civilian chief administrator directly under him. He was prominent among the pro-monarchist generals and in contact with Sainz Rodríguez and Gil Robles but, in the last analysis, he declined ever to challenge Franco. Orgaz told the Count de los Andes, Chamberlain to Don Juan, in July '43 that he would not join those working for a return to a monarchy "unless the restoration had Franco's blessing". Orgaz's excuse was that otherwise he feared a German reaction to any such move.[24] Franco was to reward Orgaz' perhaps crucial loyalty by making him Chief of the Army's General Staff in 1945. In a report by the British Consul-General in Tangiers in 1944 Orgaz was described as "a man in whom vanity, lack of culture and shyness combine to produce a violent bully who exacts terrified obedience from civilians and military alike".[25] This report, frank enough, to the Foreign Office was kept secret at the PRO under the 50-year rule.

General Kindelán, who had been among the "kingmakers" helping Franco become Chief of State in October 1936 after the uprising against the Republic – a fact Kindelán at least never forgot – was one of the most principled among the senior monarchist generals and had intellectual, though illiberal, interests. Kindelán's lengthy and confusing memoirs, *La Verdad de mis Relaciones con Franco*, published posthumously[26] – the general had died in 1962 – were put together by Victor Salmador, who did him a wretched service. The memoirs in fact shed little light on the relations between two key figures of the regime – Franco retaining all his quintessential secrecy and double, even triple, dealing. Kindelán, despite his sincere wish for replacing a dictatorship by a constitutional monarchy, never really reconciled this with the forms of a modern western democracy. But as a conspirator against Franco his skills were woefully inadequate. After the 64 year-old general, now increasingly pro-Allied in attitude, had lunched with Gibraltar's Governor in April, Mason MacFarlane's comment on him was definitive: "Kindelán struck me as elderly, tired and altogether lacking in pep," he reported.[27] Kindelán admitted over lunch that Germany was now in no position to open a new front in Iberia. His honesty about his intentions towards Franco and his criticisms of the regime's abuses was Quixotic – and so was his tall, gaunt figure. After his interview with Franco in Madrid in the wake of Torch, and the extraordinary speech on his return to Barcelona to local army commanders declaring for "our King Don Juan", the dictator had Asensio sack Kindelán from his post as Captain-General in January '43. Yet Kindelán continued urging brother officers to put pressure on the Caudillo to quit and was the author of the generals' petition addressed to Franco that September. Throughout 1943 Kindelán was advocating a restoration of the monarchy as the best way to shake off Spain's compromised position with the Axis, and facilitate a genuinely neutral stance before the Allied victory. Through Brigadier Torr, he was now in constant contact with the British embassy.

Antonio Aranda, then aged only 54, was the most complex of the trio and, if he had been assisted by the Allies in the way he desired, the most likely to have threatened Franco's survival. Looking at the trio of uncertain monarchist generals back in 1942, Hoare singled out Aranda alone as possessing the "personality, will and imagination to emulate the *pronunci-amientos* of the past".[28] With Serrano's overpowering presence deeply resented by the Spanish Army commanders, it was assumed Aranda would emerge as head of a military junta to push aside the dictator. Aranda had indeed an astute political mind and could be almost as devious as Franco.

Aranda, of humble origin, was something of an outsider for Spain's highly conformist top military. His brilliant military feat at the beginning of the Civil War well conveys his "cross current" status: a two and a half month-long successful defence for the Nationalist cause of Oviedo, the capital of "Red" Asturias, which had been laid siege to by Republican forces who had trusted him to stay loyal. Aranda was relieved by Nationalist forces and awarded Spain's highest military honour and promoted general. After victory in 1939 Aranda headed a military delegation to Hitler's Berlin, where he remained *un*impressed enough by Nazi Germany's might to reaffirm Spain's neutrality as the world war approached. As Captain-General of the citrus fruit-growing Valencia region, then almost the sole foreign exchange earner in Spain's ruined economy, Aranda regretted his country's economic dependence on Germany and urged more exports of Spanish oranges to Britain. While in the Valencia command Aranda had a serious confrontation in 1940 with the local Falange: he did not hesitate to challenge that pillar of the new regime and had one of their gangs, marauding and killing ex-Republicans, court-martialled and shot.

The dictator took his revenge by dismissing Aranda from his post as head of the Army's War College (ESE) after he had declined the offer of the post of Interior Minister in October '42, obviously a bid to "neutralize" him by making him accomplice in the repressive regime. But Aranda's grounds were good: that he did not know what the dictator's policies were on issues like the restoration of the monarchy or pursuing genuine neutrality towards the two belligerent camps. That left Aranda free, though on the sidelines, to watch the generals' comings and goings that summer of 1943.[29]

He did not sign the generals' *plante*, but he provided Hoare with the most reliable analysis of the event. By the autumn of '43 Aranda had effectively broken with the regime – he was anyway one of Franco's always suspect Freemasons – and was initiating contacts with underground Republicans and the moderate Left which he hoped to link up with the monarchist opposition. Here once again Aranda was manifesting his political abilities and independence of mind – and earned the suspicion of his colleagues.

A British commentator and expert on Spain's history wrote in a book published in 1943, *Spain in Eclipse*: "A change of regime is desired by a large majority [of Spaniards], sooner or later their wishes will be implemented," E. Alison Peers contended.[30] "It will be when the Army says 'go' that the Phalanx will obey and either the Republic or the monarchy will return." That was a nineteenth-century view of Spanish military men and their *pronunciamientos* and much influenced still by the departure of the dictator General Miguel Primo de Rivera in 1930. But Franco had learnt from that departure, and determined it should not happen to him.

Franco's Secret Orders

As the 18th July anniversary of the 1936 uprising came near Franco took a step to subordinate still further Spain's Armed Forces to his personal command. In Secret Orders passed to the regional Captains-General, Franco called on his subordinates in effect to spy on their colleagues, and on their "most intimate sentiments" on his behalf. They were to report to him the action taken against those generals, commanders and senior officers suspected of participating in an alleged plot against the regime. The orders[31] were drawn up by Luis Carrero Blanco, the naval officer working in Franco's office since 1941 who had now become one of his principal political advisers. (When the dictator finally ceded a measure of his personal power in the 1970s it was Carrero who became Prime Minister. He was killed by ETA in an act of tyrannicide in Madrid in 1973.) Carrero knew, and shared, all Franco's obsessions. International Freemasonry, the Communists and disaffected monarchists and intellectuals were leading Don Juan, the Pretender, astray: they were all lumped together and blamed in the Secret Orders for "a vast plan of action aimed at provoking a weakening of Spain to the advantage of foreign interests". The fundamental intent of the plotters, these Orders proclaimed, was "to work upon the Armed Forces, the discontented and the ambitious . . . Freemasonry well knows that while the Armed Forces remain faithful to their military virtues and stand firm as a rock around the man who led them to victory Spain will be the Spain the heroes and martyrs dreamed of who fell in the [Nationalist] Crusade."

The most striking thing is that Franco, in approving the Orders, made "corrections" in his own hand. After a passage referring to "the proven intentions of the enemies of Spain" the dictator added: "Anything which separates the Armed Forces from their loyalty to the Caudillo must be considered the gravest treason against Spain." The self-identification by

Franco with Spain was total. Those officers who denounced their colleagues to him were promised maximum discretion. Again, where the Orders spoke of Masonic action "to bring about a democratic monarchy" Franco added the words, referring to his opponents, "believing they had in Don Juan *un candidato manejable* to destroy the virtues of our Crusade". Monarchist elements in Spain were denounced in the Orders for taking advantage of the tolerance the public authorities had – allegedly – shown them. They stood accused of "seeking to install an apparently harmless monarchy which they would see became democratic and return [Spain] to the situation which prevailed before 17 July, 1936".

"Arrests of monarchists are continuing on a large scale," Hoare had reported to the FO on 24 June.[32] Franco's police had been proceeding with the arrests, as an accompanying action to the Orders, for over a month. In spite of the preposterous claims made, the Orders show Franco held the monarchist agitation in the summer of 1943 represented a real threat for his regime, which rested solely upon force of arms and victory in a civil war. The regime left a large majority of Spaniards in discontent. All except a minority, who benefited from office and favours from the regime, could see that little had been accomplished after four years of officially hymned "reconstruction".

Franco's handling of the challenge from a potential alternative regime headed by a monarchy was his characteristic blend of blandishments and repression. It is a mistake to judge that because no blood was spilled curbing the monarchists' agitation, that because no harsh prison sentences were imposed, as there always were for ex-Republicans, left-wingers and ordinary workers, there was no repression. Widespread fear of such treatment from an ill-famed police proved a highly effective weapon against manifesting public dissident, especially amongst the middle classes – the social element Franco's regime had to prevent from turning actively against it. Even the carrying, let alone distributing, of handbills about Don Juan risked for the offenders, if caught, frightening hours, or days, at the hands of police whose acts no judges dared to curb. Another of the extraordinary embellishments to the Orders was the careful adding by the dictator of the single world "*mañana*" in the passage which accused the alleged plotters of seeking to misuse Don Juan "and so prevent a true and lasting restoration of the monarchy *in the future*". The language, of course, was duplicitous: the dictator was, as he had done for long, stringing along the monarchists, appealing especially to those serving his regime while not formally breaking with their loyalty to the Pretender.

In March Don Juan had secretly addressed a letter to Franco, drafted primarily by López Oliván, which called upon the dictator "to hasten the date for a restoration" of the monarchy.[33] When later shown a copy Hoare thought it "a formidable document, if it becomes public [it will be] a rallying cry against the present regime". The urgency Don Juan was pressing for was clear. The Allied victories in North Africa had left Spain, the Pretender stressed, "identified abroad with one band" – Hitler's Germany. Don Juan's letter attacked the dictator from his most vulnerable flank – his regime was both temporary and arbitrary, i.e. Franco's personalized rule lacked any constitutional basis. Yet the dictator kept postponing *sine die* any programme to remedy that situation. Only a "Traditional Catholic monarchy" could offer, Franco was told, a national system of government for all Spaniards, and pursue a genuinely neutral policy to uphold Spain's national interests. Don Juan brushed aside Franco's appeals that he should endorse the Falange's ideology – "this would mean the negation of the virtues of the monarchical system, which is against the domination of political castes," he declared. The letter ended charging Franco with bringing about "a rapid evolution of the situation so that the Pretender could become King of all Spaniards".

Franco's Cortes

One week after Don Juan dispatched that letter Franco opened in Madrid the first reconvening of the Cortes since the Civil War. Members had all been handpicked by the dictator, all as adherents of the regime. The Cortes provided a fig leaf of constitutionality to cover the nakedness of Franco's regime which the Secret Orders had proclaimed with a starkness hitherto unseen. The new Cortes was stuffed with docile Falangists (in theory opponents of all parliamentary "systems"), but the dictator had also nominated a group of monarchist personalities who had shown a willingness to collaborate, headed by no one less than Spain's premier aristocrat, the Duke of Alba. Franco's purpose in securing a monarchist presence was to demonstrate their divisions and weaken the Pretender as much, and as publicly, as possible. Don Juan indeed chose to bow to the dictator's will, instructing the monarchists to swear the Procuradores' oath as members of the new Cortes. The Caudillo at the formal opening made an anti-monarchist speech, emphasizing his "legitimate exercise of power" as one who had saved Spanish society from Communism. "We are beginning a decisive phase of a New Order," Franco told the Procuradores. [34] The dictator rejected any talk of his heading a transitory regime when he deigned to reply in May to Don Juan's letter of March.[35] Franco attacked the Pretender's father, observing that he was not a man to renounce power – as Alfonso XIII had in 1931.

The summoning of a Cortes ushered in a period of manoeuvring all round. A group finally numbering 27 monarchist Procuradores proceeded in June to petition Franco as head of state to bring back the monarchy. This would reunite Spaniards at home and, they argued, allow Spain to participate in the new international set up "which would prevail after the war".[36] Personal regimes could only be temporary, the petitioners insisted, appealing to Franco to "complete the task of national salvation" he had initiated in 1936. The petition reflected the growing unease of more enlightened members of Spain's ruling class in the face of Allied victories. It was "indispensable", the petitioners maintained, that when the world war ended Spain should not find itself compromised by constitutional uncertainty, a euphemism for the Franco regime being completely isolated at the hour of the democracies' triumph. The formula the petitioners agreed upon was for the restoration of a Traditional Catholic monarchy, a formula Don Juan, in contacts with the Carlists in April, had again endorsed. The Pretender was being ambiguous; a Traditionalist monarchy could certainly not be squared with a liberal constitutional monarchy. Prominent among the signatories of the petition to Franco, besides Alba, were Juan Ventosa, the Catalan financier and monarchist politician, Valentín Galarza, Franco's former Interior Minister, and even Juan Manuel Fanjul, then deputy secretary-general of the Falange. But there was only one monarchist army general in active service, Miguel Ponte, hardly a leading figure.

The monarchists' démarche set the stage for the big story Hoare omitted almost completely from his published memoirs, *Ambassador on Special Mission.*

It is in his despatches from Madrid to Eden and the Foreign Office that we see Hoare following closely their moves and, at times, encouraging their cause. The sympathy he expressed for the Spanish monarchists did more perhaps than any other single issue to compound the suspicion for him at the Foreign Office which so inhibited his efforts to shake Franco in the final months of 1944.

The ambassador-politician in 1942 was, as we have seen, acting on Foreign Office instructions when, with Hillgarth as chief aide, he cultivated monarchist leaders in Lisbon. The search was still on for a political alternative if Franco threw in his lot with the Axis or Germany invaded the Iberian peninsula. Hoare, by upbringing and conviction no less a monarchist than Churchill, knew several of the monarchist figures in Madrid personally and at least one, the Infante Don Alfonso de Borbón, intimately and did not disengage – as is the way of professional diplomats – whenever national interests (as perceived by their capitals) dictate. The international uncertainties of the summer of 1943, and the fluidity of the political situation inside Spain, caused Hoare the politician to reveal his sympathies only more clearly.

Hoare's report on the dictator's Andalucian "royal progress", where he spoke too frankly of Franco's objective being "to swindle the monarchists" earned an immediate rebuke from Eden. "The Secretary of State is reminding Sir S. Hoare of the importance of maintaining a neutral line on the monarchist question," the desk officer for Spain minuted primly on Hoare's despatch.[37] The ambassador-politician had a difficult task to perform to London's satisfaction: to report day to day on events which apparently concerned the very future of Franco's regime, controversial in Spain, and yet never reveal sympathy with any of the possible outcomes. Hoare was kept constantly briefed by the chief protagonist among the monarchists, the Infante Don Alfonso; Franco took little counsel, ignored much of it, and trusted to his own skills in the leadership and suborning of men. The British politician was often baffled by Franco for, as he put it to Eden earlier that year: "No one can be sure of his intentions, not even himself. For, being a complete opportunist, they depend on events."[38]

All the Spaniards Hoare saw in the early spring had suggested that the moment the monarchists would start moves to replace the Franco regime would come when the Germans were driven out of North Africa. Germany's surrender in Tunisia came on 13 May. Hoare was reporting exactly as London understood things: Alba told Cadogan on 29 March that once the danger of Spain being drawn into the war was passed there would be favourable opportunity for a restoration. Franco would accept it, the envoy even asserted, for he was aware that his regime rested on a more uncertain basis than Hitler's or Mussolini's. "This date he (Alba) put possibly as early as the final disappearance of the Axis from North Africa" the permanent head of the FO minuted after their meeting.[39] Hoare, however, sent two reports which made clear the extent of his involvement with the monarchists. In the first, entitled "New Aspects connected with the Possibility of an Alternative Government in Spain",[40] Hoare urged London to make preparations to bring the Spanish Pretender out of Switzerland should the Germans seize the Balearics in response to the Allies taking the Azores to help win the U-boat war in the Atlantic. "If the Germans occupy the Baleares or part of the Spanish mainland, and this were allowed by Franco, we should be wise", Hoare submitted, "to help Don Juan to leave Switzerland" by plane for Portugal. The Pretender, who would bring with him " a large body of support to any movement against Spanish surrender to the Axis", the envoy maintained, had now "definitely disassociated" himself from Franco and from Axis influence.

Hoare's second report gave Eden advance notice in May of the intention of the monarchist Procuradores to petition Franco.[41] Hoare was personally informed by Ventosa, the petition's author, how things were planned to go. Timed to coincide with "clear evidence of Allied victory", Franco would be asked, the Catalan leader said, for his definite acceptance of a plan to establish a constitutional government in Spain to be in place before the end of the world war. The petition was respectful towards Franco, but well argued. "The events of war which have occurred in North Africa must have for Spain immediate political consequences . . . which it would be madness not to recognise," it declared. "In order to safeguard our national independence Spain must observe a policy of strict neutrality which the monarchy can alone provide," it continued. More directly, the monarchists told the dictator it would not be possible to realise the Cortes' proposed tasks "without resolving the essential problem of defining the fundamental institutions of state". When the war ended Spain must not still be a regime without any established legal basis. A copy in translation of the petition was later given by Alba to Churchill.[42]

Ventosa conceded the dictator might believe that he could hold on to power even if Hitler and Mussolini went. But the group, he emphasized, were looking to Spain's monarchist generals to force the issue. Great importance therefore was attached to a group of generals signing up to the petition. The Catalan politician came to sound out the British reaction. Hoare, on his guard, replied giving first London's line: the British government, he said, had definitely decided not to intervene in Spanish affairs. "Whilst we disapproved of the Franco regime we did not wish to see any upheaval in Spain in the present state of the war, and as long as General Franco kept Spain out of the war," he said. Hoare, however, allowed himself to envisage a change of government: "Naturally, if a Spanish government adopted the letter and spirit of neutrality there would be a more favourable attitude by the Allies." Ventosa quickly replied that it would be better for the petitioners' cause if there was no suggestion of any foreign backing. But they had wanted Britain to know "what was in hand". Hoare concluded the delicate *pas de deux* emphasizing success for the petitioners would depend on the weight of signatories obtained and the force with which they pushed their demands of Franco.

The Foreign Secretary's reply was a rebuke for Hoare, whatever the language used. "I am glad to note that you still consider that we should be very careful not to involve ourselves in any way in this business, nor to modify our policy of non-intervention in internal Spanish affairs."[43] Eden dismissed any idea of planning to bring the Pretender out of Switzerland: "We must not lay ourselves open to any subsequent accusation of having aided or abetted his return to Spain." Norton in Berne was also told that

British policy was "complete non intervention in Spain's internal affairs".[44] So far as Eden was concerned, British policy on Spain was another cold douche for Don Juan. López Oliván had been canvassing the British Minister about responding to the pressure from Sainz and Gil Robles that the Pretender go to Portugal to be nearer hoped-for developments in Spain. With Eden there was no place for Hoare's subtler stance: that if a genuinely neutral Spain under a different regime emerged before the war's end it would receive better treatment from the Allies.

Above all this formula of non-intervention, as it manifested itself, meant Franco coming to realize he was not put under direct pressure by Britain. The dictator was, of course, keenly on the look-out for just such signs and so too was Alba in London. Perhaps the best description of that formula, notoriously adopted by British diplomacy during the Spanish Civil War, was given by Admiral John Godfrey, the bluff head of Naval Intelligence during the world war. "Non-intervention," he wrote in his unpublished memoirs, "means that we intervene on either side in pursuit of our objectives, which are to exert a stabilizing influence." And stability was, of course, Britain's perceived national interest.[45]

A Challenger

In Madrid Hoare did not alter course for Eden, though he was regularly reporting to a suspicious Foreign Office afterwards on what he said and did. Four days after Eden's signal, Hoare had a lengthy meeting with the Infante Don Alfonso, soon to become the Pretender's principal representative in Spain. The Infante, aged 57, was one of the sincerest, and most likeable, of Don Juan's inner circle of advisers. With López Oliván, he was one of the few genuinely liberal-minded monarchists. A cousin of the former king Alfonso XIII – he was customarily called uncle by Don Juan – the Infante went to work for the Ford Motor Company after the advent of the Republic in 1931. He had personally accompanied Alfonso XIII into exile. In 1937 the Infante joined the Nationalists' Air Force, having been Spain's first registered pilot, flying as early as 1910. It was Franco, he held, who had deprived the monarchists of a restoration when the Civil War ended. From 1940 Don Alfonso was the Air Force commander for the Straits of Gibraltar region, based on Seville. Hoare was a frequent visitor in Madrid and to the Infante's home at Sanlúcar de Barrameda, near Cadiz. The two men had known each other since the 1920s when Hoare was at the Air Ministry and the Infante visited the Hendon air show. "In the dark days of 1940 he seemed to be the only Spanish general who read correctly the lesson of the

Battle of Britain," Hoare wrote in his memoirs.[46] Alfonso's wife was English, the daughter of a Duke of Edinburgh, one of Queen Victoria's sons in law. The Infante's straightened financial circumstances – his father had squandered the family fortune – made him dependent on his Air Force general's pay, and vulnerable to Franco's spite.

With such a friendship between the two it was unimaginable that Hoare should not lend a sympathetic ear to what the Infante had to tell him. He was going to Lausanne to tell Don Juan the monarchists were now convinced of an Allied victory and that the monarchy must be in place before the war's end. The Pretender ought to move to Portugal as a first step towards his taking the throne. "Whilst I feel sure that you are sceptical about the possibilities of a monarchist restoration I feel that I ought nonetheless to keep you fully informed of any developments," Hoare cautiously opened his report to Eden of the meeting with the Infante.[47] But when tested directly by the Infante on what would be the British government's view if Franco made token changes to his regime and steered a really neutral policy in the war Hoare gave him a frank enough "personal view". "I could not personally believe there was a possibility of really close relations between the democracies and a regime which seemed to run counter to so many modern movements." Hoare was here anticipating the stand he was to adopt and maintain until his departure from Spain in December 1944. He was never to succeed in getting Churchill to adopt it or be made the wartime coalition government's public position towards the Franco regime.

The Infante was frank with Hoare. The monarchists could not depend on resolute action from the generals. They hesitated to move against their commander in chief. Would Franco agree to retire from effective control of the government? The Infante also revealed to Hoare the origins of his Lausanne mission, based on a double duplicity. General Vigón, the professed monarchist but who was now the dictator's most trusted adviser, said that he had pressed for the approach to Don Juan and obtained Franco's approval. Franco, undoubtedly, was once again playing along with the monarchists to see how far they might go. The Infante knew he was on thin ice, telling Hoare that he suspected Franco "might frustrate his mission".

On returning from Lausanne Don Alfonso again saw Hoare. He told the ambassador, who carefully asked no questions ("keeping up my attitude of detachment" as he informed London[48]), only that the monarchists were determined to increase the tempo for a restoration. He would be communicating this to Franco in the next few days. The Infante had now formally been made the Pretender's representative in Spain in a bid to increase his authority. A week later the Infante told Hoare all about his confrontation with the dictator. The Infante made it very plain to Franco, Hoare told London, that his regime could not hope to survive and must make way, without delay, for a restoration of the monarchy. Franco had at first responded that he was a monarchist, ready to retire "at the right time". Don Juan had legitimate claim to the Spanish throne. When the Infante then said he was glad to hear all that, but when would the restoration take place, he was astounded to hear Franco reply: "When the totalitarian structure in Spain is completed."[49] That meant never, the Infante observed, "since an Allied victory would never allow a totalitarian Spain in the new post-war Europe." How the Infante Don Alfonso misjudged – honourably – the victorious Allied governments' attitude to Spain after 1945! The dictator was now in a mood to brazen things out – all the world, including the United States and the British Empire, would be totalitarian after the Second World War, he declared.

The Infante told Hoare he had sought to disabuse Franco of this "fantastic view", but to no avail. The dictator and Don Alfonso agreed only to adjourn their heated discussion. Hoare allowed himself a summing up: "Without strong pressure Franco will, in my view, continue to regard himself as divinely inspired to remain dictator even though Hitler and Mussolini may collapse." Hoare thereby put down a key marker for the Allies. "I am getting awfully tired of all this, particularly of Spanish generals, a most ineffective body," Cadogan had exploded to Strang, head of Central department, on reading Hoare's despatch to Eden, showing what the envoy was up against in the Foreign Office.[50]

The Infante proceeded in Madrid to sound out leading civilians and generals – his contacts reported to Franco by military intelligence and police – while the Procuradores' petition awaited more signatures. Not a single bishop had signed up. The 1941 Agreement between Spain and the Vatican covering the nomination of bishops and seminary heads, one of Franco's key steps to ensure support for his regime from the Catholic Church, was bearing fruit.

Signatures from top generals were notably missing. Perhaps crucially, there had been poor co-ordination between civilian monarchists like Ventosa and the military. Schemes to settle the monarchist generals' views on a restoration, and on pursuing a more genuinely neutral policy in the changed circumstances of the war, were "vitiated" by their personal ambitions, as Aranda told Torr.[51] Franco was meanwhile proceeding with some cunningly timed plum postings and promotions. Three of the Captaincies-General, the post of High Commissioner for Morocco and the chief of the Army General Staff, were all due to be changed and figures like Varela, Dávila, Yagüe, Orgaz and Aranda jostled for the postings. There were rumours around, which reached Sainz and Gil Robles in Portugal, that Orgaz was disposed to lead an uprising in Don Juan's favour that summer, but nothing materialized.[52] Hoare picked up at this time word that Orgaz had signed the Procuradores' petition, commenting that this addition meant Franco "will probably not dare to attack the signatories". But the claim proved untrue. Franco spent a lot of time personally courting Orgaz, and eventually kept him at the lucrative Spanish Moroccan post, despite mounting evidence of corruption. Aranda got nothing.

The dictator did show his displeasure, sacking all the signatories of the Cortes petition at the end of June for "an act of grave indiscipline" – a revealing charge. Alba had his diplomatic passport officially withdrawn, so as to prevent any contact with Don Juan in Switzerland. One monarchist leader was deported to the Canaries for collecting the signatures, described as "activities against the national cause".[53] Those like Ventosa, who did not have their passports taken back, were to be stopped at the frontier if they attempted to leave Spain. The Catalan had been in London in May. Gil Robles' diary is full at this time of complaints about the Pretender's inactivity, inveighing against "the suicidal inertia of the King".[54] The police intensified their offensive arresting lesser opponents of the regime while the Falange propaganda machine unleashed a campaign against the Pretender, insisting that a restoration would come about only as a "natural outcome" of the system based on the Caudillo. When he called on Eden to leave a copy of the Procuradores' petition Alba criticized the sackings, explaining that Ventosa had counted on the generals' backing but their rivalries had frustrated that. Eden impatiently minuted: "A monarchy under Franco's auspices with the same corrupt gang of generals would be no improvement."[55] Cardinal Segura, Archbishop of Seville, alone in the Catholic hierarchy a critic of the regime, coincided in his judgment with the Foreign Secretary. Calling on Hoare to inquire of the British government's attitude to a restoration, the prelate confessed his scepticism – how could that come about "so long as Franco and the Army thought only about sticking to their perks?"[56]

The sacking of the Procuradores, coupled with the absence of any protests against such a naked display of personal power, formed the background to Franco's seeing the Infante for a second time. Again Don Alfonso briefed Hoare fully afterwards. Don Juan's representative in Spain appealed to Franco "to avoid plunging Spain into another civil war – which the continuance of his regime would mean – and in which hundreds of thousands of innocent people would lose their lives".[57] The Allies, who were now obviously winning the war, would, he pointed out, when it was won, "either directly or indirectly eliminate totalitarianism from Spain." Franco remained quite unmoved, the Infante reported. The Allies might win the war, but that "would not affect his position", the dictator declared. Britain, "greatly weakened by the war, would not be able to injure his regime". It was his mission, Franco went on, to establish totalitarianism in Spain; he would only allow Don Juan as King when the totalitarian system was "complete and irrevocable." All the reports he received, Franco brazenly added, showed that he was "more popular every day". Only resounding victories by the Allies, the Infante suggested to Hoare, would now shake the dictator from his "self idolatry".

Franco took up his sacking of the monarchists when addressing the Falangists' National Council on the anniversary of the 1936 uprising. The dictator had absented himself from a meeting of the Cortes the day before. Calling on Spaniards to show "indispensable discipline", the dictator observed: "This will explain why we have landed from our ship those who, breaking faith at the prospect of possible storms, attempt to show distrust in the pilot. The ego must be sacrificed to the unity which is the corner-stone of our fortress" – the ego of the monarchists, not Franco's evidently.[58] Franco's speech had been largely written for him by the Falangist secretary general and included pro-Axis rhetoric. The "liberal capitalist system" would not return to Spain, it declared. The monarchists were dismissed as "futile and supported by foreigners".

Such was the mood in which the Spanish dictator faced the fall of Mussolini on 25 July. Franco may have been in tears, as aides maintained, when he gave the Cabinet details of the events which followed the Fascist Grand Council meeting in Rome, but he remained utterly determined not to relinquish his power, his *mando*. He had taken his well-timed measures with the Secret Orders to assure himself of the Army's top leaders' obedience to his person and by ordering a fresh wave of arrests of civilians. Worse, there was a new round of executions: 14 in Málaga alone on 28 July, most of them *politicos* who had long been in prison, Robert Goldie, the British Consul, told Madrid. In a vivid despatch, he sketched the local reactions to Mussolini's fall.[59] Málaga newspapers reflected the uncertainty about the future prevailing in official circles; censors had "lost heart," he said, and allowed details of the collapse of Mussolini's regime to appear. The local Falange had felt obliged to order members to wear their blue shirts and to denounce any member suspected of "democratic tendencies". Arrests, beatings and fines were meted out by the police to anyone who expressed satisfaction with Allied successes in Sicily. Copies of the Procuradores' petition to Franco circulated widely in Andalucia, the consul said. Unfortunately such reports as Goldie's, though of discernment about the situation outside Madrid, had little impact on those making policy in

London. From elsewhere in Spain there came reports that groups of the "Blue Shirts" were arming themselves fearing revenge attacks might now come from ex-Republicans. Rejoicing in Spanish prisons at the Duce's dismissal gave the Ministry of the Interior, Hoare was to note in his memoirs, "the chance of saying that a Red plot was in progress, with the result that many harmless and respectable individuals were immediately arrested".[60]

Reacting to events in Italy in a personal letter to Eden[61] (suppressed under the 50-year rule until 1993), Hoare argued that the fall of Fascism's founder imposed an urgent need on the British government to re-examine its policy towards Franco. "I feel that it is necessary to disabuse him of the idea that Falangism and the Allies can jog along happily and indefinitely . . . and to leave him in no doubt as to the feeling of British public opinion," he observed. "Ought we now to seize the opportunity given us by our military successes and the fall of Fascism to make some issue with Franco with a view not only to obtaining a genuine Spanish neutrality but also with the future objective of shaking his dictatorship?" Hoare wrote, posing the key question as diplomatically as possible to his masters in London. As Franco had asked to see him before the summer break, he therefore sought instructions directly from the Foreign Secretary. Hoare emphasized he had hesitated to "trouble" Eden amidst his many other preoccupations – another indication of the lack of ease in the two politicians' personal relations. Hoare's submission contained a highly important caution against the FO's invoking their favourite "chaos" argument, i.e. that heightened pressure risked provoking worse evils than Franco. The Spanish Left and ex-Republicans were elated by the Duce's fall, but, Hoare went on, "if they attempt any movement against the Franco regime it would be easily suppressed by the Army and the immense force of the police that dominate Spanish life". Carlton Hayes, who got to see the dictator on 29 July, and then briefed his British colleague, found Franco "so completely self-satisfied that in spite of the collapse of Fascism he believes his regime is unassailable". Reporting this to the Foreign Office, Hoare reiterated his view of the "dilemma" the Allies now faced. If they did seize the opportunity to make firm demands of Franco they risked losing certain practical advantages – Hoare instanced non-interference at Gibraltar – but "if we go on as if the collapse of Fascism in Italy has made no difference we enable him [Franco] to say that as he is on excellent terms with the Allies there is no justification for any change of regime".[62] Hoare told the FO that before his interview with Franco, set for 20 August, he "must clearly know how far you wish the status quo to continue, and, if you wish it changed, in what precise form". This was not the kind of challenge the policy-makers under Cadogan in London enjoyed, but the dilemma was well expressed.

Churchill's Assurances

It was to take more than a fortnight before Eden replied – and there was no discernible politician's input. The Foreign Secretary merely approved instructions at this important juncture drawn up by a 31 year-old second secretary, Michael Williams. Before that reply came there had however been a highly significant conversation between Churchill and Alba at a social event late July. The Foreign Office only found out belatedly about the encounter because the Spanish ambassador, besides the tête-à-tête, had handed the Prime Minister a copy of the Procuradores' ill-fated petition. The FO inquired of No. 10 about the conversation, but was told that no record had been kept, with the lame addition it was presumed monarchical affairs had been discussed. Hoare was also in the dark but not on the essential message conveyed by Churchill: it was not monarchical affairs but another of the Prime Minister's personal assurances. The Spanish Foreign Minister, who had enlightened the British ambassador, said that Alba's report on his talk with Churchill had "greatly pleased" Franco.[63] We know of the Foreign Office's deep concern by way of a memorandum which Cadogan prepared for the Prime Minister for what was to be the next tête-à-tête between him and the duke late October. "I think you should know that Hoare has reported that certain remarks which you are alleged to have made to the Spanish ambassador had a great effect on Franco, who used them to bolster up his own position," the FO's permanent head warned Churchill.[64] "Alba apparently has you as saying that England had nothing against Spain and no demands to make of her; that we were satisfied with the policy of the Spanish government and that Spain had nothing to fear from us after the war." Churchill simply wrote in a large hand in the margin: "Not true." Cadogan's memo, entitled "Outstanding Problems in Anglo-Spanish Relations", went on: "It would, I think, have a very useful effect if on this occasion you were to indicate to Alba that we are not prepared indefinitely to tolerate the hostile activities of the Falange." Cadogan's "rectification" stops short of requesting the Prime Minister to disabuse Franco, via the Spanish ambassador, of his personal position.

Coming after the Duce's fall the value of Churchill's reassurances to General Franco, however imprecisely reported by Alba to Madrid, cannot be over-estimated. Gil Robles, when he got to hear of them, commented in his diary that Franco, though initially very depressed at Mussolini's dismissal, "felt encouraged when he received a report from Alba of the conversation he had had with Churchill".[65] The Spanish politician went on to observe acutely: "The worst thing is Franco treats this as a life-long assurance policy for his remaining in power." Eden in the Commons made remarks which again would have "greatly pleased" Franco. Asked by a Labour MP what views the British government had on a possible restoration of the monarchy in view of recent events in Spain – *The Times* had reported the sacking of the Procuradores – Eden reiterated the line this was a matter for the Spanish people. "We do not propose to express a view either one way or the other." Amidst the shock on Labour benches, another MP invited the Foreign Secretary to make clear the government was not indifferent to Franco's authoritarian regime, installed with the help of Axis powers. Eden took refuge in silence.[66]

The Foreign Secretary's remarks were, of course, an especial blow for Don Juan who, only two days before, had felt sufficiently aroused by Mussolini's fall to send Franco a telegram reiterating his demand in March for a prompt restoration. "Recent events in Italy can serve us as a warning," the Pretender told Franco, arguing that the Cortes could serve as a bridge for an urgent transition to another regime.[67] Franco rejected comparison with Italy when he replied on 8 August. War weariness and military defeats explained events there. Spain, however, owed to his regime its present revival and keeping it "far from the [world] war". The dictator warned the Pretender not to do anything to lessen Spain's prestige abroad – "that would be bad for you", he said darkly. Don Juan's initiative had failed again and he became increasingly frustrated in his Swiss exile. He must, he felt, somehow get to Portugal, despite the British refusal to help, and be nearer events in Spain. In September the Pretender did attempt to reach Italy, and the shaky Badoglio regime under King Victor Emmanuel III agreed to admit him. But the whole affair was bungled as Don Juan delayed. When he did reach the Italian frontier he found the Gestapo had already closed it.

Defence of Hoare

The constant suspicion of the Foreign Office Hoare felt he was under upset him and he began to think seriously of throwing up his post. Hillgarth, who had become a close confidant, knew of all this and wrote a remarkable letter to Churchill defending Hoare and criticizing the Foreign Office for "looking askance at his work". "I am bound to say that I have noted it myself," the naval attaché told the Prime Minister. "Though the FO give him what he asks for, they appear to want the onlooker, or the general public, to regard our Spanish policy as <u>his</u> [AH's underlining] policy and not that of His Majesty's Government. This is particularly so when he [Hoare] is attacked in the press or the House of Commons . . . My ambassador finds himself pilloried as hand in glove with Franco, whom, in point of fact, he abominates. He feels the FO has reached a tactical position from which they can safely lay upon him the blame if anything goes wrong and yet claim any credit when things go well, as if Whitehall were constantly and only by great skill preserving a balance threatened by this amateur diplomat."[68] Hillgarth then laid it on for the Prime Minister, saying he knew "how very much you value the brilliant way in which the ambassador has implemented the government's policy in Spain" and would not wish for Hoare's departure. "I have written about it without reserve. Probably it is none of my business to make suggestions, but I have made so many about Spain in the last three years that I feel sure you will not mind one more." Hillgarth recommended a public endorsement should be made of Hoare's work by the government and an honour bestowed – "the detractors will be silenced and political enemies obliged to forget politics when judging his qualities as His Majesty's representative abroad," he added, deftly hinting at Conservative party circles, now at Churchill's entire command, harping on Hoare's past as an appeaser and at the Foreign Secretary's personal enmity. The Prime Minister took up the matter with Eden. "This absolutely private letter by Captain Hillgarth, of whom I think very highly, should have your attention. I want Sam to stay on in Spain for I do not see any other work for him at the present time. He will find it very difficult to get over the Hoare–Laval [Pact of 1935] and the "Golden Age" [speech] so far as British politics are concerned." That aside over – Hoare's almost forgotten speech of March 1939 had praised Chamberlain's policy "to save Europe from the scourge of war" – Churchill conceded Hoare had "done very well in Spain".[69] The Prime Minister's personal note went on: "I am impressed by the way in which he evidently commands the admiration of men like Hillgarth, who has seen his work at close quarters and is an extremely independent person, wealthy, well-married, retired from the Navy before the war and largely resident in Spain or Majorca." Churchill told Eden he would submit Hoare's name for an honour "if you think it would help". Hillgarth received a "many thanks" acknowledgement from the Prime Minister.

Eden rejected any idea of a decoration before the end of Hoare's mission as "hardly fair to other ambassadors who have had harder tasks". In answer to Hillgarth's charge the Foreign Secretary told the Prime Minister: "I can assure you that there is no truth in the suggestion that Hoare [sic] is not fully supported by the Foreign Office."[70] But Hoare never received during 1943 any public endorsement that the policy he pursued in Madrid was the government's and the honour came only when his mission was almost over. Hillgarth's defence of Hoare is damning of Foreign Office tactics. When replying to critics on the Left in London the diplomats could say, "That's

Sam Hoare, you know he's always been an appeaser." Yet they were constantly curbing him when he was trying to bring on the monarchists as an eventual alternative to the Franco regime. Hoare appealed directly to Churchill that autumn for public endorsement against his critics and went unaided by either the Prime Minister or Eden. Churchill and the Foreign Secretary were moved by personal limitations – Spain revealed Eden's unimaginativeness to an extraordinary degree – and by bitter past policy differences with Hoare.

Hoare was intrigued by the situation after Mussolini's fall. Italy was, in contrast to Spain, a country he had always loved. He knew the Duce personally, then a journalist when the envoy was a captain serving in British military intelligence in Rome during the First World War. Hoare itched to play a role, parleying indeed with an Italian Army general sent secretly to Madrid by the Badoglio government to press for an armistice of the Allies. Since Eden chose to adopt a very cautious approach towards the Italians Hoare's swift-footedness heightened the distance between them. Eden felt a strong disposition "to let Italy stew in its own juice", Hoare commented, when reminiscing many years later.[71]

Resignation thoughts by Hoare, Hillgarth's protest about the FO and Eden's dissatisfaction with Hoare over Italy thus all troubled the atmosphere before Hoare's interview with Franco in August '43. When his instructions came Hoare got only a single sentence inserted by Eden – that was the limit of the Foreign Secretary's input to his officials' draft. He topped the instructions with the observation: "The Spanish government have made no secret of their hope that the Axis would win the war"[72] – a petulant flourish, the essential "dilemma" Hoare had posed for Allied policy towards Franco Spain went wholly ignored. Cadogan and William Strang naturally had their line on Spain followed obediently by the junior diplomat in the instructions Hoare received. The attitude of Strang, as head of central department, is vividly revealed by his handling of the fracas provoked by BBC Spanish service commentator, Antonio Torres, who drew the obvious morale for Spaniards of Mussolini's departure. "We must not let our *Realpolitik* in regard to Spain be upset by ideologues. It would not be in our interest," he minuted. Cadogan was almost apoplectic: "It is outrageous. The BBC is stuffed with ideologues, always of the extreme Left [sic] who defy instructions. "[73] Torres was the pseudonym of the independent-minded Spaniard Rafael Martínez Nadal. After another clash with the FO, who controlled the war-time BBC, he was dismissed.

The instructions for Hoare temporized at the crucial moment when Franco was watching how the Allies would treat his regime after the Duce's fall. They also showed a poor knowledge of Spanish affairs. Franco had asked to see the ambassador. The junior, Michael Williams, argued that any alternative government could not be established without "serious disorders". This flatly contradicted Hoare's despatch which had stated Spain's armed forces could easily suppress any opposition. Hoare had observed that it would be "suicidal" for the Left to attempt a coup. But the instructions ploughed on: "Should the present government be overthrown I know of no alternative government which in the long run could guarantee the maintenance of a less corrupt, inefficient and oppressive regime than the present one" – an amazing blanket judgment by a very junior diplomat which provoked a protest from Clement Attlee, Labour leader and deputy Prime Minister, when he read the draft. Orme Sargent, Cadogan's deputy, came to Williams' rescue: the argument was the same, of course, since the second secretary had only been expressing his superiors' line. "Serious" became "very serious" disorders when the deputy permanent head answered Attlee. Sargent, who had the rare distinction for a senior diplomat in London of not having served in a post aboard since the Versailles settlement, based himself on unspecified intelligence sources. Attlee returned to the corruption, inefficiency and repression charges, telling Sargent tartly by way of reply that any alternative regime would "find it difficult to equal the present [one] in these respects".[74]

The deputy head of the FO took care to temporize with the Labour leader, holding out "the possibility of accelerating the fall of the present regime [in Spain] when land communications between Spain and the Axis have been severed by the liberation of southern France". This exchange between the deputy Prime Minister and the FO defending one of its own from the politician's prying so embarrassed the "weeders" that they suppressed it from public knowledge for 50 years. Eden approved the instructions to Hoare which finally got sent off on 13 August and omitted any reference to British public opinion and Franco Spain.

Just before Hoare got to see Franco on 20 August Hillgarth had erupted with a high-powered signal that a group of monarchist generals, including Orgaz and Kindelán, had "decided on a military coup between 20 and 30 August". The top generals would force a military junta upon Franco, Hillgarth said, basing himself on reports from "my three best sources". One was clearly Aranda. The Falange would be immediately suppressed, relying on the infantry and the paramilitary Civil Guard. If Franco offered no resistance he would be allowed to stay on as Head of State.

Hillgarth's blunder, contained in a file again suppressed from public knowledge for 50 years,[75] shows nonetheless how fluid the situation was that summer of 1943, and the difficulties of reporting on a near-hermetic military regime to foreign governments. Cadogan saw himself confirmed in his view that the attaché was "rather a charlatan", and Eden's contempt for Spain's monarchist generals was, if possible, augmented. When nothing happened, and Franco had, as in years previously, taken himself off to his summer retreat in Galicia trusting to the Secret Orders and his commanders in Madrid, the dictator's stature grew with a Foreign Office which had opted for "no change". The diplomatic mindset was frightened by the perceived power vacuum left by Mussolini's fall and felt reassured by Franco's cool display that he, at least, had things under control.

The analysis of the situation prevailing in Spain by Hillgarth, so often and justifiably trusted by Churchill in the past, is worth examining. "This is serious, the chances are that something will happen at last. The fall of Fascism [has] had a prolonged effect on everyone except Franco, but it appears to have penetrated to him now," the naval attaché and station chief for all British intelligence in Iberia, observed. "Franco is at last stirring from complacency and prepared to disembarrass himself of the Falange to save himself. Actually, it is too late. The Falange is his only real support. Alone, he cannot last long." There was now "great nervous tension" prevailing in military and political circles, Hillgarth noted, though Franco was boasting to everyone who would hear him of "what excellent terms he is on with the Allies". Rumours are, of course, not facts, but Gil Robles, when informed by his principal aide in Madrid, noted on the same day as Hillgarth's signal in his diary: "Despite the summer pause political circles enormously worried . . . There's a lot of talk of military government. Franco telling his supporters that Churchill is very content with him and [has] received 'assurances'."[76]

We do not know the Foreign Office's reaction to Hillgarth's signal. Roberts asked Hoare for urgent comment when the ambassador returned to Madrid from his interview with Franco, observing that the signal, initially to the Admiralty, had "aroused considerable interest here".[77] But with this file on the monarchists' opposition to Franco, which already suffered suppression until 1993 under the 50-year rule, come three reports to be kept secret indefinitely under the provisions of Paragraph 3/4 of the Public Records Act. They probably recycle the rejection of any heightened pressure on General Franco we already know of from the instructions to Hoare, though in language too compromising for officials to admit to the public's gaze. The Foreign Office put on a display of sang froid, waiting out the days from 20–30 August. But, in view of Hillgarth's privileged access to Churchill, Sargent sought Attlee's agreement that Hillgarth's alarm signal should not be forwarded to the Prime Minister, at the Quebec Conference with President Roosevelt.[78]

Hoare's account of his visit to the Pazo de Meirás, "the Berchtesgaden of the Spanish dictator", is one of the *bonnes feuilles* of his memoirs.[79] But that cannot hide the fact the ambassador-politician was outsmarted by "this small, quiet, fat *Gallego* [Galician]. His complacency was almost overpowering. Here was the dictator of Spain, 400 miles from his capital at a moment of European crisis, sitting in a comfortable smoking room as ready to discuss the crops and the weather or the prospects of the shooting season as the tremendous events taking place in the world, and all the time self-possessed, complacent and seemingly confident of his own future. My strong words fizzled out . . . Was it, I asked myself, worth protesting at all?"

Apart from Churchill's assurances via Alba there was, however, a second and major reason for Franco's "complacency". Only days before the interview, Jordana, on whom Hoare had built hopes, had signed a secret agreement under which Hitler's Germany promised an arms delivery programme worth 216 million Reichsmarks ($85 million). Here were substantial means to ensure his regime's survival, and Franco had intervened personally with Berlin to obtain them. Under the impact of the Allied landings in North Africa, the Germans had said they would accord Spain special treatment for arms deliveries during the first half of '43, fearing an Allied attack on Southern Spain. With the Germans' increasingly desperate war needs deliveries had slackened however, while the prices, often for older supplies, had been inflated. Two days before Franco met Hoare, an additional protocol signed in Madrid gave Spain improved access to German capital equipment and industrial know-how.[80] This time the Germans delivered. Spain's imports of war materials, essentially from Germany (on official figures re-worked by Viñas), grew from 8 per cent in 1941 of all Spain's imports to over 20 percent in the first half of 1944. They jumped 50 per cent between 1943 and '44. Imports of foodstuffs and manufactured goods all declined during the same period offering clear evidence of how Franco was building up his regime against the war's end at the expense of the population.[81]

Franco asserted Spain was showing "genuine neutrality" towards the Allies, Russia excepted, Hoare reported to London after the interview.[82] He got nothing but Franco's empty protestations when mentioning a series of Allied wartime grievances – the burden of his instructions from London.

But the dictator had a trick up his sleeve for Hoare. The envoy had requested the FO should permit more notice by the press than was usual if they wanted him to make progress on the grievance felt over Spain's still favouring the Axis. Franco's propaganda machine went one better, putting out a statement, via the Washington embassy. The Caudillo's talk with the British ambassador had been friendly and the two, it said, were "in accord to do everything possible towards continuing the good relations between

Spain and Britain". It even claimed that British assurances about Spanish territory had included the ex International Zone of Tangiers, seized by Spain in 1940. Eden had to correct these claims in the Commons, giving a list of the wartime grievances which Hoare had raised in the interview. To his officials the Foreign Secretary commented of Franco's performance: "There are some vague promises, it remains to be seen whether any one of them is fulfilled."[83]

No Harder Policy on Spain

At the Quadrant Conference held in Quebec in August, Churchill opposed the British and American armed forces' chiefs when each submitted that the time was now ripe for a shift in Allied policy towards Spain. The Prime Minister's opposition was clearly to Franco's advantage for any Allied pressure on his regime for a shift to genuine neutrality would as clearly have sent a message to all Spaniards outside official circles that his regime was increasingly prejudicing Spain's national interests and risking its position post-war.

The US Chiefs told Roosevelt that for the more efficient prosecution of the war "a frankly more demanding policy" of Spain was now required; the British Chiefs, after recalling Britain's "conciliatory attitude towards Spain" in the past, advised that full advantage of the Allies' present position in the war should now be taken to "intensify pressure by economic and political means".[84] The price for continuing the economic assistance accorded Spain since 1940 should now be shifting the bulk of her defence forces from Morocco and southern Spain into northern Spain, i.e. face the Allies' enemy Germany, and no longer tie up forces to protect the Straits of Gibraltar, "our life line", the soldiers argued. "We should welcome, and encourage, the formation of a less anti-Allied government" in Madrid, the Chiefs advised the politicians. It would not, they held however, be of military interest for the Allies "openly to promote the restoration of the monarchy". They recommended political and economic pressure directed to stop the Franco regime supplying Germany with war materials and obtain the withdrawal of the Blue Division fighting the USSR.

Churchill and Roosevelt had many more important matters to deal with in Quebec – about the invasion plans for France in 1944 and meetings to lay the basis for the future United Nations Organisation and the International Monetary Fund. Hoare's interview with Franco was discussed, but what really exercised Eden, and Cadogan, was preventing the two Allied war leaders from endorsing the policy recommendations of the Chiefs on

Spain. "The Chiefs of Staff are plunging into politics when they suggest these innovations in our policy towards Spain," Cadogan advised the Foreign Secretary, seeking to place his hand firmly on the tiller. "Yes, this is pure politics", Eden wrote in the margin in his customary red ink.[85] The FO's permanent head asked that Churchill be minuted "on the above terms". The Prime Minister ruled: "We cannot agree to include this harder policy [towards Spain] in the final report of the Chiefs of Staff Committee."[86] A matter for political decision indeed, but the absence of approval by Churchill for a harder policy towards Franco was highly political as well. Churchill's mood towards Franco at that time was unambiguous. When he heard about the publicity accorded Hoare's meeting with the Caudillo the Prime Minister let fly to Eden: "I do not understand why it was necessary to make any public reference to Ambassador Hoare's interview with General Franco. It certainly seems very offensive to Franco and would I think harden him against any reasonable measures."[87]

Churchill's appeasement of Franco's humours when considering the recommendations of the British and American service chiefs cannot be justified. It was certainly not Strang's *Realpolitik*. All British policy towards Franco Spain from the beginning of the Second World War, and especially after Churchill had taken over, was determined by the defence chiefs' recommendations. The politicians always gave them priority in formulating policy and they paraded their advice and requirements eagerly to silence any critics. Now their advice was being rejected by the Prime Minister himself. It was always in terms of their changing military needs in prosecuting the war that the Service Chiefs sought a change of policy. Throughout 1943 up to that August, the chiefs had been advising Churchill how the risks of Germany seeking to take advantage of eventual heightened pressure by the Allies on Spain had lessened and now practically disappeared. In June, and at the Prime Minister's request, the chiefs had told him: "In point of fact, we can inflict far more damage on Spain than the Germans . . . The Spaniards are well aware that we have a much stronger economic stranglehold upon them than the Germans."[88] In July the Chiefs had noted the Prime Minister had agreed with their analysis about the "unlikelihood of Germany being able to react and do the Allies harm in Spain".[89]

The Foreign Office's complacency at this time was considerable. "The tide is flowing nicely in our favour in Spain at the moment . . . We do not wish to encourage any speculation or suggestion for drastic changes in our policy," Roberts asserted.[90] How far Whitehall minds were from the kind of war Britain was publicly fighting is well shown in the reply given by Torr, the quick-thinking military attaché in Madrid, when he saw Jordana late in August. The Foreign Minister, who had just signed that arms deal with Germany, urged the British government to help modernize the Spanish Army. A strong army was the best way to maintain security and order in Spain and so prevent a recurrence of civil war: would Britain assist? Torr replied that he had no instructions on that, but Spain had still not re-oriented its policy in favour of the Allies. Speaking personally, the British Army man went on: "I felt there would be a strong reaction against the suggestion that we should supply arms to maintain internal order which public opinion [in Britain] would interpret as a measure to assist a Falangist, i.e. Fascist, regime to crush those very elements in Spain which were most friendly to us and looked to the United Nations as their hope for the future." When Jordana regretted a "lack of understanding" by British public opinion, Torr replied that there appeared to be "a still greater lack of understanding on the part of Spain as to what we were fighting for".[91] Herbert Morrison had in June warned Eden that Labour would block in Cabinet any arms deals with Spain. The idea got nowhere in 1943.

Hoare took some revenge over Franco's exploiting the 20 August interview when, back home, the ambassador-MP addressed war workers in his Chelsea constituency, and, like Torr, distanced himself from the prevailing professional diplomats' complacency. Although Hoare's speech criticized Franco's police state, the Spanish embassy in London took Hoare's "Chelsea Message"[92] as expression of the real, British attitude towards Franco. All there were quite convinced, the FO's research department man who kept close contact with the embassy, reported, the speech would be read in Madrid as aimed "much more at the Spanish government than the Chelsea constituents".[93] Taking Franco and the Falange in his sights, Hoare observed that just as he did not believe any human being could safely be entrusted with absolute power so he was convinced that no state, however well-meaning its officials might be, could be safely be allowed a monopoly of power. He tackled the "Red Peril" argument, hammered out unceasingly by Franco's propaganda. "If you fear it, you should so set your house in order that your social and political condition will silence any demand for its introduction," Hoare advised Spain's ruling elites, showing once again his more liberal conservatism than Churchill's. After the war it would be the duty of every Continental people "to do their utmost to remove the causes of social and political discontent".

The mood of Spain was that autumn without doubt one of widespread expectancy towards the Allies – and of uncertainty by the regime. Starkie, head of the British Council office in Madrid, toured Spain to gauge that mood for the BBC. Mussolini's fall, he found, had produced "a remarkable swing of opinion in Spain. The nation expected from us a frank statement of the British point of view". Britain, he warned, would lose "respect and friends if we do not speak our minds".[94] The report from the Spain beyond Madrid was passed to the FO where its tenor was unwelcome. Goldie, the Málaga consul, also spoke at this time of "innumerable rumours circulating about impending political developments". Monarchist slogans were going up on walls, apparently left there by a police force uncertain of the local mood and who had to be punished. Goldie linked the public mood to Hoare's interview. "Many Spaniards," he observed, "appear to be convinced that HMG made certain requests [to Franco] which amount to an ultimatum with time limits."[95] Churchill's secret assurances to the dictator via Alba frustrated the growth of such trends.

August 30th passed without any of Hillgarth's intelligence coming true yet in Madrid the rumours continued unabated about the generals' restiveness. "Something [is] being hatched by the military," Farquhar, the Consul-General, reported from Barcelona.[96] Kindelán had given Ventosa a rendez-vous in Madrid for 6 September. All eyes were on General Orgaz, including Franco's, Yencken, the chargé in Madrid, observed.[97] The Caudillo was thinking of bringing Orgaz back from Morocco and making him Army Minister in place of Asensio, having satisfied himself of the general's "loyalty". But Yencken also learnt that a military government, eliminating the Falangists from the Cabinet, was "expected shortly". A few days later he even gave London a Cabinet list: Orgaz would replace Jordana as Foreign Minister, the latter becoming Prime Minister, Varela, with all his prestige, would take back the Army Ministry Franco had deprived him of after the Begoña incident and Ventosa would be Finance Minister. Its complexion was unambiguously monarchist. "As always, we can only remain sceptical about such changes," Roberts commented, but he showed Eden the list.[98] Such an administration, he advised, would be "anti-Falangist, neutral, moderate and pro-monarchist". Exactly the kind of government the British and American Chiefs had wanted, but which had failed to encounter Churchill's favour. Arrese, the Falange's secretary-general, also got wind of these proposed changes. In a speech at Burgos, the leader of the Blue Shirts distanced the Falange publicly from its Italian and German models. Somewhat naïvely he observed: "Perhaps this speech will appear to many an opportunist way of the Falange re-positioning itself."[99]

The Failed *Plante*

With Franco back in Madrid from his Galician retreat where Hoare had found him so complacent, General Varela, the most decorated Spanish general, went to the Pardo and handed the dictator a petition on 15 September. It asked for Spain to be given a stable regime in the form of a restored monarchy.[100] The petition was signed by Varela and seven other lieutenant-generals among the most prestigious and authoritative judged by their exploits in the Civil War – Orgaz, Kindelán, Fidel Dávila, José Solchaga, Andrés Saliquet, José Moscardó and Miguel Ponte. Among the generals whose signatures were missing were Jordana, Vigón – both currently Franco Ministers – and Aranda, as usual cast in the role of outsider.

The petition, dated 8 September, was respectful in tone asking General Franco whether he did not agree the time had come to replace the existing regime by a monarchy in the Spanish tradition, "a loyal appeal from his old comrades in arms who were acting," the generals emphasized, "with maximum discipline and in sincere adherence to his person". The text had been drawn up by Kindelán, who had consulted the Infante Don Alfonso, who, in turn, tried to obtain Vigón's signature.

The petition reminded Franco that the signatories included those who had invested him with maximum powers in the armed forces and authority in the Spanish state after the Civil War broke out. The Army was posited as the ultimate authority, and arbiter, well capable of putting down any internal disturbances and not afraid of what the generals described as only the Communist "phantasm". A more aggressive version of the petition had been prepared, telling Franco how a totalitarian regime, favouring the Falange, had been installed. The Army leaders had been neither consulted nor had they ever approved such a regime. These observations were deleted to obtain the signatures of two generals who objected to any personal attack on Franco. The generals' *plante* was, of course, secret emanating from the Army's Superior Council. (A plante is the term in Spanish for a stand adopted by a group of subordinates who refuse to obey a superior unless he accedes to some of their demands.)

Franco reacted with all his mastery of men and of himself. He did not even manifest anger as, initially, he had done over the Procuradores' manifesto. He received each of the signatories individually. None of the generals who signed was disciplined; the respectful tone, one could argue, ruled that out. Dávila was actually promoted shortly afterwards Chief of the Army General Staff. Professing to agree to a return to the monarchy at the opportune time, Franco urged the generals to withdraw the petition. The dictator even had a message conveyed to the habitually well-informed Portuguese ambassador asking him not to tell Salazar of the generals' step.[101] To the generals Franco made much of the Allies' support, as he saw it in the continued supplying of Spain with the essential elements for its economy. One general reportedly broke down under

Franco's questioning and, in tears, said that he had been pressured into giving his signature.

Before the *plante* Kindelán had written to Asensio urging him to "help Franco, out of patriotism, to find a sound solution to the grave problems of the moment".[102] Kindelán had realized that Franco's Secret Orders made the role of Army Minister and head of the Army's Superior Council, the body from which a junta might eventually emerge, crucial. But Asensio stayed loyal to Franco, not signing and, when shown handbills from Madrid streets in mid October referring to the petition by eight top generals, wrote to Kindelán asking him to deny any such "letter" to Franco had ever been sent. An appeal by Gil Robles at this time urged the Army Minister, and the Army under him, to act now to avoid "the abyss" Spain would otherwise face at the end of the world war. Asensio's reply touched upon the consideration which prevailed in all conventional-minded Spanish Army officers like himself: nothing must be done which might set members of the "military family" one against another. Here was one of Franco's assets; those like Kindelán argued in vain for a kind of discipline which was not blind, subordinating everything to the generalísimo's person.

Orgaz, whose role might have been decisive but who had stayed sinuously "loyal" to Franco, justified his attitude after the *plante* in a communication to Gil Robles. The younger generals and majors were "with Franco, making things difficult for a pro-monarchist uprising".[103] Varela wrote to Kindelán : "What is certain – and it is very sad – is that nothing has been achieved by the paths of honesty and *compañerismo* which we have adopted to help Spain's situation and that of Franco himself. What is worse, the most authoritative voices of the nation are ignored and lose therefore prestige."[104] Franco was now determined, Kindelán told Orgaz, to "dismantle slowly, and without any strident steps, the dangerous mechanism" threatening him. He confided to Torr his analysis of the dictator's dispositions,[105] the fullest account of the British embassy had of the *plante*. Control of the country meant foremost control of the line of command from Madrid and Castile: here Asensio was the subservient Army Minister, Raphael García Valiño, the Army Chief of Staff and Agustin Muñoz Grandes, relieved of his Blue Division command in Russia, was now chastened head of Franco's military household. Of the troop commanders in the field, Yagüe, the tough pro-Falangist former Air Minister, now held the Burgos command, which meant he had charge of Navarre, home of the Requetés. Despite his signing the petition, Moscardó was obliged to demonstrate his "loyalty" in Barcelona and Saliquet required to do likewise under the suspicious eyes of his superiors in the Madrid region. Asensio, García Valiño, Muñoz Grandes and Moscardó only thought of their personal interest and ambitions, Kindelán told Torr. All four owed their posts to Franco. At a meeting at Kindelán's Madrid home with Orgaz, Solchaga, Dávila and Ponte it was decided they would not undertake any further action until early 1944. Not only did Kindelán lack the conspirators' operational skills in manipulating men, he often told the dictator of his sincerest feelings to his face. "Loyalty has been a mania for me," Kindelán was to write later in an autobiographical sketch.[106] That need not, of course, have been a fundamental impediment, but Franco was never one to respond to such a human quality. This personal chemistry at the top of the pyramid of power in Spain's military regime was an essential factor and not *petite histoire* at all.

Thus ended the 1943 generals' petition to Franco; in the words of the Chinese proverb "there is a lot of noise on the stairs, but nobody comes into the room". Eden and Cadogan felt satisfied, contemptuous of the generals whom Britain had earlier in the war spent millions to bribe. "All Spanish generals are undependable; I wouldn't even rely on them for a correct account of their interview with Franco," the permanent head of the FO minuted on the despatches from Madrid. "I agree," the Foreign Secretary added. "They are wretched lot and unworthy of any consideration from us." In July Eden had already decided "a monarchy with the same corrupt gang of generals would be no improvement".[107] Roberts drew the obvious conclusion: "Franco is clearly far ahead of his fellow generals in political shrewdness."

The moderates' way to solve Spain's pressing problem of an Axis-compromised regime, when the United Nations, fighting under the banner of democracy, were evidently going to win, had been twice rebuffed by Franco. He would in no way facilitate the approach of either the civilians – the Procuradores' petition – or the eight brother generals' *plante* – to restore the Spanish monarchy and so end an interregnum based on force. Spain's internal position that summer of 1943 was best characterized by the dictator's ringing refusal to hear the plea of the Infante Don Alfonso at their second interview. Franco was determined to stay in power by all and any means of repression, and even blood-shedding on the scale again of the Civil War if required.

Don Juan was the biggest loser by the generals' failed *plante*. His telegram to General Franco after Mussolini's fall had brought only the dictator's defiant reply. The Pretender's urgings that the professing monarchists in high places in the Franco regime should now quit their posts had to be abandoned for lack of a favourable response. Above all, General Vigón, Don Juan's former tutor, who had projected a visit to Lausanne, opted with utter clarity after the *plante* to abandon it to demonstrate he preferred to stand by General Franco and the existing regime.[108] Cambó, the Catalan leader, had shrewd comments on both the Procuradores' and the generals' moves. Franco, he wrote in his diary, was "a master of the art of pretending not to hear what he did not want to hear": he would make to the generals individually promises, threats and even a few concessions.[109] Yet Franco's conflicting problem would find no solution: the setting up of a constitutional monarchy alongside the maintenance of a personal dictatorship. In another diary entry Cambó tackled the monarchists' ambiguity – what kind of a monarchy were Don Juan and his supporters intending to set up – an "aristocratic" or a "democratic" one? "The monarchy will not be able to consolidate its position unless it is of everyone, and, equally, if it fails to obtain the backing of intellectuals, the middle class and the sympathy of the people," he wrote.[110] His prescience anticipates what Don Juan's son, King Juan Carlos, was to achieve after 1977. The Procuradores, Cambó thought, criticizing his own protégé Ventosa by name, should never have launched their petition without having decided to act against General Franco in the case that he refused their pleas.[111] But, in fact, there had been no co-ordination between the civilians and the military men. This was the fatal flaw.

The situation posed for the Allies, and British diplomacy especially, the question how to respond. The fruits of the Foreign Office's *Realpolitik* were proving meagre indeed. "The policy of HMG remains one of strict non intervention in Spain's internal affairs and, in return, we expect strict neutrality from the Spanish government," Cadogan was still maintaining in a memorandum he prepared for the Prime Minister's Mansion House speech that autumn.[112] The FO's permanent head knew better than anyone, however, that with Churchill's "assurances" to Franco that expectation was getting nowhere. Spain's situation at that juncture was one of frustration. "The truth is the monarchy went farther away from the Spanish political horizon inspite of Allied progress on all fronts . . . Franco refused to make concessions, yet played along skilfully with the United States and Britain," Laureano López Rodó, the politician and historian of the Spanish monarchy's restoration writes, lucidly summing up that period.[113]

Franco stage-managed his triumph over the generals who signed the *plante* at the opening of a new term at the Army's Escuela Superior in November and also cocked a snook at the Allies' war effort. The dictator had all the assembled generals form up an avenue through which the Generalísimo walked on arriving and they welcomed him, as instructed, with the Falangists' salute and shouting in unison "Franco".[114] Kindelán, as director of the academy, made a humiliating speech "obviously intended to curry favour with the Generalísimo," Hoare told London, basing himself on the British military attaché's eye-witness account. "Greatly as we deplore them, I fear we must expect such apparent recantations . . . No individual general is strong enough to stand up to against Franco. This makes me more sceptical than ever of an army coup in the near future," Hoare went on. The dictator seized upon this gathering of young aspirants to the generalcy to declare that in future the Spanish Army must be one million strong. Many army officers had been fearing for their jobs when the world conflict ended. Now they were reassured about the real job – shoring up the Franco regime. Franco spent most of his time looking at the numerous photographs and busts of himself, Torr reported, and dropped the observation: "You see, gentlemen, at the end of this war Spain will be counted *the bride of Europe*." Hoare called it "shattering complacency".

But Portugal was different and on 12 October Churchill announced to Parliament that "certain facilities", i.e. the use of naval and air bases, had been granted Britain in the Azores. These facilities would allow air cover and refuelling for the Atlantic convoys. Here was a real shift of policy by Salazar – from now on cooperating with the Allies. Secret talks had opened in Lisbon in June and Roberts came out to negotiate personally with Salazar. Britain in return for the facilities would supply Portugal with economic aid and arms. Roberts went over to Madrid to consult with Hoare to make sure about any negative response by Franco. The successful conclusion of this accord, kept secret till October, brought Roberts the prestige he enjoyed in Central department and helps perhaps to explain his attitude of determined optimism, however unjustified, towards the entire Iberian peninsula that autumn. Using as framework the 600 year-old alliance with Portugal, the British government achieved by collaboration what Roosevelt and the American Service Chiefs had, back in 1941, envisaged seizing by force. Eden and Cadogan had, however, to work hard upon Churchill earlier in '43 restraining the Prime Minister from using force. "Talk with Eden about the Azores. The P.M. has got on to this again with great vigour. Agreed we might ask Salazar for facilities, but must *not* [Cadogan's italics] seize them. Defence Committee confirmed," the FO's permanent head confided to his diary.[115] Cadogan got his way. For the first year of the agreement the Americans were in fact involved, but dressed in British uniforms. By November 1944 the senior partner took over, helping with the construction of the bases which post-war became Portuguese.

Salazar took care to explain the shift to the Spaniards, going personally by car in early October to meet Jordana just across the frontier and give the details. Spain's Foreign Minister made no objections, only voicing surprise that Britain had not made such a request for base facilities long before.[116] Franco subsequently let the Portuguese know he saw no reason why their concession to the Allies should affect Spain's "neutrality". Reporting from Madrid to Churchill, Hoare said Franco was backing Jordana's determination to accept the Azores agreement and to ignore any German complaints. This was due to "the general conviction that Germany is now too weak to retaliate," he observed.[117]

But Portugal's policy shift, engineered by the always subtle Salazar, only underlined Franco's continuing hostility to the Allies as much as to all moderates inside Spain. Hoare's word that the Germans were now too weak to retaliate really signalled to London that the view previously accepted as gospel by the diplomats, that stability for the Franco regime was the best guarantee for Spanish "neutrality", had by the autumn of 1943 no longer validity. Professing to believe his Spain would be "*la novia de Europa*" at the war's end, why should Franco change course? It was clearly time for a fresh approach. It came from the Americans.

5

The Wolfram War
November–December, 1943

The Azores agreement with Portugal was the last hurrah for British diplomacy so far as the Iberian peninsula was concerned in the Second World War. Increasingly, the weight of the United States in the Allied war effort brought on its role in foreign policy-making towards Franco Spain. This led to British resentment, fuelled by a quickly emerging trade rivalry. Perhaps because there was no need to manifest unity on any battlefield the economic strains in a war effort going beyond Britain's means showed up early in Spain.

By the autumn of 1943 the Roosevelt Administration decided for itself upon a toughened approach on economic issues: a suspension of petrol supplies for Spain was envisaged unless the Franco regime agreed to put a stop to the highly lucrative export trade to Germany that Spain had developed in wolfram, the ore from which the alloy tungsten is derived for producing armour-piercing projectiles of all kinds.

At the root of Allied difficulties over the wolfram "war" lay the policy, initially devised by Britain to forestall the Germans getting the raw material, of so-called pre-emptive buying. Wolfram had however by 1943 become the Franco regime's single most important means for economic survival, as well as cornerstone of the "get-rich-quick" economy of the favoured few. Under the unscrupulous, but skilled supervision of Demetrio Carceller, Franco's economics "supremo", it contributed notably to rebuilding Spain's gold reserves depleted by the Civil War. The two belligerent camps must therefore be kept competing for the wolfram as Spain both drove up production and prices to benefit the state coffers and so enabled to buy yet more gold. These reserves, at dangerously low levels at the beginning of the world war, reached by the conflict's end more than 120 million dollars. Carceller, in one of his rare public statements on economic policy which were true, had declared in January 1943 the build up of reserves was vital "to avoid the paralysation of the nation's economic life if difficulties should arise in future times " – he meant, the uncertain outcome for the Franco regime of the war. Proof of Carceller's value for the regime came after 1945.

The regular war-time purchasing by Spain of gold lingots from Switzerland, often in origin the tainted "Nazi gold" taken from European Jews and central banks of the occupied countries, was controversial. Carceller's January statement defied the spirit, if not the letter, of a warning to the neutral countries 17 United Nations governments issued then that they would take measures to combat such plundering by Germany.

Yet the paradox lay in the fact that it was Spain's trading surpluses with Britain and America, to which wolfram contributed so substantially, which gave Franco the means to build up the gold reserves. Germany's trade, though bigger than Britain's in 1943, was by contrast on the basis of bilateral compensation agreements. Spain provided the wolfram in return for arms deliveries from Germany. Carceller, in addition, paid off large tranches of Spain's Civil War debts to Hitler to facilitate Germany's taking the wolfram away from the Allies. The massive purchases going to Spain's reserves, and not to extra purchases of food to relieve the often near-starvation conditions of many ordinary Spaniards, underlined the harshness of the regime.

The Allied economic "weapon" had by 1943 achieved a hitherto unseen degree of control over a neutral's economy. But here was the underlying issue: was it to be used, as proclaimed, in effective pursuit of war aims to pressure Franco or, in fact, to strengthen his regime and his hold on power? Wars, as is well known, often develop a dynamic of their own.

American policy was also undergoing a subtle, but important, evolution from a principled opposition to a pro-Axis, because anti-democratic, Spain to a hard-nosed perception of the opportunities winning the war would afford the United States both economically and strategically. A significant part in finding a way to this new role for America in Spain was played by Carlton Hayes, the US ambassador in Madrid, with the clash of personalities between the right-wing Catholic Yankee professor and the British Conservative elder statesman, Hoare, symbolizing and, at times, aggravating the two nations' rivalry. Spain's leaders quickly, and cleverly, exploited their differences. Roosevelt, in his third term as President, increasingly eclipsed the State Department which also found itself challenged by new US government departments set up to wage the war. In a parallel development, the Foreign Office was overtaken in policy-making by the Ministry of Economic Warfare, which substantially breached, so far as Spain was concerned, the economic blockade policy it had initiated in 1940. Under Eden, the FO did not fight back against the newcomers, unlike the State Department. The prolonged crisis over how to prevent Spain's mounting wolfram exports from reaching Germany in the end defeated British diplomats and revealed a serious ignorance of economic affairs.

Herbert Feis, the senior State Department official who had charge of the US Iberian Peninsula Operating Committee, the body responsible for handling the wartime trading with Spain, posed a crucial question when he asked sceptically in his memoirs after the war – how far a government should go with economic measures "to gain the easiest victory that might rob the victory of ultimate and lasting meaning?"[1] But that dilemma, so well expressed by Feis, one of the finest minds on either side of the Atlantic concerned with Spain during the world war, was beyond the perception of his contemporaries while waging it.

Economic Rivalries

It was the United States government which seized the opportunity forged by the Allied invasion of Sicily and the fall of Mussolini for some fresh thinking about Franco Spain. The Foreign Office had plenty of warning. "As the military situation improves the political pressure for treating Franco more in accordance with what are felt here to be his deserts will certainly increase," Halifax already told London in July.[2] He caught the perception by public opinion, political circles and inside the Roosevelt administration that successes on the Mediterranean front had reduced the strategic arguments for economic leniency to Franco Spain. Americans held, he reported, that Spain must stop its economic aid to Germany and give more favours to the Allies. The FO was advised by the ex Foreign Secretary, to "update" its policy objectives on Spain. But London was seeking desperately for ways to increase exports to Spain to pay the ever mounting bills for wolfram purchases, and not how to use the economic weapon to bring Spain to heel.

By October two US government departments launched policy initiatives – Robert Patterson, the Under Secretary of War, called for tougher policies towards all the neutrals, including Spain and the Office of Economic Warfare declared that the time had come for the Allies to "utilize their economic bargaining power" so that Spain and Portugal limited, or prohibited, the export of strategic commodities to Germany.[3] US intelligence, Patterson said, showed that vital war materials were being supplied by Spain in significant quantities to the Germans. To shorten the war and save American and Allied lives, all the neutral governments should now be required to curb dealings with Germany. Allied supply/purchase programmes for Spain and Portugal were the place to apply the screws.

The US Joint Chiefs endorsed exerting economic and political pressure on Spain and Portugal, though it should be applied gradually. That was enough for Patterson: "There is an opportunity for effective economic action," he urged, suggesting reducing the Allies' overseas supplies to Spain beginning with petrol and cereals. Hull, the Secretary of State, as an old Wilsonian idealist, was mindful as well of American public opinion and the press.

Economic rivalries with the US now heightened Britain's problems waging the economic war. During 1941 and '42 cotton, for example, from the sterling area, chiefly Egypt, had supplied all Catalonia's needs. Carceller secured the regime, and himself, by maintaining minimum living standards and staving off labour unrest in Spain's key industrial region. This had given the British leverage at the highest level. But from the beginning of 1943 the Roosevelt Administration was offering Spain American cotton, in response to pressure from US southern states. By September the British share of the Spanish market for cotton was being seriously squeezed. London had again to insist that phosphates from conquered French North Africa – vital to Spanish agriculture – were kept under joint Anglo-American control as a source of much-needed peseta revenue.

Even the cinema was a field of rivalry as Spanish audiences, so long supplied by the Germans and the Italians, were by 1943 eager for British and American films. The British embassy came to the rescue of a British representative, who had been doing well, but now found an American muscling in, offering Spaniards British films as well on the black market. The embassy made one of its forays into the "parallel market" to obtain pesetas for sterling at a favourable rate and so subsidize the undercutting of the American. "We have never considered it necessary or desirable to disclose our financial arrangements or sources of black market pesetas" to the Americans, Yencken told the Foreign Office afterwards, "nor do we expect to be told of their transactions". For obvious reasons this file[4] too was suppressed under the 50-year rule. Leslie Howard, star of Alexander Korda's *The Scarlet Pimpernel*, visited Spain and Portugal to give a propaganda boost that summer and so stimulate box office returns for British films, and help peseta needs. On the homeward journey he perished when his aircraft was shot down over the Atlantic by the Luftwaffe after a tip-off from German intelligence.

Petrol became ground for serious divergences between Britain and America over markets as well as over how to utilize the petrol "weapon" over Spain. British companies had been well established on Spain prior to the Civil War for petroleum and for fuel for ships in the Canaries, then one of the largest bunkering stations in the world. Shell had managed to get itself re-admitted to the Spanish market in 1942. But subsequently, although Spain's state oil concern Campsa wanted to diversify its sources, the British oilmen found themselves squeezed by Standard Oil/Esso. By 1943 British officials were obliged to play a secondary role in running the network, set up the year before by a corps of US oil attachés, for the control of oil imports to Spain and their distribution around the country. In petrol as elsewhere it was no longer an affair between allies as equals: one of the starkest statistics of the Allied war effort shows that of the nearly seven billion barrels of petroleum produced for wartime use between 1942 and

'45 six billion came from American producers.[5] Although the British
looked more favourably on supplying Spain's expanding oil requirements –
for the sake of the peseta revenue – the Spaniards knew the Americans were
the bosses and showed them gratitude accordingly.

What level to set for the Franco regime's oil needs was a constant topic
of debate between the two Allies. With the oil attachés, and the navi-certs,
the Allies enjoyed a degree of control over Spain's economy which contra-
dicts the Foreign Office's profession of non-interference in Spain's internal
affairs. The judgment Allied war-time controls over the Spanish economy
were indeed "unique" is made by a team of Spanish post-Franco economists:
they quote a confidential report by General Fernando Roldán, the Petrol
Commissioner, complaining Spain was being kept in a state of permanent
insecurity. Spain could never obtain written guarantees from American officials on fuel supplies, he told the Foreign Ministry.[6] By mid 1943 the US
Chiefs of Staff estimated, and the British Chiefs endorsed the view, that
Spain's minimum petrol requirements would be met by supplying 100,000
tons a quarter. Both countries' soldiers specifically stated they saw "no military disadvantage" in restricting Spain in view of recent Allied successes.[7]
The chiefs' figures are important for they strongly suggest American and
British politicians had a margin for cutting back on Spain's imports without endangering the Franco regime or provoking the disorders or "chaos"
the diplomats believed, or professed to believe, threatened. Speaking in
Barcelona in February, Hayes had bluntly told the Spaniards they were
enjoying higher levels of civilian petrol consumption than in any other
European country.[8] His remarks caused an uproar in the US where public
opinion was incensed by the thought American-produced petrol was bene-
fiting Franco's anti-democratic regime – and, thanks to his duplicity, the
Axis as well. In 1942 Spain's consumption for the whole year amounted to
330,000 tons. The Spaniards had been pushing to obtain more petrol, sending more of their tankers to the US and, of course, the oil majors would not
refuse more trade: the "nominated" vessels might even be on the high seas
before the State Department reacted. By May '43 the quarterly figure for
Spanish oil imports had reached 135,000 tons, i.e. 540,000 tons annually.

"Fantastically Costly"

The Allies had got themselves into a fundamental contradiction: they
wanted to sell more petrol to Spain to be able to go on with the stagger-
ingly expensive policy of pre-emptive purchases of wolfram. "Our great
difficulty is to find goods [from the sterling area] to balance Allied

purchases in Spain. Petroleum is one of our greatest assets," as Roberts had confessed that spring.[9] The wolfram pre-emptive buying had handed the Franco regime the opportunity to augment the production levels at Spanish mines.

By the summer of '43 that trade had reached crisis proportions for the Allies. The Americans first tried upping the price for Spanish oil imports in a bid to obtain more pesetas for the pre-emptive buying. But for Britain, which had first initiated that will o' the wisp policy and then persuaded the Americans to join in, that ploy was not enough – and by a long way. Wolfram had become by 1943 Spain's biggest single foreign exchange earner. It helped Spain significantly to increase its imports of petrol which went from £2 million in 1942 to $4.2 million in the following year.[10] Such figures give a measure of the contribution wolfram made to the build up of the Franco regime economically – and of failures in Allied policy.

"We are faced with a very serious financial situation," Hoare had to report to London in July.[11] "What's all this?" Eden minuted his officials, as if almost instinctively wary of Hoare's signals. But Spain had vastly augmented its production of wolfram which the Allies had to buy. Before the Civil War some 40 tons a year came from Spanish mines, selling at around £300 a ton. Production was of only marginal character.[12] It was German buying in Portugal, which also produced the mineral, after the world war began which first alerted the British to the significance wolfram was playing in Hitler's war effort. By 1942 the US government agreed to embark upon pre-emptive buying of strategic war materials with Britain, with their newly set up Commercial Corporation (USCC) working alongside the UK state trading concern (UKCC). The Americans found Spanish wolfram production and prices rocketing: by November 1942 it had reached a level of 3,000 tons a year and the Spanish prices were well over ten times those of Bolivia, another wolfram producer. By the next year production was running some months at a rate of between 4,000 and 5,000 tons annually. Prices by May had reached £6,200 a ton, plus a £2,000 production tax the Spanish Treasury had slapped on from February. By July, when Hoare startled London, prices went even higher to £8,000 a ton – "fantastically costly," as Selborne, the Minister of Economic Warfare who in peace-time had made money in the cement business, admitted.

Projections in London, when preparing for the July–December supply/purchase programme for Spain, were that wolfram purchases would in 1943 account, alone, for £9,300,000 of the total of £10,868,000 to be spent by Britain on buying war material in Spain. Wolfram was providing extraordinary revenue for the Spanish Treasury, handsome profits for many hundreds of smaller, and some big, mine-owners, the middlemen and a living for thousands of labourers in the impoverished region of Galicia – and all due to a battle between the Allies and the Axis over who should get the raw material.

British policy-makers aggravated the problem by making the wolfram supply from the Iberian peninsula in 1943 into the overriding objective of the economic warfare policy. Between October '42 and September '43, the figures later showed, Britain purchased 2,397 tons of wolfram in Spain at a cost of £9,688.000.[13] This was without a further £4,574,000 Britain was liable for with the Spanish Treasury. Britain's entire exports to Spain for 1943 were, however, expected to reach only £13,390,000. In June '43 British exports to Spain were only worth £266,000, whereas they were supposed to reach £1 million a month. A very serious financial situation indeed. In June and July the British found themselves purchasing record amounts of over 500 tons of wolfram a month: according to projections made previously by Hugh Ellis Rees, the Treasury's man seconded to war-time Madrid, these should have been 240 and 400 tons respectively.[14] Carceller had simply "allowed" them to buy more. By August a perplexed Ministry of Economic Warfare official in London conceded: "Spanish production [has been] going up by leaps and bounds, thanks solely to our purchasing . . . We see no prospect of financing expenditure of this magnitude at £8,000 a ton indefinitely."[15] Britain and the United States were doing nothing more than purchasing Spain's greatly increased wolfram supply, and not reducing their enemy's purchases. A document in the form of a copy to the FO of a telegram from the State Department, suppressed under the 50-year rule until 1994, contains reluctant admission by both the US Office of Economic Warfare and the MEW of these facts.[16]

In this payments crisis, for that is what it was, Britain and the US felt there was no alternative but to sell Spain gold to get the pesetas – not withstanding the Inter Allied Declaration aimed at the neutrals. The British pressured the Americans who reluctantly agreed to joint operations from August.[17] Carceller told the friendly disposed Ellis Rees that Spain's gold deposits were needed for "post-war problems" – frank admission enough. The deposits, it was agreed, were to be transferred in part physically to Spain and the rest to be kept in the Bank of England's vaults, and become available to Spain "as soon as cessation of hostilities between the UK and Germany or circumstances permit".[18] In the wake of the "Nazi gold" controversy in the 1990s more light was shed regarding Spain's war-time gold purchases from Switzerland. The gold reserves of the Instituto Español de Moneda Extranjera (IEME), the state body which controlled all foreign exchange transactions by Spaniards, and deposited with the Bank of Spain, stood by 1945 at over 75 million dollars. Expressed by countries purchased from the 5,661 lingots held by IEME at the war's end 3,181 were from the Swiss National Bank and 1,226 from the Bank of England.[19] When dealing with IEME, whose board meetings were chaired by Carceller, London sought to keep the Spanish Foreign Ministry in the dark "to avoid publicity". One transfer in October, worth £2½ million, was routed via Seville where the consul was pronounced "accustomed to dealing with special transactions".[20] At the beginning of 1944 the FO signalled to Madrid a transfer of gold worth £1 million was coming. This was in answer to a request for further tranches of gold by Hoare in order to pay almost £600,000 (at the official sterling/ peseta rate) still outstanding on wolfram purchases, plus taxes, from the previous August and September.[21]

"The more we bought, the more there was to buy" was Herbert Feis' succinct summing up, post-war, of the Allies' wolfram "war".[22] But the most remarkable aspect of the battle has not been mentioned – from April to August 1943 the Germans absented themselves from Spain's wolfram market for large-scale purchases because of the Spaniards swingeing export tax. The Germans limited their purchases to three sources: the fossickers, working for themselves, clandestine purchases from a well-developed smugglers' network and to supplies obtained with connivance of the Spanish military, the Consejo Ordenador de Minerales de Interés Militar (COMEIM). This body could requisition wolfram supplies or obtain them from existing stocks without any outside supervision, even the US attachés were barred here. A meeting of the Anglo-American economic committee, the joint body which was supposed to decide tactics in the wolfram "war", calculated in December that Britain in the first 11 months of 1943 purchased 2,563 tons of wolfram while Germany had obtained 1,186 tons in spite of being absent from large-scale purchases for over three months.[23] Taken with the 2,000 tons allotted by Portugal for the year, that was enough for German needs.

The position of Portugal, over the whole war actually a bigger producer of wolfram, is interesting for it underlines how obsessed the British policymakers became with Spanish wolfram. In contrast to Carceller's freeing prices as the Allied embarked on ever bigger purchases, Salazar had from 1942 set up a quota system for official supplies, with allocations for both Germany and the Allies, to which he kept despite British pressure. Many of the mines in Portugal were British-owned and prices, though inflated to take a neutral country's advantage of the two belligerents, were less than the Spanish free-for-all: That encouraged smuggling across the frontier into Spain to take advantage of the higher rewards. Britain preferred to turn a blind eye and, by 1943, to concentrate on obtaining the Azores bases agreement from Portugal.

"I am fully alive to the importance of continuing with the wolfram purchase programme," Eden wrote in response to Hoare's sounding the alarm.[24] But the Foreign Secretary gave no detailed attention to that summer's acute wolfram payments crisis, nor did he make any policy input. The Foreign Office knew at that time from a senior Ministry of Production official that Britain "could probably manage with less wolfram from the peninsula than we are now getting under the pre-emption programme". With those record purchase levels by Britain in June and July, and while the Germans were still absent from the main markets for wolfram, that was a highly significant admission.[25]

Hoare, who had swiftly perceived how Spain's Commerce and Industry Minister would respond to Britain's "stick and carrot" policies in 1940, made a serious misjudgment about him in the wolfram battle. Carceller was only turning the screw. With his participation in the Santa Comba mine, opened in 1942 and which became Spain's biggest single wolfram producer, Carceller personally stood to gain from the bonanza as well as the Spanish Treasury.

During that summer and early autumn Ellis Rees became the British embassy's man handling all the intricate financial and trading operations with Spain. An Inland Revenue inspector recruited by the Treasury at the beginning of the world war, he rocketed to the same temporary importance Eccles had achieved, though in the difficult days of 1940–41. With the MEW's backing, Ellis Rees sought to make policy in a big way and the Foreign Office, and Hoare, let him. "It was agreed that ordinary orthodox blockade considerations must not be allowed to stand in the way of increased sterling earnings," one senior official at the MEW had briefed him. [26] When Rees broached the highly political issue of talking post-war trade with Carceller it was the Board of Trade which stepped in to rebuke him. It was "quite out of the question to discuss post-war commercial policy with a neutral, and least of all Spain," the Foreign Office was told.[27] The British government had not yet opened discussions with even the USA on the matter. The Board of Trade man had shown the greater political acumen. Carceller had eagerly taken up Rees, lunching and meeting him frequently, since he had gone naïvely to Spain's economics supremo and told him "frankly" of Britain's peseta needs for the wolfram battle. Spain was prepared, Carceller said, to grant "generously" the licences now needed. But Rees' proposal went farther, asking Carceller to arrange peseta credits for Britain to spend on wolfram against a promise of deliveries of British manufactured goods to Spain post-war. The US stepped in to veto any such deal.

As he ventured deeper into Carceller's spider's web Rees was pressed by José María Lapuerta, the Minister's deputy, to get the British government to agree to supplying arms to Spain.[28] The Under Secretary at Commerce and Industry indicated the Franco regime needed well-equipped armed forces for keeping internal order. Hoare squashed that suggestion, despite the desperate search for pesetas, for obvious political reasons. Herbert Morrison, the Labour Home Secretary, had already got on to Eden, warning against any such idea[29] after he had spotted a reference in a telegram from the British Consul-General in Tangiers to a local Spanish official's soundings on Spain's need of weapons "to put down internal troubles" as the end of the war approached. Pursuing a policy to take a neutrals' advantage of the war to acquire foreign assets, Carceller sought to buy out the shareholders of the British company which had owned the Santander-Mediterranean Railway, seized by the Franco regime in 1941, and, a much bigger plum, the Barcelona Light and Traction Company. Only the former deal went through by November '43.

Sometimes the Allied efforts to stop the Germans getting their hands on Spanish wolfram reached ludicrous proportions. To stop the clandestine passing of Portuguese wolfram across the frontier, "selective smuggling operations" were secretly set up and financed by the official British and American purchasing corporations, managing to whisk away some 20 tons a month from Portugal by sea to Gibraltar. It was estimated some 60 tons of wolfram were crossing into Galicia from Portugal. The FO file on the meeting between Rees and his US counterpart which decided on the "official smuggling" was suppressed under the 50-year rule.[30] Among the skulduggery countenanced was the use of black market pesetas – previously only the Allies' secret services risked frequenting such dealers – to bribe Spanish officials working with the Axis to permit sabotaging the lorries transporting, or warehouses holding, the wolfram as well as rewarding anyone reporting on Germany's smuggling plans. A Foreign Office document, also kept secret under the 50-year rule, shows the British embassy seeking to get rid of blocked sterling, by-passing the War Trade Agreement clearing accounts, for pesetas on the black market – and haggling with shady dealers for a favourable rate. As the FO told Rees,[31] who was to supervise the operation: "To take any unfavourable rate for a substantial quantity of pesetas, which cannot be justified to the Spanish authorities, is rather like getting the worst of both worlds. We should much prefer not to use this kind of source, with its attendant risks, unless the rate is attractive i.e. 60 or better [pesetas to the £]." The official exchange rate was then only 41 peseta to the £. The official rate set by the Franco regime for sterling against the peseta was widely recognized as discriminatory, compared to that for the dollar and the Reichsmark. Britain had to bear it until, after a two-year-long fight, the Spanish government agreed to 45 pesetas to the £ in November '43.

Arms from Germany

The secret August deal Franco had personally fixed up with the Germans to supply Spain with modern arms and equipment was of major importance for securing the regime against those future "internal troubles" Spanish officials had talked about. Spain's armaments purchases went from £3.7 million in 1942 to £7.9m.in '43 and were to reach over £11m. by 1944, according to calculations on IEME figures.[32] Security through repression was General Franco's No. 1 priority.

The Allies only found out about the arms deal in mid September. The upcoming arms deliveries would clearly put the Germans in peseta funds if they wanted to re-enter Spain's wolfram market in a big way. That autumn Carceller arranged for the repayment of a second tranche of Spain's Civil War debts in order to make sure the Germans had an extra RM 100 million to continue its buying rivalry with the Allies. Three-quarters of this sum was immediately passed to the German state trading organization Sofindus running the wolfram purchases programme.

When Yencken, the British Minister, saw Jordana that autumn he asked: "Was prolonging the world war really in Spain's interest?"[33] Wolfram had become a "vital issue" in the war, the Minister emphasized, and Spain was no longer in danger from the Germans. He got nowhere when he also saw Vicente Taberna, the Foreign Ministry official in charge of economic affairs. Taberna was another of those Spaniards in high places believed to be friendly towards Britain. He had been buttered up by the MEW seeking to send him "a few suit lengths and shirt materials from Bond Street". But the Board of Trade allowed only the suit lengths. The MEW maintained the suit lengths would create "a very favourable impression" among Spanish officials.[34]

With evidence of Franco's refusal to adopt a more friendly attitude towards the Allies here was an opportunity for Eden, ever suspicious of Franco and exploding earlier in the year over "that stinging jellyfish Spanish gratitude", to order his officials to make some robust response. An important internal shift in Britain's trading policy to Franco Spain had in fact occurred, but was submitted to by the Foreign Office. "We are doing very much more than supply Spain's minimum economic needs, which has been the political objective hitherto," the desk officer for Spain observed, going on revealingly: "In future, the case must rest on the needs for funds for essential supplies and pre-emptive purchases. The political case is no longer strong." The FO was letting the MEW have the driving seat and push other departments – a complete reversal of what had happened in 1940. Eden did not seize the opportunity, and from the papers on Spain's arms deal with Germany there is no evidence that he even read them. So Roberts, without any input from his Foreign Secretary, lamely minuted: "Let's ask the Treasury and MEW." With things now under its sway, the MEW instructed the Madrid embassy directly: "We do not think we should be frightened . . . by the possibility of Germany re-entering the [wolfram] market." Under Selborne, two senior posts at the MEW were held by British bankers, yet surprisingly little sense was shown of the vulnerability of Spain's economy. The search was always on for any signs of Spanish "goodwill" towards the Allies. The MEW was telling the Foreign Office the Spaniards would turn "mulish" if economic pressure was applied. "Yes, but if the Spanish government turn mulish there will be no obligation on HMG to feed the mule," Eden did this time minute his officials.[35] Though the Foreign Secretary's personal feelings were sometimes quite clear, he unfortunately failed to clothe them in policy – or then get his officials to implement it.

With MEW views prevailing in London, Rees could go on searching for ways to stimulate Anglo-Spanish trade. He chose Spain's traditional orange exports. This was in its way symbolic, for oranges, which made up 70 per cent of Spain's agricultural exports, had gone largely to Germany in the early war years as the Axis was winning. Rees responded eagerly to Carceller's suggestions – who clearly had the future, i.e. post-war, considerations in mind. The MEW took the view that Germany's economic pressure on Spain had been heavy-handed and had got them nowhere. It followed, simplistically, that the "right" policy for Britain would be to maintain the flow of supplies without making the Spaniards any conditions.[36] After a visit that autumn to London, where his repetition of Carceller's arguments showed how far he had become the Spanish economics supremo's mouthpiece, Rees returned with word the Ministry of Food wanted to buy "large quantities" of Spanish oranges, onions and dried fruit. He held out to Carceller the prospect of £4 to £5 million to be spent by Britain – though, of course, it could not "at present" find exports to Spain on a corresponding scale.[37] As Rees put it, when talking to the head of IEME, London's trade policy had been "to give Spain the chance of an independent economic existence, we would continue to do so and I saw no reason why we should not do so after the war".[38] Rees was venturing deep into making foreign policy again. Both Churchill and Eden were still backing the policy Britain "had pursued for the last three years". Britain had "a permanent interest" in having Spain "undisturbed", this war-time Treasury official contended in a memorandum he wrote for the MEW's chief representative in Washington that October.[39]

As negotiations began for a British purchasing programme from December '43 to March '44 of oranges and onions worth £2m. an internal report leaked to Rees by Valencia's orange-growers pleaded with the Spanish authorities that the English market represented "the only possible hope" for that region now the Germans were taking much less. The low purchasing power of Spaniards meant the growers could not look to the internal market to save them, they contended. But when the deal was concluded the prices of Spanish oranges, already above those for South African or Jaffa oranges, had been jacked up still further, and was knowingly accepted by the British government. There was "appeasement" even for Spanish oranges. Spain's Banco Exterior, in which Carceller had an interest, was moreover made the designated bank for the oranges transaction, replacing the Bank of London and South America.

The Roosevelt Administration disliked what it saw of the British turning to "traditional trade", perceiving the longer-term significance of that policy. It was helping to build up the Franco regime. Several prominent officials in the State Department still wanted to keep Spain on a tight leash. The Secretary of State had himself stated in May, and the policy remained unchanged, that the US would not supply Spain beyond her "minimum essential needs" and he had instructed Hayes in Madrid to act accordingly.[40] Halifax had to report what he saw and heard in Washington: there were wide divergences between the two Allies; the American government had never been wholly satisfied by the economic arguments alone, he said, which MEW in London had pursued. Wolfram purchases had been seen as a way, though expensive, to reward Spain's abstention in the war; by the autumn of 1943 they were no longer necessary, or affordable, in Washington's view.

Immediate Embargo

On 10 November the Americans demanded an immediate embargo on all wolfram exports to Germany by Spain.[41] The emphasis was put on Allied war needs. America's resources were directed to winning the war in the shortest possible time and its "economic programmes with neutral countries must contribute to that objective", a statement said. Then came a direct warning to Spain: purchases of wolfram could cease at any time; they were not required by the US for arms production. Wolfram purchases had, "attained such figures that the USA finds it necessary carefully to weigh whether it can also permit entry of those other Spanish commodities which enter into traditional commerce, none of which are essential to the present wartime economy of the US".[42] A substantial increase in Spain's exports of non-essential commodities had occurred in recent months, yet the US had hesitated to impose controls "which would adversely affect several branches of the Spanish economy". Hayes advised Jordana an immediate prohibition of wolfram exports to all countries would make it "unnecessary to restrict imports from Spain".

None of this was really a surprise to either Jordana or Carceller. Seeing the Foreign Minister in mid October the US envoy had emphasized how Spain's economy had experienced a substantial improvement from its wartime trading arrangements with the USA, Britain and other countries in the Americas. "If it desires to continue trade with the US, it should take steps to reduce its trade with Germany, especially in foodstuffs and strategic materials," Hayes warned. [43] For the first time, the US envoy referred the Spaniards directly to the petrol supplied by the Allies and always kept under strict review.

When seeing the Spanish ambassador in Washington later in the month Hull emphasized how "extremely important" it was that the Madrid government "act at once favourably to US requests".[44] Armed with the US statement, Jordana warned Franco's Cabinet that Spain's wolfram bonanza might be coming to an abrupt end. Many of the Ministers were still pro-German, but Jordana told them the political aspects of the wolfram business were, in the light of Allied victories, getting "every day more delicate". Carceller spelt out Spain's huge vested interests in the business, boasting earnings for the year up to November '43 from wolfram exports totalled 1,500 million pesetas (£33m. at the adjusted official exchange rate). This figure included 600 million pesetas to the Spanish Treasury alone. The minister might well have also spoken of the massive profiteering since the Spanish authorities had never done anything to curb prices.

The Americans' demand for a wolfram embargo was admission the pre-emptive purchasing programme had failed. The Franco regime had to be obliged to stop the exports. In November Germany had re-embarked on large-scale buying operations. That meant "all the more need for us to stop the wolfram business", as Hayes observed.[45] Thanks to the massive increase in production by Spanish mines, the Germans obtained 927 tons in 1943, against 254 tons during '42.[46] The Allies had in '43 to buy, regardless of their needs, 3,035 tons of Spanish wolfram, plus their share, of course, of Portugal's production. When the "wolfram battle" came to be reviewed by cooler heads post-war, the pre-emptive programme was seen as a massive waste of Allied resources. Spanish economists and historians of the post-Franco era, as well as at least one US senior war-time official in retrospect, Dean Acheson, are unanimous that until the land frontier with France was sealed after D-Day 1944 Germany was not stopped from obtaining the minimum necessary quantities of wolfram. [47] Even after that small consignments went from Spain by air to Germany, often with Spanish military assistance. At the end of the war the Allies found the Germans had an estimated one and a half years' stock of unused wolfram. Worse, much of what Britain had purchased from Spain during the war was pronounced by the Ministry of Supply post-war as of such poor quality it was simply uneconomic for British smelters in peacetime.

The US government knew the Franco regime was at that juncture facing severe difficulties over food supplies. The harvest had failed and Madrid had approached the Americans in October about delivery of 100,000 tons of US wheat. At first the State Department thought of linking delivery to Spain's embargoing wolfram exports to Germany. But that idea fell through and the US government took the harder line with the Hayes démarche after the so-called Laurel incident. Franco's Foreign Ministry had sent a congratulatory telegram to the head of a Japanese puppet government in the Philippines, incensing American public opinion at such an unfriendly act by an evidently still pro-Axis regime in Madrid.

Franco, though wrong-footed by this absurd gesture recalling Serrano's days at the Foreign Ministry, played characteristically for time over the Americans' demand for an embargo. After telling Hayes not to "point a pistol at the Spaniards' head", Jordana got down to discussing with Franco and Carceller the underlying problem of being obliged to choose between petrol from America and wolfram for Germany. Spain was anxious to reach a decision, as Jordana put it euphemistically to the US envoy, "not impairing the Spanish economy". [48] The Foreign Ministry argued that the "vigilant neutrality" Spain had officially switched to early October meant that stopping wolfram exports solely to Germany would be an unneutral act. More frankly, Carceller confessed to Ralph Ackerman, the US Economics Counsellor, with whom he was having lengthy conversations, how troubled he was about the effect on Spain's public finances if the embargo were implemented. He knew, of course, the situation of the mines as well: several Spanish mine-owners were already seeking to sell out to German or Allied buyers; one of the biggest owners was looking to starting up tin mining in Bolivia on his profits. Yet the Allied purchases of wolfram from Spain still went on, and amounted that November alone to 353 tons, i.e. at an annual rate of 4,000 tons. [49]

The reaction in London to the Americans' demand came down to temporizing, rather like Franco. The MEW went on repeating the mantra that any conditioning of trade with Spain was counter-productive. Rees had already volunteered to Ackerman (and subsequently informed London) "not to count on us in any way [for] a reversal of policy on the supply programme" to Spain.[50] The FO concurred, Roberts minuting he preferred the Treasury man's views on the tactics for handling the Spaniards "to those of his less experienced and less subtle US colleague".

Hoare's own reaction in Madrid was more subtle. He let Rees play his hand while the Treasury man had London's backing, but the ambassador-politician had his reservations that summer, though he kept them almost private. By November, however, and reacting like the sensitive politician he was to the Americans' move, he told the MEW directly of his doubts: in a word, the futility of the pre-emptive programme. "The Spanish government," he wrote,[51] "obviously wants the belligerents to go on buying [wolfram] . . . It is disturbing we are having to deal with new production . . . we are still obliged to buy considerable quantities without reducing the amounts falling into German hands. Without any contrary advice from you or Washington, we have felt obliged to continue with these purchases." Hoare added, pointedly enough, that it would be "of great value" to hear the Foreign Office's views. A few days later, and as the US government waited on a response from Spain, the ambassador probed again, reminding London of a policy statement which had gone disregarded that Britain, like the US, had no supply interest in wolfram. Hoare had evolved, after cynical handling by the Franco regime, from his initial hopes of success for a pre-emptive programme. But the Foreign Office had not, and when it saw the Roosevelt Administration was in earnest about the wolfram embargo temporized. After hearing out Hoare, London instructed Halifax: "Agree for the time being you should in consultation with US colleagues keep up the pressure on the Spanish government to return a favourable reply to the US memorandum. When reply received we can reconsider the position."[52]

A Dissenting Voice

There was, however, one dissenting voice among the band of self-satisfied diplomats and officials in London who decided policy towards Franco Spain. John Alexander, junior to the rest in the strict hierarchy Cadogan demanded at the Foreign Office, became even more of an outsider with his awkward criticisms of the MEW's wolfram policy. Alexander was just come back from

a first secretary's posting in Washington, where he had picked up something of America's principled dislike of Franco Spain. He was soon to leave
London to join in May '44 the nascent United Nations Relief and
Rehabilitation Administration (UNRRA). In the debate on how to react to
the Americans' demand of an embargo by Spain his comment was clear-cut.
"We have no reason to be so tender with Spain," Alexander submitted, "if
the Americans get what they want, so much the better; if not, at least we
shall have another complaint to chalk up on the debit side for the day we
come to settle accounts [with Spain]."[53] Hoare, he recommended, must
support the US move "vigorously" in Madrid.

Alexander had already attacked the muddled thinking on "pre-empting"
Germany's purchases of wolfram from Spain. If the Germans were shunning
large-scale purchases it must mean they did not want it so much; if, on the
other hand, they were to show that they needed it badly it would be "essential to stop them getting it by all means in our power. This should include
withholding wheat, petroleum, etc. and making up our supply [needs] from
other sources".[54] Present British policy, Alexander argued, had the ultimate
effect of leaving the choice of lifting, or not lifting, vast quantities of
wolfram from Spain . . . to the Germans. There was a row between the
unconventionally-minded young diplomat and Roberts, acting head of
Central Department, full of confidence after the Azores Agreement. When
Hoare reported mid December there was still no reply by Spain to Hayes'
move, Roberts tackled Alexander's complaint of British "tenderness"
towards Franco Spain head on: "Carceller, thanks to judicious handling by
Ellis Rees, has done much more for us than for the Germans over the past
three years. The simple American approach to the Spanish problem has yet
to register a success in Madrid."[55] Roberts overlooked the fact Spain's
exports to Germany in 1943 attained almost double the value of those that
year to Britain.[56] An export drive had taken place, despite all the Allied
economic appeasement, to supply Germany with foodstuffs and raw materials for its war. In view of Carceller's connivance with the Germans his
praise borders on the absurd.

Alexander pointed his finger at a more serious issue for British policy-
makers. "The great danger seems to be in antagonizing the Americans,
which is far worse than the Spaniards, or even the Portuguese, and this point
might be made to MEW," he minuted.[57] Roberts was provoked beyond his
habitual cool – perhaps that "even the Portuguese" was too much for him.
The department head at the Foreign Office produced one of the vividest
expressions of diplomatic rivalry with the USA, before the post-war re-
dimensioning of British foreign policy set in. "The fundamental difficulty
with the Americans is that we know much more than they do about Spain

and Portugal, and they rather resent having to play second fiddle, particularly locally at Madrid and Lisbon." Roberts went on serenely: "We always do our best to respect their point of view, when it is not calculated to harm our – and their – interests in the peninsula. There is no danger of a major clash between us – at all events at present." The "Yanks" following Britain's lead was the role the FO always dreamed about, and still tried to pursue in spite of the seismic changes in power the war was bringing.

To puncture that "the British always know best" pose there came a rebuke from a most unexpected quarter – the Ministry of Economic Warfare. On Christmas Eve a top official wrote irately to Roberts: "The Spaniards have done nothing to keep exports of Spanish wolfram to Germany down to a low level. HMG have managed to keep them down to a fairly low level by pre-emption at an immense expense."[58] In reality, that was admission of defeat of the policy to put down no conditions when trading with Carceller and his business cronies. The UKCC had taken 2,563 tons of wolfram in the first 11 months of 1943, 353 in November alone. Rees' efforts to get the Spaniards' production curbed, and to be more "vigilant" over smuggling the wolfram for the Germans into France, had got almost nowhere.

When therefore on 30 December Halifax reported Washington's belief, based on Hayes' reporting from Madrid, that the chances of the Franco regime agreeing to an embargo on all wolfram exports were now "very faint unless some further action [be] taken"[59] there was simply no alternative for the Allies but to throttle back those petrol supplies vital to the Franco's regime's survival. With the food crisis unresolved, the prospects looked good for applying such pressure. But would the British agree?

6

Churchill Intervenes I
January–September, 1944

A major diplomatic dispute over Spain between Britain and the United States occurred in the first half of 1944, the second of the pivotal years for Franco and his regime. The dispute gave one of the first clear expressions of policy differences between America in its rise to world power status and Britain's corresponding descent. Economic interests meant far more was at stake than the Iberian peninsula. The chief of these rival interests, oil, was at the heart of the Allies' disagreement as the Roosevelt Administration at the end of January stopped petrol supplies from reaching Spain in a bid to force Franco to embargo all exports of wolfram to Germany. The British government sought to "mediate" – appease in American eyes – and so win advantages for what were held to be British interests in Spain.

The Allies' dispute, which was only settled in a messy way by May, may have been played out in departmental memoranda and diplomatic feints between London and Washington, but it was tough enough to be remembered keenly in the protagonists' post-war memoirs. The extent of Churchill's differences with the Americans was laid bare. "All of us bitterly resented the British refusal to cooperate," Dean Acheson, the former Secretary of State, then Assistant Secretary, at the State Department, recalled years later. "The 'Former Naval Person' {Churchill} could be as stubbornly set on retreat as upon standing fast," the American judged unambiguously. Because of the determination of the Franco regime, which introduced petrol rationing with uncharacteristic swiftness, the dispute ended abruptly when the British Prime Minister outsmarted Cordell Hull, the US Secretary of State. Churchill committed himself, alone, to resuming petrol shipments to Spain. He secured in return only a grudging reduction by Spain of exports of wolfram to Germany – the legal exports that is, for clandestine smuggling of the war material continued with Carceller's connivance right up until France was liberated in August. When the petrol re-started, the Americans had to scramble to re-assert their control over supplies to the Spanish market – which were largely American-produced anyway.

Churchill's personal intervention with Roosevelt had lasting, adverse consequences for Britain. The settlement gave further incentive to an America already seeking to promote its own economic interests in Spain and elsewhere in the world. The American oil majors led the way. The defeat of the US policy-makers like Hull and Acheson over Spain helped to bring on a shift of power in Washington, which was entirely unfavourable to Britain. The Prime Minister initially told Eden to go along with the American demand for a complete ban on wolfram exports by Spain, and Eden even suggested adding exports of cotton, vital to the Catalan textile industry, as further means to bring pressure on Franco. It was the Foreign Office which readied the arguments for whenever Churchill's mood changed, as it often did where Spain was concerned. Britain's diplomats resented an American policy lead over Spain. Hoare this time worked in agreement with Churchill, instead of standing aside, and soon got caught up with the dispute within the Spanish government between the Foreign Minister Jordana and the still pro-Axis ministers, headed by Asensio, the Army Minister, over how they should handle the "no petrol unless no wolfram for Germany" imbroglio. Hoare was finally instructed by the FO to go behind the back of his US colleague Hayes on the excuse that the American professor was often in disagreement with his instructions from State. The British statesman showed a lack of nerve throughout the petrol crisis in contrast with his striking performance in Madrid in the summer of 1940. The "wolfram war" in '43 had worn him down, and he had grown, erroneously, to trust Jordana.

The Foreign Office's counter-argument of Britain's requirement of raw materials from Spain suddenly became an overriding consideration when seized upon by the Prime Minister. Distracted by the diplomatic battle, no one in London perceived that neither Franco, nor Carceller, could have any interest in augmenting the regime's already severe economic difficulties by further losses of revenue. Franco's stopping of the wolfram exports to Germany immediately after the Americans suspended petrol supplies, represented admission of the economic vulnerability of his regime vis-à-vis the Allies, whose eloquence ought to have been sufficient for any policy-maker. Here were economic facts which Britain's leaders of the day were untrained to appreciate.

The British Prime Minister's speech in the House of Commons on 24 May when, as one American commentator put it, Churchill "celebrated" publicly his satisfaction with the settlement he had engineered, provoked another round of suspicion about Britain and its empire in the US, both within the Administration and public opinion. Eden did not share the Prime Minister's satisfaction, and was correct when he commented gloomily to Hoare of Allied disagreements: "Our recent troubles over Spain are by no means unique."

Wavering Support

Churchill was uncertain how to handle the Americans' "suspension" of petrol exports when it was made known to the Spaniards on 28 January. In a personal minute to Eden he observed: "It is not an unreasonable position for the United States to take that if the Dons want American oil they should stop sending wolfram to Germany. I am not at all sure that they may not give in."[1] In the light of his subsequent stand, and how determinedly he argued with President Roosevelt over the matter, that initial assessment shows how Churchill's judgments on Spain could waver. "I am sending you this," the Prime Minister indeed added, "because on the telephone this morning I gave rather an opposite indication." Of course, as a master-politician, Churchill found the words to justify his switch. "I am coming round to the view that the US have now come so far out into the open against Spain that it is too late and would be a mistake to try and upset their rough treatment . . . Anyhow, I see great disadvantages in the 'blow hot, blow cold' process."

Hoare in Madrid was instructed by Eden to support the American position. The Foreign Secretary declined a suggestion Churchill volunteered that, as Prime Minister, he might "say something" to Roosevelt. Nonetheless, Churchill did get on to the President, observing that now the US had taken "such decided action" Britain would give all the assistance it could and Hoare had been told to "align himself with your representative" in Madrid.[2] The promise was to be soon forgotten. Even Cadogan apparently agreed about supporting the US suspension when he saw Alba[3] after the news was out. Acheson, the Assistant Secretary of State, had told Spain's ambassador in Washington no loadings would be allowed for Spain on 11–12 or 21–22 February. Churchill, though his fingers itched to get in on the matter, was prepared to wait and see whether joint Allied pressure through the cut-off of oil supplies might actually persuade Franco to "give in".

The Spanish government had procrastinated throughout December and continued doing so during January. When the oil suspension came, Jordana feigned surprise to Hayes,[4] even though the chief US petroleum attaché in Madrid had sensed that General Roldán, in charge of all Spain's requirements and supplies of energy, had "some inkling" when meeting him six days before.[5]

The Franco regime had given no signs since the autumn of 1943 of any real shift in attitude despite the course of the war. By January disappointment, exasperation was perhaps not too strong a term, had become acute in the Foreign Office. A series of wartime grievances showing how the dictator was still sympathizing with Nazi Germany festered; the uncurbed activities of German agents in Spain against Allied interests was the most flagrant. An explanation for Franco's conduct was given the Americans "off the record" in Tangiers by the political adviser to Orgaz, the High Commissioner in Spanish Morocco. The Spanish government was "a government of generals notoriously unfamiliar with the world outside; their primary preoccupation was maintaining themselves in power". Many of them could not see how, in the event of an Allied victory, they could survive.[6] An evolution towards the Allies had been much slower than he had hoped, the Spanish diplomat confessed. Franco's ambiguity was well expressed in his handling of German spies. They would be ordered to leave Tangiers, say, as the Allies had long demanded and then the most experienced among them would be identified, having slipped back into Spain with the connivance of Franco's police. In a new development explosions at Spain's ports would damage the ships loading the oranges for Britain. Under its Germanophile permanent head, José María Doussainague, the Spanish Foreign Ministry, had ruled from November '43 that "firm resistance" must be the stance towards heightened Allied pressure.[7] Here was further justification for the American decision to put a stop to Spain's aiding the German war machine.

Eden was foremost among those indignant about the Spanish attitude. Seeing Alba twice in January he put the pressure on. "We all wanted to end the European war: the Spanish government should make their contribution by delaying or refusing supplies of wolfram [to Germany] to the uttermost," the Foreign Secretary urged.[8] Because of the duke's rapport with Churchill, Eden stressed that the Prime Minister also regretted how things between Britain and Spain had "deteriorated" over the past six months. In both interviews Alba, defending Franco, pressed a series of complaints – about British press coverage of Spain, delays in deliveries to Spain, which only made Eden more irascible. He, too, he said, had long series of complaints to make about Spain's conduct and they were "more serious ones [affecting] the future of Anglo-Spanish relations". As the American suspension began Eden summoned his officials to coordinate policy, commenting: "What next? Looks to me like another turn of the screw. Cotton?"[9]

Carceller was again the key figure. Desperately anxious to secure the supplies of cotton for Catalonia's textile mills, he had asked the Americans for an immediate dispatch of 15,000 tons. But the economics supremo was battling on an even more acute front: cereals for those Spaniards who could not afford recourse to the black market. In a rare admission on paper by any senior figure of the Franco regime of its vulnerability during the world war to popular unrest driven by hunger, Carceller told Jordana: "There exists no problem in Spain so grave, even approximately, as the absolute necessity to carry on importing a minimum of 50,000 tons a month of wheat. Without it, hunger would deal a devastating blow to the great mass of the Spanish people."[10] Spain had just concluded difficult negotiations with Argentina for supplies of cereals, in return, steel exports would go to the South American country despite Spain's own needs.

Carceller during January was desperately pressing the Germans, now in funds, to take more wolfram.

Spain's economic reality was bleak indeed: acute problems with cereal and cotton supplies, loss of wolfram exports revenue and now the cut off in petrol. It is this economic background which should above all be kept in mind when judging how the diplomats, soldiers and politicians from America, Britain and Spain handled the crisis.

On 1 February the Franco regime introduced petrol rationing: all private motoring was forbidden and in Madrid taxis were only allowed to ply on alternate days.[11] Spanish fishermen, among commercial groups, were particularly hard-hit, but, as the US envoy noted, "not the high officials of the Spanish government".[12] Food shortages resulted in Spain's bigger cities and industrial shutdowns in already discontented Catalonia. The Allied diplomats brought in their petrol supplies, and some foodstuffs, from either Gibraltar or Lisbon. Nothing had been done by the regime to prepare the public so, as John Marks, *The Times* correspondent, reported, the restrictions were felt "like a slap in the face", something the regime quickly manipulated as "patriotic indignation". But the regime from 2 February did stop all "official" exports of wolfram to Germany, the centre of the dispute.[13] This step, though it concerned a major economic interest, shows crucially how the Franco regime responded when there was sufficient Allied resolve.

Left No Threat

Under the impact of the Allies' suspension of oil supplies and its implications for the regime, General Antonio Barroso, the politically astute acting Army Chief of Staff, called a meeting of all the heads of Spain's armed forces and the police. General Franco was pronounced "the best man for the job", Barroso afterwards informed Torr, the British military attaché.[14] The monarchy, the generals judged, was "not yet in a position to govern" – a fair comment on Don Juan's immobility. The British Joint Planning Staff were then taking a less flattering view of the Spanish generals. "They are all doing very well financially out of the present regime and have little wish to see it changed until the last possible moment. We suggest we should wait to see the effect on Franco of the economic pressure now being applied before any further steps are discussed."[15] Until 'Overlord' [the Allied landings in Normandy due in June] looked like being a success, the planners argued, there would always be generals ready to support Franco through thick and thin, and neutralize opponents. The planners saw "no solid military advantages in attempting the fall of Franco at present" since no alternative government could be counted upon to be in place before Overlord was launched. After seeing the Spanish Chief of Naval Staff the British naval attaché likewise signalled: "A certain rallying to the regime of otherwise apathetic, if not hostile, opinion is taking place." The telegram, which may have been seen by Churchill, quoted Admiral Arriaga as maintaining the oil embargo showed "a lack of appreciation of Spanish psychology".[16]

Both the British and Spanish Service heads were agreed on one cardinal point at least: the regime was not vulnerable internally to any threat from the Left. There was no evidence, the British planners observed, the Left was "strong or organized enough to take advantage of Franco's weakening position". The Spanish generals could sleep safely at home; their worries concerned, rightly, the regime's vulnerability to external pressure. As in August '43, Britain's military men were less inclined to regard Franco as some kind of inviolable object, or to appease him, than the diplomats. They had kept to their basic anti-Franco views expressed after Mussolini's fall, which Churchill had disregarded. The soldiers' judgment is important and should be balanced against Foreign Office worries of eventual "chaos" down the road if economic sanctions, which is what the petrol suspension was, were continued. It strongly suggests those worries were unfounded.

Eden went into the oil crisis deeply resentful of the uncooperative Spanish attitude and he remained supportive of the Americans' stand until Churchill intervened. Eden's hostility cannot be doubted – as Cadogan clumsily put it in his diary a few days into the crisis: "Talked with Anthony about Spain. He is still infected with his anti-Franco views."[17] There was indeed antipathy towards Franco Spain on the part of the Foreign Secretary, but no input from him in consequence. Eden had genuine anti-Fascist credentials, and could parade them when arguing with Alba, but he never imposed a policy on Spain consistent with his views on his officials. They first temporized, and then found in Churchill decisive backing for their views. The clearest expression of Eden's personal view came in a letter to Hoare mid February instructing him to support the Americans. Eden wrote of his wish "to take more vigorous action . . . to clear out the Falangists and the Germans and, if necessary, Franco himself". Yet he cautioned himself, adding that such action was not desirable "in the present circumstances". "When, as we hope, the Second Front has been successfully established we can consider the whole question afresh."[18] That puts down a significant marker about Franco's prospects by the British Foreign Secretary which we shall have to consider when, by the autumn of 1944, the Second Front had changed the relations of forces in the strategic triangle made up by Britain, France (now liberated) and Spain. Eden had added a further personal reservation on taking action in the spring of '44 – that there existed little prospect "as yet that any alternative regime would be satisfactory policy". Here again was his distaste for that "corrupt gang" of Spanish generals, as he had put it without subterfuge in '43.

Eden had somewhat improved – publicly at least – his relations with Hoare, praising him in the Commons. But when the ambassador-politician wrote thanking the Foreign Secretary for his "kind personal reference", but injudiciously adding a complaint about how the Americans were handling the petrol/wolfram crisis, Eden's patience snapped again. He minuted his private secretary: "You, and the department, may like to draft a reply to this querulous refrain."[19] Handling the petrol crisis with the Franco regime proved to be one of Hoare's worst patches in Madrid. He misjudged Spain's economic vulnerability that spring of '44. Though from an old East Anglian banking family, Hoare's grasp of economics, as the wolfram "battle" had shown, was slight. He was content to be guided too much by Rees, a narrow technician and devout Catholic who lost his heart to Spain – in the judgment of Tom Burns, another Catholic in the wartime Madrid embassy[20] – and developed a dubious sympathy for the Franco regime. As things ended up, there was no logic in the British scheme of things. After battling throughout 1943 and buying, like a sorcerer's apprentice, ever growing quantities of Spanish wolfram, the Madrid embassy in early '44 worked to resist the Americans' new policy.

Hoare had started out backing the Americans over an immediate and complete ban, signalling to Eden on 19 January: "Have asked for early interview with Franco. To have maximum effect US measures should be put into operation without delay."[21] Hoare's interview with Franco was however completely overshadowed by the Americans' embargo announcement the same day. Franco made the preposterous assertion that wolfram was "only a commercial matter and did not affect Spanish neutrality".[22]

In a bad temper – because he had not been informed beforehand of the Americans' ban – Hoare reacted negatively to Acheson's blunt words to the Spanish ambassador in Washington. Hoare's resentment had at least this justification: the US government had previously agreed with London that the suspension would be unannounced, in order to put the Spaniards at a tactical disadvantage. They would run into the suspension of the routine petrol shipments and have to ask what was afoot. The Foreign Office had striven to keep the British press muzzled and got a question in Parliament postponed. No purchases by Britain had been agreed with Spain for the next six-month period under the supply programme, Hoare noted. This was "part of our plans for preparing the Spanish government for our demands", the quiet diplomacy he preferred.

Hull sought to calm the waters disturbed by America's brusqueness, but Roosevelt came in, tackling the bigger issue of Spain's stubbornness. Only two days after Churchill had promised all possible British support the President signalled his unease. "I believe that as a result of our suspension of tanker loadings the Spanish situation is developing satisfactorily," he told the Prime Minister, going on however: "If both our governments hold firm we can obtain a complete and permanent Spanish embargo on the export of wolfram to any country. I see no danger that our joint insistence upon a complete embargo before resuming loading of Spanish tankers will produce any serious reaction in Spain, which would adversely effect the Allied position. I hope you will send instructions to Hoare to stand firm as we are doing to Hayes," the President urged.[23] The US Chiefs backed him up: there was "no reason," they said, "why we should be deterred from using the oil sanction to the full for fear of the consequences in Spain." Eden echoed the President's line. "I doubt whether we should have got . . . as far as we have without a show of American firmness," he observed.[24] In the Commons, answering a question on Spain, which could not be delayed any longer, the Foreign Secretary went so far as to emphasize publicly that, now there was no danger of German troops entering Spain, "a stricter view [was] required of her neutrality obligations". Neither of the Allied governments had really kept to a co-ordinated strategy on pressuring Spain and each often acted alone, engendering additional mistrust. Public expression of such differences was given by the *New York Times* when it reported on 21 February that Washington was preparing further economic sanctions against Spain for March but that the British government favoured "a face-saving compromise offered by General Franco". "This is a bad leakage, adding suspicion State when it really wants to maintain secrecy can prevent," was the sour Foreign Office comment.[25]

Churchill's reply to Roosevelt's stand-fast message claimed that, if the Allies acted quickly "a settlement I should myself regard as eminently satisfactory can now be reached [with Madrid]".[26] The President replied at his most Olympian. "It is very pleasing to know that a settlement of our current controversy with Spain promises to be accomplished quickly." "Cryptic" Eden minuted of Roosevelt's words.[27]

Franco was adamant, wanting to continue to draw economic benefit from both belligerents in order to continue with building up his regime. For almost a month things stalled. He let his Foreign Minister go down to defeat at a Cabinet in early March, where the pro-Axis Ministers simply said "no" to any giving in. Spanish sovereignty, Asensio, the Army Minister maintained, was at stake and with that argument won the day. Asensio was protector of Sofindus, the German concern which organized the wolfram and other raw materials trading. Jordana threatened to resign. Carceller maintained that since export licences had been promised the Germans for some 200 tons of wolfram, in addition to the 300 tons supplied in January, the deal must be "honoured".[28]

Switching tack from how he had argued in Cabinet, Carceller went to the Allies behind Jordana's back. The British embassy listened, in spite of the State Department's demand for no compromise. "Whatever may be his moral obliquities, [Carceller] is the ablest minister in the government and has Franco's ear. It is essential that we should have him on our side if the impasse is not to continue," Hoare advised London on 20 March.[29] It did not apparently worry the Foreign Office, or Hoare, that the offer was extremely vague – "any formal or written agreement should be avoided for obvious reasons" Carceller had told Rees. The minister envisaged interest-free loans to enable Britain to purchase whatever Spanish goods it desired. The British should "request" facilities to acquire Spanish wolfram, but everything else would depend upon "private undertakings which would be kept so far as he was concerned". The Treasury man, who reported all this unblushingly to London,[30] was assured of Carceller's confidence that he could get his scheme through Cabinet with the argument it was the Allies who could supply the petrol, cotton, and rubber Spain's economy needed, and the Germans could not. Berlin "must accept that Spain had therefore to send wolfram to the Allies and not to them". After discussing Carceller's wheeling and dealing with the MEW, Roberts minuted: "These developments offer a much better chance of a satisfactory practical settlement than the diplomatic exchanges of the past few months. Señor Carceller is certainly unscrupulous and out for his own interests," the FO man allowed, but the Spanish proposals amounted "to directing the Spanish economy into mainly Anglo-American channels". Almost as an aside, the British diplomat added that the Americans "will have to find most of the supplies" to fulfil the deal.[31] Eden approved Robert's recommendation.

Carceller had approached the British side knowing that as the weaker partner they would most likely assent. But he also saw Hayes. "Carceller expressed contempt for Jordana's lack of business sense," the US envoy wrote in his memoirs, "and made direct overtures to the British and to us, indicating that he had an inside track with General Franco. We should negotiate with him rather than the Foreign Minister . . . The British made it clear to us, and more or less to the Spaniards, that they wanted an early settlement."[32] Jordana also criticized the all-powerful Commerce Minister to Hayes. The soldier-Foreign Minister observed there were "important private interests, as doubtless in most countries, which would strive to block a settlement in order that they might continue to line their pockets", Hayes reported.[33] That was a rare admission at the highest level of the inner workings of the Franco regime.

Helped by Carceller, as it fondly believed, the FO pressed Washington to give Hoare a free hand to negotiate a settlement. Hayes' suspicions about the British were well founded. "The US ambassador is certainly not capable of handling matters, more particularly as he does not enjoy the confidence of his government," Roberts was minuting.[34] Hoare must remain in Madrid, and not come on leave, until the government knew whether the Roosevelt administration would "permit us to carry out the negotiations on the lines we desire", Roberts continued. Halifax was told to take up matters directly with Hull, but got nowhere. Hull and Acheson were firmly in control of the dispute with Spain. The Americans, Halifax had to report, were "determined on no account to agree oil shipments [resuming] as long as any wolfram moves over the frontier [into German-occupied France]".[35]

Although Franco had bowed to the Allies, stopping the wolfram exports to Germany, he did nothing to curb a Carceller determined they should continue by illegal paths. Trade by the self-styled autarkic regime had often been supplemented by all kinds of clandestine means. In early February the German ambassador invoked to Jordan his country's "right" to take as much wolfram as it desired under the August 1943 arms agreement. Carceller, while talking to the British, saw to it the Germans were kept supplied. Hans Dieckhoff, the envoy, who was also Ribbentrop's brother-in-law, signalled in April to Berlin that black market purchases of wolfram had only been possible "thanks to the collaboration between us and Carceller".[36] This included meetings by the Commerce Minister with the Nazi head of Sofindus, in Madrid. Some 500 tons of wolfram, it has been estimated, reached Germany by clandestine routes during the first half of 1944.[37] This was on top of the 300 tons exported legally in January. One of Carceller's meetings occurred in May after the Allies' "settlement".

Unaware of such machinations, Churchill had meanwhile joined in, even though he was going against the State Department. "I have no doubt," Churchill messaged Roosevelt late March, "that by increasing our economic pressure we can eventually bring the Spaniards to heel. In fact, with reasonable people the mere threat should be enough. The Spaniards are not, however, reasonable and they have a capacity for tightening their belts in resistance to foreign pressure."[38] Against the Americans' complete embargo – "what I understand you are now expecting of Spain" – the Prime Minister advocated what he called "some small compromise" over wolfram. Preparing the ground with the President for dealing with the unreasonable

Spaniards, Churchill dismissed outright Carceller's schemings. "I do not think we should be well advised to enter into any long-term commitments with the present regime," he declared. That was already some way from his assurances, and reassurances, to Alba, yet the Prime Minister then went further, much further indeed than he was to go in the autumn of 1944, adding for Roosevelt's eyes: "When we have, as we hope, established the Second Front successfully the whole picture may change."

Churchill could now deploy the argument the Foreign Office had long kept in a bottom drawer as a supposed clincher. If the deadlock over wolfram continued, Spain, the Premier asserted, would apply economic counter-measures against Britain. There existed "serious risks" Britain would lose Spanish iron ore – Churchill gave a departmental figure of 42 per cent of Britain's requirements coming from Spain – and Spanish potash, essential, he argued, for the maintenance of Britain's wartime agriculture. "I would venture to remind you that we have gone along with you in Argentina," Churchill claimed, " [and] we feel entitled to ask you to take our views seriously into account in the Iberian peninsula where [our] strategic and economic interests are more vitally affected than those of the United States. I earnestly hope that you will give your consideration to our appeal without which we shall be in very serious difficulties." Churchill then added: "I could not support in public the policy which is now being enforced upon us." The language is that of political blackmail. Britain had recently baulked at seconding US moves against a generals' putsch in Buenos Aires because of the need of Argentine beef. The Prime Minister was on weak ground, thinking only of national interests as he perceived them.

Roosevelt did not give way. "I have studied with considerable care your message," he replied, "I am most reluctant to accept any compromise on this matter with the Spanish government."[39] It would not help, the President pointed out, with negotiations going on with Portugal, where the Germans were still obtaining larger, and more regular, quantities of wolfram. Churchill had overlooked that, and did not put any pressure on the Portuguese until writing to Salazar in mid May.[40] The Portuguese dictator had judged the Azores agreement was enough to placate the Allies and declined to stop the lucrative wolfram trade with Germany. Hull had made a speech warning all the neutrals they were facing their "last chance to join the winning side with credit". The Allies had scrupulously respected their sovereignty in the conflict, but would no longer tolerate their prolonging the war by sending resources – often obtained from the Allied world – to Germany. The speech had been toughened in tone by Acheson with the President's approval.[41] Roosevelt told Churchill he could only recommend a fresh effort by State to work with the British embassy on "a mutually agreeable line to take with the Spanish".

Churchill's reply covered up a defeat. "Thank you so much," he signalled, going on to claim, perplexingly: "I am entirely in agreement with you on the principle, but I think we can get more out of it by the method you now approve."[42] The FO did not relish further talks with American officials "against our better judgment" as London put it. Roberts, when shown a draft of the reply, minuted: "I think the P.M.'s message is a little too gushing. We do not agree with the President's principles (1) that there should be no compromise with the Spanish government or (2) that our compromise would not be helpful in negotiations with the Portuguese." Roberts was overruled by Eden and Churchill's gushing reply was sent.

Churchill wrote again on 17 April, making his fourth appeal to the President on the wolfram problem so far. The Prime Minister urged acceptance of a Spanish offer of 60 tons of wolfram for Germany between April and the end of June and then a further 240 tons spread over the remaining six months of 1944. Madrid officials were meanwhile plying the Treasury man Rees with prospects of Jordana obliged to resign and Germanophile bogeymen taking charge. No British diplomat could evidently grasp that a "threat" by Spain of taking counter-measures flew in the face of economic reality. Neither Carceller nor Franco could have any interest in augmenting the regime's grave economic difficulties now that the dictator had stopped all "official" wolfram exports to Germany, by stopping exports of iron ore and potash to Britain as well. The Spaniards, certainly the hard-nosed Commerce Minister, knew that the many other Allied supplies were essential to the regime's survival, and cheaper than Germany's eventual substitutes.

Roosevelt replied declining once again, and with perceptible sharpness. "We have gone a very long way to meet your difficulties," the President began, "will you not therefore reconsider an instruction to our two ambassadors to join in a determined effort to settle the matter on the basis of a suspension [of wolfram] during the first half of the year? I do not believe we have done all that is possible along this line," he told the Prime Minister.[43] Roosevelt simply ignored Churchill's new-found Spanish counter-measures gambit and endorsed Hull's "get tough with all the neutrals" approach. Compromising on wolfram to Germany by Spain would frustrate efforts with Sweden, Switzerland and Turkey, as well as Portugal, to curb all kinds of supplies for the German war machine. "Our public attaches the greatest importance to Spanish shipments of wolfram [to Germany] and is most critical of oil supplies going to that country while these continue. They are most insistent upon a policy of firmness and a contrary course on the eve of military operations would, I believe, have the most serious consequences," the President advised Churchill, tempering the British leader's *Realpolitik* with a breadth of fresh air – American public opinion. "A tiresome telegram from President Roosevelt" was Cadogan's comment.[44]

Churchill answered the same day. He got around the President's point on US public opinion in the simplest, and roughest way – though he well knew how this exercised Hull. The British government would sponsor – the Premier's term – resumption of oil shipments to Spain on the basis of "our special interests in Spain".[45] The US would not be directly concerned in this arrangement Churchill maintained, seeking to justify Britain's going it alone in appeasing Franco Spain. "I am convinced the present Spanish offer is a good one which I shall be glad to sponsor as a practical and prestige victory over our [German] enemy. I am also sure that it is the best we can get," the Prime Minister asserted. This was followed by even weaker arguments. Only negligible quantities of wolfram, "a few lorry loads" he claimed, would be going to Germany before the end of June. His information was that Jordana would resign if this offer was not now accepted. The Foreign Minister stayed in his post until dying in office in August '44.

The Whole Responsibility

The Spanish offer which the Prime Minister espoused was for 60 tons a month of wolfram to go to Germany till the end of June – the period during which the Americans had battled since January to have a complete embargo and on which Roosevelt had urged the British government so many times to "stand firm". Churchill got off two quick telegrams, one to Halifax to tell Hull expressly in the Prime Minister's words that he would "take upon myself the whole responsibility for this settlement"[46] and, the second, to Hoare to inform the Spanish government of the agreement reached as soon as the Americans had indicated acquiescence. Halifax replied, however, that he anticipated Hull and Roosevelt would "stall" – in plain English, the Prime Minister was jumping the gun.[47]

Churchill made a fifth appeal to Roosevelt and his threat to go it alone worked. The Prime Minister had outsmarted the US Secretary of State. "We all feared that to announce the British were going ahead alone would result in repercussions detrimental to our united front towards the neutrals. The President agreed," Hull wrote soberly in his memoirs.[48] Churchill's telegram was "so insistent", Hull advised Roosevelt on 23 April, the wisest course was to accept the Spanish proposal "which the British had espoused".

The President signalled "the Former Naval Person": "I have today author-ized Hull to accept Halifax's proposal." [49] "We are all greatly obliged for your consideration," Churchill slammed back the same day, elated at having imposed his will upon the Americans concerning Franco Spain.[50]

The Prime Minister's triumph was an illusion. It went down badly in Washington. The unvarnished pursuit of Britain's perceived interests in Spain was to be exploited by US business to Britain's longer-term commer-cial disadvantage. What was clear, and above all clear in Madrid, was, with Britain's lack of nerve and weakness, that Spanish stubbornness had paid off. Churchill's "We are all greatly obliged" was not true. When the Foreign Secretary came before the Commons to announce the settlement on 3 May he was far from enthusiastic. Eden knew that no decisive shift in Spain's course had been wrung from Franco by Britain pushing hard against the Americans. The Foreign Secretary spoke only about an agreement "we can broadly regard as satisfactory for the immediate future". The much-needed petrol for Spain would start crossing the Atlantic again – Eden claimed the amounts would be "only just enough for the bare needs of the Spanish economy" – and wolfram exports again to Germany. Spain's concessions had been that the "official" exports at least would be in smaller amounts, "dras-tically reduced" in Eden's words when compared with a peak month of '43 of 500 tons. If rivalry was now the name of the Allies' game, the US ambas-sador then went one better, obtaining from Jordana a last-minute further reduction on Churchill's claimed "best offer we can get", down from 60 tons a month to 40.[51]

How Churchill's course to appease Spain was seen in the United States, and especially by the State Department, has been fully mirrored in the memoirs. Although Hull's language was measured, his resentment over the Prime Minister's conduct is obvious. As the Secretary of State told Hayes, when informing the envoy of Churchill's unilateral threat: "It would obvi-ously be necessary to issue a press statement which could not but clearly indicate a break in the united front of the United States and Great Britain." Agreement on less than a total embargo, Hull's guidance stressed, was "on the urgent request of the British government".[52] Four days later, the US Secretary of State observed to Hayes: "With full British support we could have achieved our objective, i.e. a total embargo."[53] He was convinced, Hull said, that "a large section of the public here might well have the same impression". Franco Spain was "not popular with the American press, public and press alike would regard anything less than the complete attain-ment of our objective as a compromise. No compromise with Spain would be well received," Hayes was told roundly. Hull ends his treatment in his memoirs of the wolfram battle contrasting Spain unfavourably with

Portugal, which, in response to Allied pressure, did implement from June '44 a complete embargo on wolfram exports to Germany. To manifest his discontent to Madrid over the wolfram settlement, Hull tried again to obtain "immediate fulfilment" of other Allied demands, chiefly the promised expulsion of German agents, which, of course, Franco ignored.

Acheson, who in his memoirs proudly describes himself as "sound on the Spanish issue", is less formal. "Economic warfare [over Spain] ended in a flare up of tempers between Washington and London . . . Churchill out-bluffed Hull by assuming personal responsibility for sponsoring oil shipments to Spain," he recalled.[54] Acheson paints a picture of a "mutinous" State Department, only obeying orders from Roosevelt with the most considerable reluctance. "All of us bitterly resented the British refusal to cooperate," he observes, going on: "The role played by Mr Churchill in deflecting our economic pressure was my first experience of a relatively weak ally by determined, sometimes reckless, decisions, changing, and even preventing, action by a much stronger one charged with ultimate responsibility." The future US Secretary of State places Churchill in the same unflattering category as De Gaulle and Syngman Rhee of South Korea as America's "relatively weak" but headstrong allies. Acheson manifests contempt for the laboriously negotiated figures on monthly wolfram exports. Franco's officials' statements were "mendacious and their statistics falsified", he wrote. With justified scepticism about the settlement of the Allies' wolfram war against Germany, Acheson's verdict was: "Exports from the Iberian peninsula probably moved in the minimum necessary quantities [for Germany] until military measures stopped them"[55] – with the liberation of France. According to a German historian's estimate, stocks amassed of wolfram were enough for one and a half years' wartime needs, so there was no substantial disruption of the Nazis' war efforts, he judged.[56]

Herbert Feis drew in his memoirs an even more telling conclusion from the Allies' missed opportunity to agree at that juncture on a viable policy towards Franco Spain. Hull was "angry at the British desertion," Feis reports on the crisis, "and thought Spain would have given in long since were it not for British protection".[57] The best-informed US official on Franco Spain's war-time economy, later turned its historian, judged Britain and America chose that spring of 1944 "to let events evolve in Spain rather than to dictate them . . . Spain could not have gone without oil much longer. By summer a crisis would have come," he held. The oil suspension had severe results, drastic rationing, food shortages, industries shut down, the economy was near collapse. Feis speaks of Washington's deep sense of "a job half done". The American asked poignantly: "Was it not the knowledge that the crisis had come and gone and left 'the Spanish problem', not the wolfram

problem, unsolved? Germany and Italy would fall, but Franco would stand
... We were committed, and in some ways more fully than ever before, to
continue to supply Spain with the means to maintain its economic life. But
no documents of the time record such thoughts," Feis, the historian,
concluded.[58]

No Allied wartime documents, but the Spanish elder statesman Cambó
did capture in his diary the real import of Eden's announcing an end of the
oil embargo. "There is no doubt at all the arrangement consolidates Franco,"
he wrote.[59] It was Britain, he pronounced, which had obliged the
Americans to accept that settlement. Churchill's responsibility in helping
the Franco regime's efforts to survive economically in 1944 is well conveyed
in the Spanish politician and financier's words. Cambó, though in self-
imposed exile in South America, maintained close contacts with Spanish
and other European business circles throughout the world war thanks to his
great wealth and wide-ranging interests.

The time for any dispute with the Americans by a weakened Britain was
singularly ill chosen by Churchill. There were two disputes of greater
importance already going on between Washington and London. The first
concerned the limiting of Britain's gold and dollar reserves and the conditions surrounding the US Lend-Lease, that vital lifeline that Roosevelt had
accorded Churchill, but which was also "the main instrument of America's
foreign economic policy" according to the biographer of Keynes, the man
much involved in Anglo-American wartime economic negotiations.[60] The
Prime Minister was well informed of what was at issue. The Chancellor of
the Exchequer, John Anderson, minuted him starkly that February: "If we
were to accept the President's proposal we should lose our financial independence as soon as Lend-Lease comes to an end, and would emerge from
the war victorious indeed but financially . . . with reserves inferior even to
France and Holland."[61] The second weighty issue involved petrol and in a
world context far beyond Spain. Arguments between the American and
British governments about the carve-up of future oil resources and markets
for the post-war troubled relations seriously throughout that first half of
'44. Here again it was no longer an affair among equals. Spain showed up
the reality of trade rivalries underneath Churchill's public rhetoric on the
wartime alliance. The Prime Minister's private pleas to the President for
special consideration for British interests in the Iberian peninsula were part
of government efforts to maintain market shares in Spain for British oil
companies or, at least, not to lose them when peace came. A senior official
from the Ministry of Fuel and Power visited Spain in April with that aim
just as Churchill was at work on his wolfram "compromise" against
American wishes. As the Foreign Office informed the Madrid embassy

before the official's arrival, Fuel and Power were anxious when the oil embargo was lifted "to strengthen British oil representation in the peninsula . . . careful handling [would be] required *vis-à-vis* the Americans". The British government was concerned not only about supplying Spain "but also with the maintenance of British distribution outlets".[62] London was manoeuvring for Spanish oil purchases from the sterling area, against their American rivals.

Churchill's ruse of "sponsoring" oil shipments to Spain brought on more naked expressions of that rivalry. Hoare, Hayes told the State Department, had "cheerfully assumed the oil shipments would come from British sources and be under British control. I assured him they would be our special business in the future as in the past".[63] As the US envoy argued in his memoirs: "If oil control should pass from American to British hands any incentive for the British to act jointly with us would disappear. We would lose basic influence and power not only with the Spanish government but with the Spanish people. Now we had joined, and even led, Britain in the final settlement," Hayes went on, "there was no reason why we should surrender oil control and every reason why we should retain it." The force of the petrol "weapon" was laid bare. State informed London on 5 May that the situation obtaining before the January oil embargo had been restored. Nevertheless, it took a month or more of pressure on Hoare and the Foreign Office, Hayes recalled, to ensure the newly appointed British petroleum attaché was "subordinate . . . and to restore full American direction of the petroleum programme".[64] "Trade rivalries resumed", Feis summed it up laconically.

Dissatisfied by Eden's unenthusiastic announcement of the settlement with Spain, Churchill seized the opportunity when he made a wide-ranging review of the situation in Europe before the Allied D-Day landings in the Commons on 24 May. "I look forward," the Prime Minister told Parliament, "to increasingly good relations with Spain and to an extremely fertile trade between Spain and this country which will, I trust, grow even during the war and will extend after the peace. As I am speaking here today kindly words about Spain, let me add that I hope she will be a strong influence for the peace of the Mediterranean after the war." Churchill had more to add, observing: "Internal political problems in Spain are a matter for the Spaniards themselves. It is not for us to meddle in such affairs."

Such remarks, announcing publicly the policy to be pursued towards Franco Spain, even into the peace, were a major blunder. Harold Nicolson, the diplomat, writer, and parliamentary secretary in Churchill's 1940 Ministry of Information, who spoke immediately after the Prime Minister in the foreign affairs debate, noted in his diary that night what was wrong. "To our surprise he [Churchill] went miles out of his way to shower roses and lilies upon Franco."[65] The Associated Press man in Madrid, Charles Foltz, caught precisely where the Prime Minister had blundered. The evening of the speech he witnessed groups of Falangists in a Madrid main street with cans of black paint putting up on walls in Castilian: "Internal political problems are a matter for Spaniards themselves – Churchill."[66] Foltz reported the Franco establishment was made "first incredulous, then suspicious, next jubilant" by the British Prime Minister's words.

The moment for Churchill to speak about increasing trade with Spain was certainly inappropriate. Long-established British interests in Spain, notably mining concerns like Rio Tinto, were at that time subject to constant bureaucratic hassles and threats of nationalization from Carceller. The four-fifths British-owned Orconera Iron Ore Company was actually appealing to the relevant British government departments to come to its aid over a new Spanish Mining Law unfriendly to foreign companies. Orconera, responsible for one-third of all Northern Spain's high-grade ore for the steel industry, believed it was being deliberately bankrupted by the Spanish authorities, through a pricing policy kept below production costs, to engineer a takeover. From 1940 Orconera had been stopped by Franco Spain from all exporting to the UK.[67] Yet Churchill in the Commons had singled out the Bilbao-based iron export trade for Anglo-Spanish development. The Prime Minister had not bothered to let himself be adequately briefed.

Evidence suggests Churchill's remarks about Spain were, to some extent at least, extemporized. The Prime Minister was famous for taking the greatest pains preparing his wartime speeches. Cadogan's diary shows us the FO did see a draft that morning before the Prime Minister opened the debate. "A good mad-house in Anthony's room at 10.30. A [Eden] and the other people fluttering pages of the PM's draft speech, looking over each other's shoulder and all talking at once," he wrote.[68] "When asked my opinion I said that if I could have a glance to read the damned thing I might express one." In view of the Foreign Office's reaction to Churchill's remarks in the Commons, and the repeated efforts in Madrid, through Hoare and other channels, to "put the record straight", it would seem surprising no one from Eden downwards spotted the blundering "kindly words", if they had indeed been in the pre-delivery text.

The objections to Churchill's "kindly words" on Spain are manifold. Less than one month before, when pleading with Roosevelt for his wolfram compromise, the Prime Minister had described Franco Spain as "the most pro-German among the neutrals".[69] It was not advisable to look to long-standing agreements about trade with Spain. Churchill's words were as changeable as his moods about Spain. What alone mattered for Churchill was Spain's serving Britain's strategic interests in the Mediterranean.

Best Card

Two of the weightiest objections to Churchill's impromptu policy-making remain to be mentioned. The Prime Minister by that speech gave away one of the Allies' best cards for influencing the course of Spanish affairs as the victorious democracies extended their sway in Europe. Churchill hindered a growing isolation of the Franco regime: reluctant half measures from "the most pro-German" of the neutral states in Europe had been declared "enough" by Churchill. The Prime Minister seems to have been pleased to celebrate his satisfaction at outsmarting the Americans. He was in a defiant mood. "I have always worked for good relations with Spain," Churchill roundly told Eden when showing him a telegram about to be dispatched and instancing his remarks about Spain in an October 1940 Guildhall speech.[70] But here is exactly the point: Britain's desperate efforts in the autumn of '40 to keep Spain from joining the triumphant Axis powers, and acceptance even of Franco's *malevolent* neutrality, had become strategically unnecessary – as the Service Chiefs had repeatedly advised – and ought to have been unacceptable by the summer of 1944 to a Britain victorious in the name of democracy. Those words to Eden had, again, been better not said.

Secondly, the effect of the Prime Minister's words on the other side of the Atlantic was little short of disastrous. "A pat on the back for Franco", as many Americans saw it, brought letters of protest pouring in daily at the British embassy in Washington. Isaiah Berlin, in his wartime *Washington Despatches* for the British government, reported Churchill's remarks had "profoundly upset" Acheson.[71] For US journalists, Berlin observed, the passage on Spain had overshadowed all the rest of the Prime Minister's speech. When pressed by newsmen for his views, Roosevelt emphasized that the American government's attitude towards Spain was unchanged, and carefully added that he did not think "any of us is satisfied with what Spain is doing".[72] Spain's curtailment of wolfram supplies to Germany was "insufficient", he remarked – public criticism enough of the settlement Churchill had pushed through. The President's wife, Eleanor, seized upon Churchill's ambiguous observation in Parliament that as the war progressed it became "less ideological in character". She asked whether the Prime Minister was "trampling the Atlantic Charter into the dust".

The American press and radio refused to allow Churchill's remarks to drop and there was public comment on the two Allied leaders' serious differences over Franco Spain. Churchill felt obliged to telegraph Roosevelt: "Our friendship is my greatest stand-by amid the ever-increasing complications of this exacting war," he began flatteringly.[73] "I see some of your newspapers are upset at my references in the House of Commons to Spain. This is very unfair as all I have done is to repeat my declaration of October 1940 . . . I do not care about Franco but I do not wish to have the Iberian peninsula hostile to Britain after the war." Churchill's old-fashioned perception of the strategic interests of an imperial power is vividly expressed – even though Roosevelt could hardly be thought a sympathetic recipient for such views. Once again, the Prime Minister judged no policy shift was required, might indeed be dictated by the difference in Britain's war fortunes between 1940 and '44. As the criticisms continued of his "kindly words" Churchill sought to explain himself to the Foreign Secretary. "I very strongly desire to see a friendly Iberian peninsula to us after the war, which I think will be of great importance to the United Europe for which I look and also to the Mediterranean which will be entrusted to our care," the Prime Minister minuted.[74]

Official Madrid may well have been in doubt what the British Prime Minister's speech meant exactly. Alba, however, in London grasped its full significance for the regime and asked Eden for an appointment on 26 May to "express appreciation".[75] Franco was to keep a tight hold on the talisman Churchill had handed him. He had a copy, it was said, with him in his pocket of a translation of the Prime Minister's precious remarks, and pulled it out whenever challenged by doubters. The dictator pointed it as definitive proof that he and the British Premier were "the best of friends". According to an anecdote told Roberts by Antonio Pastor, a member of the Spanish banking family, a relation in Galicia had ventured in the dictator's presence that summer to question Britain's real intentions towards Spain and received the full quotation read out.[76] Roberts' recording of the anecdote, which showed the force of Churchill's error, was suppressed under the 50-year rule at the PRO. (Pastor held a teaching post at King's College, London, and enjoyed a rare personal entrée to the Foreign Office. All ex-Republicans exiled in wartime London were excluded from the FO.) Cambó, too, picked up the full significance of Churchill's Commons speech. "He went too far and the excessive spontaneity of his words will possibly give him some trouble in Britain and, above all, abroad. He had exaggerated praise for Franco and his regime, which will have upset the great majority of Spaniards and all of Britain's allies," the moderate Spanish leader judged. "Where has this sudden enthusiasm of Churchill's for Franco come from?" he asked in his diary.[77] Roosevelt had "disauthorized" Churchill's remarks as to the Allied position on Spain, Cambó wrote.

Throughout the wolfram dispute with Washington Spain's purchases of gold for its reserves had continued and this in the face of the Gold

Declaration signed by the US Treasury Secretary, in February. Switzerland and Spain were clearly in its sights when denouncing Germany's practice of refounding gold and seeking to sell it to countries "which maintained diplomatic and commercial relations with the Axis".[78] The US Embassy drew Madrid's attention to the declaration, but, under Carceller's guidance, the IEME reiterated its policy was "to acquire gold as Spain's trading surplus allowed". Only two days before V Day in Europe in 1945 did the Franco regime formally agree to the Bretton Woods reaffirmation of the declaration on pillaged gold.

Hoare was on leave in London when Churchill spoke in the Commons. His remarks about Spain came just as the ambassador saw how a contrary attitude was steadily gaining ground in parliamentary and wider, politically aware circles in London, as victory for the Allies came nearer. It was based more on public opinion than on one based exclusively on old-fashioned perceptions of national interest. The British Labour party had publicly disassociated itself from Churchill's "kindly words" and even looked forward to "a great act of self liberation" by the Spanish people.[79] The month Hoare spent in London heightened his sense of the unpopularity prevailing in Britain for the regime to which he was diplomatically accredited. He became fully aware of how much informed opinion in Britain – he addressed a private meeting on Spain attended by several hundred MP's during his stay – disliked Franco and all his works. There was, above all, resentment over how Spain's dictator had sided with the Axis powers, even publicly pronouncing the Allies had lost the war in 1941 when Hitler's strength was at its zenith.

Hoare's despatches from Madrid had kept the Foreign Office regularly informed about Franco's brutal repression, maintained despite the passage of years since the Civil War had ended with the sole purpose of preventing any opposition from organizing. By way of an answer as to what the future of Spain might be, Hoare gave expression to his own views in an address to his Chelsea constituents on 31 May. He had begun his final evolution from collaborating with Churchill at the time of the wolfram battle, and appeasing the Franco regime, towards opposing it because of the changed fortunes of war.

More forcibly than in his "Chelsea Message" to war-workers in 1943, Hoare repeated his rejection of a police state for a post-war Spain and spoke of answering "questions put to me by Spaniards in Madrid as to the British position in Europe at the end of the world war". Hoare observed that he was drawing on his four years' experience of living in continental Europe. He thereby not only paid Spaniards the compliment that they could look to having a place in post-war Europe like the others, but sketched political ideas that were to find expression in post-war European Christian Democracy, most notably in Germany and Italy, each with their experience of dictatorships which had been Franco's model. There is self-criticism: "We are often ignorant and misinformed about the European point of view," the politician-envoy declared, arguing that Britain must not fail to play a part in continental affairs in the critical first years of the post war. The whole tone is aware, sensitive and quite un-Churchillian.

"When totalitarianism finally crashes a great void will be left over many parts of Europe . . . We must reintroduce the basic and essential principles of European civilisation, human personality must count, state idolatry must be dethroned," Hoare declared.[80] He offered a prescription of liberties for the development of the human personality, all of them denied by Franco's police state: security from arbitrary arrest and imprisonment, freedom of association, liberty of discussion, regular process of law with no executive interference and religious toleration. "Let all European countries set up a minimum standard of personal rights for all their citizens," Hoare urged. There should be "no caste that is above the ordinary law or possessed of special privileges" – here was a direct attack on the Falange and Spain's armed forces, the twin pillars of the Franco regime. All such liberties were needed in a Europe which had been devastated by anti-European totalitarianism, they should be Britain's goals "throughout Europe" for the post-war, he emphasized. The speech was a politician's attempt at an input for future British policy-making. The Foreign Office had no comments on the deeper issues Hoare had raised. Their only contribution would be a negative one – to correct him if he got "out of line" on the routines of diplomacy.

But the mood in Britain was decidedly forward-looking and idealistic and Churchill by his remarks on Spain and contention that the war was becoming "less idealistic" had misjudged the mood of his fellow countrymen and their war effort – a foretaste of the 1945 General Election result. Hoare was more abreast of his country's feelings. He was sent back to Madrid with clear instructions at least to rectify the Prime Minister's Commons speech. Cadogan endorsed this distancing from Churchill's remarks: "I approve your language and agree that you should bring these points home to General Franco," the permanent head of the FO signalled after Hoare's preliminary meeting with the Spanish Foreign Minister on his return.[81] Hoare found Jordana eagerly asserting that "a great change" had come about in their countries' relations thanks to the Prime Minister's remarks. Hoare rebutted the "misunderstanding", giving a skilled re-interpretation of the remarks. The Prime Minister, Hoare observed, had made abundantly clear that British policy was for non-interference in Spain's internal affairs. "It was therefore altogether untrue to suggest that we were supporting a particular regime in Spain. As a matter of fact, almost everyone in Britain, including the Conservative party, detested Falangism . . . The Spanish government should take this detestation into account. It was idle to think the British and American governments would not be influenced, as the war's end approached, by this very strong feeling," Hoare warned.[82] To rectify the Prime Minister's error to a wider audience Hoare issued instructions to British consuls in Spain. "Your line should be to insist that it is well known to everyone that British public opinion detests totalitarianism wherever it may exist. Spain must settle its own affairs, the attitude of Britain to any Spanish government will depend entirely upon the policy, attitude and behaviour of a particular government," he wrote.[83] By referring to any Spanish government Hoare had disowned Churchill's kindly words for the Franco regime and yet not got out of line. "Very good", Harvey, Eden's closest aide at the FO, minuted.

Seeing Franco on 12 June Hoare, as ambassador, had to be more diplomatic to a head of state. But, to instance London's mood, he reported his meeting with several hundred MPs. How was it possible the British politicians had pressed him, Hoare told the dictator, to have good relations with a government which had in the past been "so closely identified with the principles and policies of our enemy in Europe?"[84] Hoare spoke of the hatred of the Falange and "deep-rooted doubts on fundamental issues". Many people in Britain were "very suspicious of closer relations between the two countries in present conditions". Franco of course grasped the illusions to his regime's totalitarian principles and practices. But Falangism was "materially different", he claimed, from Fascism. Though the Normandy invasion had begun six days before, Franco took up much of the interview urging Britain to lead a western bloc against Russia, showing himself, as the envoy testily reported "as obsessed as ever with the Communist danger".

"I was very glad you spoke to Franco as you did, and that you have been taking every opportunity to remove the false impressions formed in some Spanish minds by the Prime Minister's recent reference to Spain," Eden wrote to Hoare.[85] The Foreign Secretary was keenly aware how Churchill's appeasing the Franco regime rankled in Washington. But the subtle, yet vital, shift of emphasis on British policy would only be effective if it was maintained. Hoare rammed home the message on Churchill's clumsy words when he called on Jordana a second time: "So far from being evidence of support for the Franco regime, they should be regarded by all wise Spaniards as giving them an opportunity to set their own house in order without dictation from the Allies."[86] "Good" Eden minuted on reading Hoare's despatch.[87] The Foreign Secretary and the Prime Minister were in clear disagreement over Spain and Eden at that moment was backing Hoare's more forward-looking approach. The Spanish Foreign Minister took copious notes, but there in reality things rested. Hoare's strategy was based on the false supposition the Foreign Minister, whom he believed pro-Allied by now, would be able to convince Franco to carry out an effective re-orientation of Spain's policies. Hoare was counting on General Jordana to initiate change from within. He grasped at him, as he had grasped at Carceller, but each in their different ways served only Franco. A contemporary Spanish insider, the physician-author and now cautious opponent of Franco, Dr Gregorio Maranon, dismissed all Franco's ministers as lacking in the stature needed to "hold high position in any healthy political set-up".[88]

Churchill's frustrating an offensive when Washington was minded to bring effective pressure on the Franco regime had a boomerang effect for British interests in Spain. Outsmarting Hull over the oil embargo was to mean the loss of a restraining influence by the State Department over the brash go-getting US ambassador and, more importantly, over the American businessmen who were now increasingly visiting Spain in search of post-war markets. They had much to offer a backward country. The British diplomats who had naïvely thought they were ingratiating themselves in Madrid saw their hopes quickly dashed.

The personal rivalry between the two Allied envoys had been exacerbated by Churchill's "settlement". Hayes was annoyed that his part in securing from Spain's Foreign Minister a further reduction in wolfram deliveries, thus "trumping" Churchill, had gone unappreciated in Washington. The British had got all the credit. Hoare had returned to Madrid in a special flight by the British Overseas Airways Corporation inaugurating a weekly direct service from London to the Spanish capital instead of via Lisbon. This flight was a source of particular satisfaction to Hoare, who had been interested in air travel since his days as Secretary of State for Air in the 1920s, when he helped pioneer the air route to India. It contrasted with his uncertain arrival in Franco's capital in 1940. Hayes, however, had the week before started negotiations with Spain on future landing rights for American airlines.

Barcelona was the public forum for these Anglo-American trade rivalries. Hayes attended the Barcelona trade fair in June, though the only other countries present were Sweden, Switzerland and Chile. Big US firms represented included Ford, General Motors, Chrysler, General Electric, Westinghouse, Rand and Singer. America's publishers were alone, out of principle, against displaying their books in Franco's Spain. Banners proclaimed the American "Way of Life" to Spaniards eager for contact with anything so modern from abroad. Spanish cinemas, Hayes boasted, were showing "many more American films than from any other country".[89] Carceller, who opened the trade fair, made a combative speech. Spain, he declared, had "nothing to learn from the democracies", boasting that its social services were the best in the world. Spain would respect all foreign countries but they, in turn, "must understand there would be no toleration of interference in Spain's internal affairs". The Commerce and Industry Minister, speaking evidently to please his master, attacked both the Allies and Catalonia's former ruling class, notably the monarchists. Britain and America were publicly blamed for Spain's difficulties over obtaining a sufficient level of imports – meaning the navi-cert system – "so badly needed by the poorer sections of the community" Carceller, who had greatly enriched himself during the world war, declared.[90] The Catalan *haute bourgeoisie*, growingly sensitive to Allied successes in the war, were roundly told by Carceller that "the only road to follow was that fashioned by the Caudillo", the British Consul-General who was present reported. This included, Carceller said, the regime's autarkic economic policy. The speech's defiant tone highlighted the errors of Churchill's 24 May speech and ignorance of how differently Franco Spain's rulers viewed things, including trade.

Hayes ignored Carceller's broadside and staged a lavish Fourth of July celebration, bringing to the embassy, as he noted in his memoirs, "the biggest crowd yet – practically all the Foreign Ministry, the Spanish Chiefs of Staff, numerous representatives of the Spanish Catholic Church, university, press, etc. It was a beautiful day."[91] Hayes was marking a burgeoning American ascendancy. When the ambassador saw Franco two days later the dictator charged him with a message for President Roosevelt which asserted that the USA could "count on the sincerest, continuing cooperation of himself and of Spain". Striving not to be outdone, Hoare was in Barcelona that month, but it was to rejuvenate a British Chamber of Commerce all too obviously set in its old ways. In a speech Hoare mentioned ideas from his Chelsea address, including "individual liberty [as] the foundation of European civilisation".[92] His difference with the Churchill of the kindly words for the Spain of Franco was thus made evident to anyone with a fine enough ear. Hoare rejected Carceller's demagoguery about the regime's autarkic policies, offering instead Keynesian economics, then the height of fashion. The politician-ambassador's words: "We have seen the dangers of capitalism drifting into an excess of profits" must have hit the Spanish business class attending with their British hosts, who had been so protected by the Franco regime.

When Hayes returned from a lengthy stay in Washington and New York in August '44 it was clear a more business-friendly attitude had taken over in large parts of the Roosevelt Administration. The envoy set about encouraging full-scale American economic penetration of Spanish markets – and British diplomats on the spot were deeply worried. Early September Franco, dressed in the uniform of the Falange, told Hayes without subterfuge that Spain "needed more American investment".[93] The dictator agreed to negotiations to settle the long-running dispute over ownership of Telefonica, Spain's national telephone network which had been built by American engineers. Carceller was put in charge of the Spanish negotiating team. By the year's end this matter was settled, as was the US airlines arrangement under which the Americans were to help build up Spanish airports. The United States thus acquired two key economic bridgeheads into Spain – with the petrol supply again firmly in their hands, three. America would be supplying post-war the technology of modern communications and of air transport.

An Astute Basque

Jordana's sudden death in San Sebastian, Spain's summer capital, on 3 August was a blow for Hoare and the hopes he had nursed that the Foreign Minister could influence the dictator. Even worse in Hoare's eyes was Franco's choice of José Félix Lequerica, Spain's ambassador to Vichy – at that moment collapsing – as Jordana's successor. "A notorious collaborationist with the Germans" was how Hoare judged him.[94] Once again, however, Franco's judgment of men proved helpful for his regime's survival. Lequerica, intensely ambitious and quite unprincipled, was a highly skilled operator in high places. He was destined indeed to become Franco's No. 1 representative in Washington after the Second World War. Lequerica was a wealthy man and on his mother's side an Urquijo, owners of the Basque bank. He was a prominent member of the Basque financial and industrial establishment which, unlike the Basque people, had thrown in its lot with Franco in the Civil War and profited from the connexion thereafter. He had been one of the early paymasters of the Falange.

Lequerica, who became one of the grandees of the regime, represents a far more important element in Franco's struggle to survive in the crucial period while the world war was still on than the external "window dressing" which the pseudo-Christian Democrat, Alberto Martín Artajo, Lequerica's successor, indulged in at the dictator's orders when the war was over. Lequerica, who had spent four years at the London School of Economics before 1936, had been a close friend while in France from 1940 of Otto Abetz, the Nazis' ambassador in Paris. In 1944 it was only thanks to the

Germans escorting him that Spain's future Foreign Minister could avoid the Free French Forces and get safely through to the Pyrenees. In choosing him Franco had calculated that if the Germans defeated "Overlord" Lequerica, with his past in German-occupied Paris, would stand well with them – in other words, he could face all ways, exactly as the interests of the regime required.

Hoare's loss proved Hayes' gain. Knowing that he started with a very weak hand Lequerica began by flattering Hoare's sense of importance. But the swift-witted Basque soon found that in Hayes, eager to seize the economic advantages American business might reap in Franco Spain, he had a more congenial partner with more to offer. The new Foreign Minister sensed it was vital for the regime to seek a new backer as the Axis' fortunes declined. It was to be the United States, the emerging world power, that Spain must look, if Lequerica had his way, with Britain seen as a declining force. Lequerica was to treat Hoare according to that shrewd perception.

The Basque saw he could exploit the personal rivalry of the two Allied envoys in Madrid, the aggressive, brash and self-opinionated Yankee and the Briton, so obviously the elder statesman attuned now to the moral issues the survival of the Franco regime posed for the victorious democracies. American diplomacy was still evolving: while Hayes in Madrid was now opportunistically pressing for "all essential supplies" to be afforded the Franco regime, in the State Department there were still those who desired the dictator's overthrow and others with shades of opinion somewhere in between. But the Americans were, and unanimously, determined to answer Britain's short-lived pursuit of its perceived national interests in Spain and much better equipped as an emerging world power. Hoare was among the first to express his concern. Hayes, he complained, was disposed to offer the Spanish government economic advantages "without our knowledge or at our expense". Any concessions would be used "to prop up Franco's government, and run contrary to my statements to Franco, Jordana and Lequerica that we detest the Falangist regime," Hoare observed.[95] Roberts thought Hayes was "rapidly becoming one of General Franco's staunchest supporters".[96]

Hoare's relations with Lequerica quickly deteriorated, the Foreign Minister perceiving that the envoy was not following the line of Churchill's Commons speech. "Everyone in England, the Prime Minister included, detested the Falangist regime," Hoare declared at their first in-depth meeting.[97] Spain should consider what action to take so as to avoid "isolation after an Allied victory". On wolfram, the envoy protested that clandestine exports continued on a substantial scale to Germany. Before he left for London in October Hoare had what he described as "a very heated final interview" with the Foreign Minister. Insiders in Madrid at this time did not rule out that Lequerica was nursing secret ambitions to become Spain's Prime Minister, eventually ushering in some kind of political transition from within. "Why couldn't the Spanish government start putting its own house in order?" Hoare asked pointedly. He communicated to Lequerica the political message he had absorbed in London: the ordinary Englishman could not distinguish the Franco regime from what it had copied from Fascism and Nazism. At present, Hoare went on, there existed no individual liberty in Spain, arbitrary arrests occurred frequently, men were imprisoned and kept for months on end without investigations; there was a parody of justice, particularly by the military tribunals. "Our discussion became very heated, he insisting on the need of order, and I on the need of individual liberty," Hoare reported to London.[98] It was Lequerica, the subtler diplomat, who lowered the temperature, referring yet again to Churchill's May speech. The Foreign Minister asked Hoare to give Churchill and Eden "assurances" that Spain was anxious to follow Britain in the role the Prime Minister had foreseen for Spain post-war in the Mediterranean.

"I had spoken as an Englishman who knows much of public opinion," the politician-envoy explained to Lequerica as he disengaged from their encounter – revealing the scars on him left by the Abyssinia crisis of 1935. Roberts minuted that the ambassador had spoken well, but added slyly: "I cannot help thinking that his constant comminations are only irritating the Spaniards without achieving their purpose." Hoare was a lonely figure at this time. But if this exchange had become known outside the chanceries the consequences might have been different in both Spain and in Britain, markedly strengthening the veteran statesman's hand. Spain's new Foreign Minister resented Hoare's words and wrote a long letter to Alba in London, who called to inform Cadogan of its contents, thus outflanking Hoare. Lequerica professed that Spain would act at all times with absolute frankness and loyalty towards Britain, but it would also say 'No' where the circumstances did not admit of an accommodation. Evidently that meant Spain's internal affairs – and Cadogan was in accord with that line.

In Churchill's mind, Hoare had been sent to Spain in 1940 to attempt to keep Franco from joining the war on the Axis side, and after Overlord was successfully launched his mission was over. With the wolfram dispute settled on his own terms, the Prime Minister felt his old rival in Conservative party politics of the 1930s could come home. But Churchill's attitude was ambiguous when he and Eden discussed the matter of according him a peerage – Hoare was already the second baronet – to mark the end of his mission. He would be leaving the Commons after serving as MP for Chelsea uninterruptedly since 1910. Making Hoare Viscount Templewood in July '44 – the title he chose after the home he had built himself before the war in Norfolk woods near Cromer – was thus almost a routine matter for such a long-serving MP "At any time he can go to the House of Lords if he does not wish to go back to Spain," he told Eden that May. There followed a rare, though still only private, acknowledgement by the Prime Minister of Hoare's achievement in Spain, but with a sting in its tail: "He has rendered very good service and my only desire is to make him as comfortable as present circumstances and his own record allow."[99] Eden, who had blocked the matter in 1943, talked with his advisers and there was more venom. "If Overlord goes well Spain would become a country of secondary importance, not requiring a political appointment such as Sir Samuel Hoare's," Eden's private secretary recorded of the discussion in the FO. "I would not put it like this," Eden subsequently commented to his officials, "diplomatic representations can be better than political ones".[100] So much for appreciation of Hoare's wartime services. With foes like that in London's high places one of Hoare's motives in "coming home" was precisely to attempt to obtain public recognition for his wartime efforts abroad, and to rehabilitate himself politically for his errors of political judgment pre-war. Hoare in that autumn of '44 had not abandoned hopes for a continuing political career.

Don Juan's Labyrinth

While Franco had, with Churchill's aid, weathered the spring storms of '44, how far had the Pretender advanced his claim to provide Spain with an alternative regime? The generals' petition of September '43 had failed to make any inroads on Franco's will to stay on in untrammelled power. Don Juan must present himself as Spain's alternative more in line with the victorious Allies, his advisers urged. Here was the dictator's weakest flank, they told the Pretender in Lausanne. Gil Robles was shaken by the last conversation he had in Lisbon about Don Juan with Hillgarth in December '43 before the attaché left for naval intelligence duties in the Far East. The diarist quoted Hillgarth as reporting that Churchill had now lost interest in the Spanish Pretender and had observed: "What a shame about that young man!" He was "the pretender who stood the best chance of reigning in Europe, and now he's lost it all!"[101] Unfortunately, there is no British source to vouchsafe for the Prime Minister's alleged words. Hillgarth kept to a promise never to write his war memoirs. But the remarks are too important completely to ignore. Gil Robles held Don Juan must make a clean and public break with the Franco regime as his only way forward.[102]

The Pretender pursued a more uncertain course. He and Franco were in correspondence for much of 1944 and it was the dictator who began it. The exchanges were, of course, secret. Franco's first letter, dated 6 January, conveyed his by now customary mixture of duplicity and vain-glorying. "We are advancing towards the monarchy, it is you who are preventing us from achieving it," the dictator asserted.[103] Yet in the next breath Franco insisted that victory in the Civil War had given him what he called "the sovereign right" to be Spain's ruler. "I only say this to combat the idea of my being a usurper which they wish to parade before your eyes," Franco explained to the Pretender, getting to the essence of what concerned him – "the supposed illegitimacy of my powers". The Pretender's pro-Allied advisers were accused of "playing the absurd card of a rupture [with the regime]". The dictator ended by giving a warning to Don Juan: "Do not listen to what those foreigners may insinuate – the promises to Peter of Yugoslavia, to Greece, to Victor Emmanuel [of Italy] . . . they will disappear before the realities of power" and for Franco these were, of course, Marshal Stalin and Communist guerrillas. Hoare was a target here, but perhaps Churchill as well.

Don Juan's reply was for once clear-cut. "You are one of the few Spaniards who believe in the stability of the regime, the support of the Spanish people and that you will succeed with the victor nations," he told the dictator.[104] "I am convinced that you, and the regime you represent, will not be able to withstand the end of the war. If the monarchy is not restored beforehand the regime will be defeated by those who lost the Civil War, helped by the prevailing international situation," the Pretender went on, attempting to play on the Spanish middle classes' fears about a so-called "second round" of the Civil War. So far so good, but Don Juan then advocated a quick restoration of Spain's Catholic and Traditionalist monarchy; this would offer a third way between, he told Franco, "your totalitarianism" and the return of a democratic republic – "the ante-chamber of extremist anarchy". Such a phrase makes it clear how far Don Juan still was from the tenets of a liberal constitutional monarchy. He claimed his kind of monarchy, if restored, would be closer to the ideals of the July 1936 uprising than the existing Falange regime of Axis inspiration.

Three days after that letter was written, a leading South American daily, *La Prensa*, published a declaration of principles from Don Juan, prepared by his advisers.[105] This repeated, publicly, the Pretender's demand for an urgent restoration of the monarchy for the sake of Spain. A restoration was required to reconcile all Spaniards and to bring about a genuine rectification of Spain's foreign and domestic policies and not to crown the existing set-up, Don Juan emphasized.

The Pretender's words appeared just as the Roosevelt administration suspended the oil shipments to Spain. The petrol crisis was to give everyone in the know singular proof of the Pretender's political gaucherie, or lack of a sense of timing. The Pretender misread the situation for he followed up the news with a telegram to Franco on 3 February, seizing the opportunity as he apparently saw it, to insist on the need for a quick restoration of the monarchy. "Tomorrow may be too late" the telegram ringingly told Spain's dictator.[106] The Pretender warned of the threat of a new Civil War, or, as he clumsily put it, of "revenge with foreign help" of those who had lost the "first round" of that conflict.

Franco was incensed, seeing Don Juan as both in the know and seeking to exploit the regime's most vulnerable moment. His reply dropped all pretence of being conciliatory with the person of the Pretender. "My correspondence has always sought to overcome your obstinacy," Franco declared, complaining of "errors" Don Juan refused to abandon. "We shall defend Spain's sovereignty to the last man and to the last Catholic, not willing to allow the world war to deprive Spain of the fruits of the victorious Crusade," the dictator continued, apparently offering defiance of the Allied oil embargo.[107] But Don Juan's language made things worse on another front too. By a quick restoration, the Pretender observed, "we should be able to defend the principles which caused us to oppose the Popular Front". Such an appeal might attract waverers amongst supporters of the Franco regime, but it went down very badly amongst former Republicans to whom Don Juan had only just offered a reconciliation in the *La Prensa* interview.

The Pretender had only weakened his position. So, in a bid to keep up the momentum, the Infante Don Alfonso decided to attempt again to get Franco to see reason, reason which, for the Infante, was grounded in the Allies' now inevitable victory. The Pretender's representative wrote to the dictator on 25 February, following this a few days later with an aide mémoire and what might be called a position paper by Don Juan. The Infante appealed to Franco for the sake of Spain as an old comrade in arms and their young days together at military academy. "I did my utmost," the Infante subsequently told his fellow monarchist general Kindelán. But the dictator was absolutely adamant. With the oil crisis then at its height, it was one of those supremely intimate moments when Spain's dictator refused to be moved by any other consideration than his belief in himself and naked desire to survive.

Don Juan's document accused Franco, by insisting that he should remain in power, of risking "pulling down the monarchy with him". The Pretender refused again to identify with the principles of the Falange, a manoeuvre he dubbed contemptuously "a marriage of the monarchy with failed national syndicalism". As to Franco's charge about seeking a "rupture" Don Juan observed that he had, till now, avoided a public break with the regime, not because he agreed with its internal workings or the foreign policy it pursued but solely in order to deprive either the Allies or the Axis of any excuse to make Spain a theatre of operations of the world war for their own ends. Don Juan also rejected the suggestion Franco aides were then canvassing that Franco should become Regent – on the lines of Hungary's Admiral Horthy – of a monarchy to be restored sometime in the future. (This "Hungarian solution" had already led to a visit by some Spanish journalists to examine on the spot the regime peculiar to Budapest after the collapse of the Austro-Hungarian Empire. It was one of Franco's more bizarre diversionary ploys.)

The Infante also saw Asensio in an attempt to get him to move the dictator. The Army Minister, usually subservient to Franco, did write a letter to the dictator, urging him to reach some kind of understanding with the Pretender for a rapid restoration of the monarchy. As Asensio saw it, this would avoid the Left's return to power in Spain after an Allied victory.[108] Don Juan's thinking is conveyed in a letter he wrote to Gil Robles in Lisbon, seeking to reply to his adviser's constant complaints about his "apparent passivity". The Pretender contended that he had to avoid alienating his more conservative supporters inside Spain.[109]

While rejecting Don Alfonso's pleas face to face, Franco had carefully approved a succession of visits by monarchists, aristocrats who had found a billet in the regime, to see "the King" in Lausanne. But all the parleyings brought on was a heightened repression by the regime and a campaign in the press against a restoration. When a group of 50 Spanish university professors took the step in March '44 – unparalleled since the end of the Civil War – of addressing to Don Juan in Switzerland a joint declaration of allegiance to his cause Franco had them all summarily dismissed from their posts. The suspected ringleaders, professors with chairs, were deported to isolated provincial towns for several months as well as suffering fines heavy for Spain's traditionally ill-paid university teaching staffs.[110]

In April '44 Don Juan made Gil Robles his official representative outside Spain – an appointment which says a good deal about the lack of any more adequate figure in the monarchist ranks to fulfil such a (potentially) important post. Gil Robles, widely hated among ex-Republicans and the Left since his days as leader of the right-wing CEDA party under the Second Republic, possessed an inordinate sense of self-importance, and was to manifest little disposition, or tact, for rallying support for the Pretender's cause. He did not go aboard on Don Juan's behalf until 1947 when any chance of dislodging Franco had passed. But the dictator struck nonetheless at Gil Robles, pressuring Dr Salazar to order the Spanish politician to leave the Portuguese capital. He was "confined" to Busaco, the beautiful, forested resort in northern Portugal. "I accept this harsh testing time . . . My great political offence is that I do not bow the knee," Gil Robles wrote self righteously in his dairy.[111]

Don Juan's growing sense of the weakness of his position showed up cruelly when he wrote in April asking for a personal meeting with Franco – and was refused. As intermediary, the Pretender chose to write to General Juan Vigón, the Air Minister, who had been Don Juan's tutor while serving at the court of Alfonso XIII. Don Juan appealed, again, for a quick restoration of the monarchy "in the supreme interest of Spain".[112] The Franco regime would have "no other successor but 'the Reds'," Don Juan asserted, for the post-war international situation would be a highly unfavourable for Spain. "No one has explained to me why the Generalísimo and his government persist in remaining in power," the Pretender went on, adding that he would willingly listen to any arguments on the matter. "I pledge now to hear from the Caudillo's mouth his arguments and, if he convinces me that I am in error, I put myself unconditionally at his orders for the good of Spain." Vigón's reply when it came in June turned the Pretender's *in extremis* appeal on its head. The regime, and its principles, were "indispensable for Spain", Vigón claimed, and should therefore be acceptable for the monarchy.[113] Don Juan felt deeply betrayed by his father's erstwhile aide-de-camp. When reminiscing many years later, the Pretender observed of Vigón to Sainz: "I have very bad memories of him. It was Franco whom he served most faithfully."[114] Using colloquial language, Don Juan went on to remark of Vigón: "What a very shifty type!"

"Many important people in England desire to see a monarchy in Spain," Gil Robles quoted Viscount de Mamblas, the Minister-Counsellor in the Spanish embassy in London, as saying that autumn of 1944 as he passed through Lisbon on his way to Spain.[115] There was "a very strong tendency" in Britain against the Franco regime, the Spanish diplomat thought and the absence of a public stand by Don Juan was lamented. All this was grist, of course, to Gil Robles' mill with his criticisms of the Pretender's inactivity. Yet one of the principal difficulties for Don Juan, when surveying his situation that autumn, was Gil Robles himself. He was the antithesis of Cánovas del Castillo, the statesman who, as a moderate conservative, had united political forces for placing Don Juan's grandfather, Alfonso XII, on the Spanish throne in the nineteenth century.[116] The Foreign Office had already made up their mind about Gil Robles in the crisis summer of 1940, feeling unattracted by his personality, and lack of political following. The FO declined a Madrid embassy suggestion that he should be included in the motley crew of ex-Republican leaders, hand-picked by Cadogan, to come to Britain for the eventuality that Franco would join the Axis side in the war and political material for an alternative Spanish regime be needed. "Not much good to us," was Roberts' succinct judgment then[117] on the Spanish right-wing leader from the pre-1936 era.

Churchill's "kindly words" addressed to Franco Spain in the Commons in May represented yet another blow for Don Juan. England's most passionate monarchist did not spare a thought, evidently, for any alternative regime and had contributed to strengthening Franco. One day in August '44 Churchill was in reminiscent mood about the many kings of Europe and the Balkans in his younger days, and spoke of what he had sought to do for them during the Second World War. Pierson Dixon, Eden's principal private secretary, listened and noted down the Prime Minister's words in his diary: "I have fought hard for George [II of Greece], and Peter [of Yugoslavia], the King of Italy slipped through my fingers," Churchill wistfully observed. He had omitted any mention of the Spanish Pretender.[118]

Don Juan was caught in the Spanish labyrinth: the Civil War had polarized Spanish society and Franco's tyranny was doing everything in its power to keep the victors and the vanquished far apart. There exists a fundamental problem close to that nebulous yet very real thing – the Spaniards' national character and the difficulty, in such polarized situations, for any leader to emerge appealing for the pursuit of society's common good. The taking of extreme positions, and not of the common ground, precludes figures emerging as true national leaders rallying many and diverse currents of opinion and interest.

7

Churchill Intervenes II
October–December, 1944

With France liberated the last months of 1944 brought on the decisive phase for the Franco regime's survival, and a series of moves by the dictator showed it. That crucial autumn three leading Spaniards made appeals to Britain, each of which in their differing ways offered Churchill the opportunity for assuming a responsibility, as Britain's leader in the democracies' fight against dictatorship, regarding the future of a regime built on force. One call came from the Caudillo himself, via the Duke of Alba, one from the Pretender, Don Juan, and the third, the most remarkable, from General Antonio Aranda, who grasped the full implications, both in power relationships and moral force, of the Allies' victories over the Axis for Europe. All three were naturally delivered secretly and kept so for many years – in Aranda's case for no less than 50 years. In October 1944 the anti-Franco's general's letter was put aside.

In the previous chapter we saw how both the British Prime Minister and the Foreign Secretary put off the question in the spring of '44 of how the Franco regime might be handled until after a successful Allied invasion of Hitler's Fortress Europe and the liberation of France – Churchill to President Roosevelt and Eden to Hoare en poste in Madrid. "When we have, as we hope, established the Second Front successfully the whole picture will change," the Prime Minister observed, even volunteering that March his view to the American President that any long-term commitments with the present Franco regime would not be advisable. With Hoare the Foreign Secretary was apparently even more explicit: "We would wish to take more vigorous action than is desirable in present circumstances," Eden explained, going on to specify what that more vigorous action he envisaged for the future would be – "to clear out the Falangists and the Germans and if necessary Franco himself". But he observed: "There is little prospect as yet that any alternative regime would be satisfactory policy." 'As yet' apparently meant the Foreign Secretary was keeping an open mind back in February as to what alternatives might emerge in Spain as Overlord changed circumstances dramatically for continental Europe. We are, apparently, back again with that "half-open door" prospect British diplomats had previously given Don Juan if he had prepared skilfully enough. It is, of course, possible to see Eden's remarks as no more than temporizing, that professional vice of diplomats left without a proper input from the politicians. Eden's record shows that his antipathy for the Franco regime, as well as for the Spanish generals, was genuine. But, though the politician with an anti-Fascist record, he never imposed that approach upon his officials who often pursued their self-styled "objective" view of Britain's interests.

When he did intervene from November onwards, Churchill took full responsibility for the formulation of British policy towards the Iberian peninsula. He faced Eden, Hoare and even the Foreign Office who, at that juncture at least, were all in favour of heightened pressure on Franco in a policy co-ordinated with Washington. The Prime Minister refused this last cardinal point yet there now existed the possibility of the Roosevelt Administration swinging away from the past tough policy of suspending oil shipments to Spain – economic sanctions in all but name.

Churchill was heavily involved that autumn in the making of post-war Europe, and alarmed as the collapse of Nazi Germany brought the Red Army and the Soviet Union's influence nearer central Europe. He travelled much – in August in Italy, in October in Moscow, in November in Paris and in December he was in Greece where he exercised, as he put it in his war memoirs, "a more direct control" in the battle to stop the Communists seizing power in Athens. The United States was alarmed at Churchill's intervening in a civil war with the aim, which the Prime Minister achieved, of restoring the Greek monarchy. In August Churchill had spelt out in a message to the Italian people what he understood by western democracy. Among the "tests" for a democracy he offered were: "Have the people the right to turn out a government of which they disapprove and are constitutional means provided? Are their courts free from violence by the executive? Is the peasant or workman . . . free from the fear that some grim police organisation under the control of a single party will tap him on the shoulder and pack him off to bondage or ill treatment?"[1] The Italians, who had fought Britain in the war, had to work their passage to democracy, but the Spanish people, who had not taken up arms against Britain but stayed neutral, were to receive less. In reality, Churchill's position was only a victor's terms to Italy in the play of power politics.

Churchill devised his own reply to General Franco, instead of following Foreign Office advice to back Hoare's proposed "final warning" to the Spanish dictator with a personal message co-ordinated with the Americans. A fundamental error in the Prime Minister's reply was the omission, which had been in the Foreign Secretary's draft, of the reason why Spain, under Franco, would not be admitted to the future United Nations Organisation: the repressive nature of the regime of Franco. Hoare's proposals, by contrast, envisaged a place for Spain in a Western Europe based upon the rule of law, with influential Spaniards possibly coming to perceive this to be in their country's national interest and acting as a fulcrum. By rejecting Eden's policy of making Spain's eventual UN membership dependent upon internally brought-about reforms, Churchill threw away one of the Allies' best cards for encouraging such change. If Churchill had applied to Spain his own tests in his homily to the

Italian people that might have had some influence over Spain's elites as the world war ended. "Power, law and freedom", which the Prime Minister had maintained were at stake in Greece, were not a concern for him in Spain.

Three Spaniards Wait Upon Churchill

In October 1944 General Franco reluctantly accepted an Allied victory over Hitler's Germany as the inevitable outcome of the world war. Fearful for his own survival, the Spanish dictator grasped the nettle and made an approach to the British Prime Minister via his ambassador, Alba. Franco's hoped-for stratagem was that the duke should convey its contents at one of his uniquely-privileged têtes-à-tête with Churchill.

Franco's "incredible letter", as Hoare called it, [2] parted characteristically from a feigned position of strength, with Britain assigned the role of seeker of a "much-needed friendship" from Spain. "Our good friend" was how Franco styled the British Prime Minister in his 18 October letter to Alba, seizing on Churchill's remarks about Spain in his Commons speech in May. Churchill, Franco thought, shared his fears of Communist Russia, or "insidious Bolshevism" as the dictator called it. The letter came direct from the Pardo, the Generalísimo's residence, the Foreign Minister Lequerica having played no part in it. Britain was unblushingly addressed as "a country long used to dealing with other countries whatever their systems of government may be". Alba pronounced that Franco's letter was in "shocking Spanish".

While the ambassador was still pondering how best he might handle Franco's message, the letter of another Spanish general, Aranda, – addressed this time directly to the Prime Minister – had reached London.[3] It had been brought secretly from Madrid to Downing Street by Walter Starkie, the ebullient Irish head of the British Institute in Madrid. Starkie had more than once sought to persuade the British authorities that "another Spain" still existed alongside the official circles of Franco's capital, deeply resentful of the regime and its inefficiences. In spite of its potential significance if it had received sensitive attention, the letter was passed by No. 10 to the FO where Roberts minuted: "We can have nothing to do for the present with General Aranda's letter."[4] For his errand Starkie got only a rebuke from his British Council superiors at the FO's instigation.

Aranda appealed to Churchill to cease the British government's support for the Franco regime. It was shrewdly devised, concentrating on that essential support from abroad; Franco had often paraded the evidence of support, he claimed, from the Americans and the British when keeping his fellow generals in line. "Señor, Once again the Spanish nation appeals to the

generosity and understanding of the English people as the sole means to end
a regime of tyranny," the appeal began, aiming to touch memories of the
Peninsula War of which Churchill was often mindful. After recalling the
British Prime Minister's famous words about "blood, sweat, toil and tears,"
Aranda declared pointedly enough: "We ask only that the British do not
support in Spain what they would reject indignantly for themselves in
England." Aranda was emphatic – and it was another key point – that Spain
was not asking for any material aid or intervention from Britain – the *coup
d'état*, by implication, would come from inside Spain. By depriving the
Franco regime of support Churchill, Aranda maintained, might open the
way for a strong, but liberal-inclined, monarchy to emerge as solution for
Spain's political problems. Eden appears never to have raised Aranda's letter
when seeing the Prime Minister. Churchill, who had taken such a close
interest in bribing the generals, passes over the Spanish general's approach
to him in his war memoirs.

The British chargé in Madrid Bowker was however sent a copy of
Aranda's letter by Roberts and asked to comment. (The chargé's reaction to
Aranda's letter was of course also suppressed by the FO for 50 years.) The
chargé was sceptical – to London's relief.

How was it, Bowker asked,[5] that a regime so generally detested survived
with Franco more powerful internally than ever before? "There has been
constant talk of a change of regime and it has repeatedly been said that the
generals or the monarchists, or both, were on the point of presenting an
ultimatum to Franco." Aranda had met with a degree of success, Bowker
did admit, liaising with centre and left-wing elements inside Spain who
could be expected to support the new regime suggested by the general. But
there was no organized opposition, nor had any personality capable of
forming it emerged to challenge Franco – "not excluding Aranda", the
British diplomat judged.

The chargé offered his overall estimate of Spain's situation. "Responsible
Spaniards", as he put it, whatever their political views, would prefer not to
take any action which might produce another upheaval, or a "second round"
of the Civil War. Fear of further class violence and even the possibility of a
revolution, supposedly led by "the Communists", did breed political inertia
in Spain. However exaggerated those fears, Bowker added, they assisted the
Franco regime to survive. The dictator could thus concentrate on preventing
any leader or forces from emerging as expression of the rest of Spain – apart
that was from an opportunist pro-Franco elite who gained so dispropor-
tionately from the regime's continuance.

But times throughout Europe were changing that autumn and winter of
1944, and this was possibly the essence of the problem. Where might

Bowker's "responsible Spaniards" turn, or perhaps be induced to turn, if Aranda's appeal had been taken into account and had led to a public shift by British policy-makers away from support of the Franco regime? Aranda's difficulty in obtaining a hearing by London in 1944 lay, in part, in the protagonism he had promised in '42 and '43, and not been able to deliver. His very political astuteness – it was an innovatory step to cultivate centre and left-wing Republicans, which Don Juan only essayed after the war's end – prevented him from becoming an alternative leader among the less politically-aware generals cultivated by Franco. In an unflattering symmetry, both the duller Spanish generals and the British diplomats preferred to stay with Franco to whom their hierarchical obligations and their accreditation bound them. "On present form, it seems to me, that the Spanish generals are no use and Aranda is not the best of them," was Cadogan's stinging dismissal of Aranda's appeal.[6] Cadogan, who had seen the letter, and Bowker's assessment, was again settling the matter for the department in the absence of any input from Eden.

It was, however, disingenuous of British diplomats to profess to believe, at one and the same time, both in the risks of "Red" tyranny taking over Spain and in an inertia paralyzing the country politically. There was no sign the Spanish generals would have hesitated for a moment against the former – and they had already mobilized fighting units against the Communist *maquis* in the Pyrenean region to prove it. As British policy towards Spain, it was contradictory.

The third appeal came that winter from the Pretender. This was directed at King George VI, Don Juan's cousin, and brought to London by his mother, ex Queen Victoria Eugenia. "Memorandum of Don Juan, given me by Queen Ena, November 1944", Hoare wrote in his own hand on the message. The Foreign Office, to whom the appeal was passed, thus getting the Pretender's démarche back on the rails in a constitutional monarchy, apparently kept no copy; one fortunately survives in Hoare's papers.[7] A passing reference to Don Juan's plea by Eden in a memo to Churchill[8] shows the two leaders were at least aware of the Pretender's move. Alfonso XIII's widow had come to England to be with her dying mother, Princess Beatrice and last of Queen Victoria's daughters. To everyone in the know it was as obvious that Don Juan's mother dearly wished to bring her son to the British authorities' attention, when the future of Spain was under active debate within the government, as it was that the Foreign Office shunned arousing suspicion by the Franco regime. Of course Alba knew – there was even gossip he might marry the ex-queen. George VI had proposed inviting the Pretender to Windsor with his aunt, but the FO instructed the Berne legation that "the inclusion of Don Juan should be discouraged".[9]

Unwisely the Pretender's memorandum tackled the British government's attitude to his cause head on. "Is the British government opposed to the restoration of the monarchy in Spain?" he asked. "Is this opposition due to the fact that they wish the present regime to continue indefinitely, or because they would be glad to see the Republic restored?" Franco maintained that the governments of Britain and the United States saw with satisfaction his continuance at the head of the Spanish state, both at present and in the future, Don Juan said. If that were true, he would seriously consider abstaining from all political activities in the future. "If on the other hand," the Pretender ploughed on, "the United Nations . . . though not wanting to interfere in Spanish political life, would be glad to see a regime restored better able to establish policies in harmony with the prevalent ideology, then the successor to the Spanish crown would re-double his efforts." "Prevalent ideology", relativizing the ideals of the increasingly victorious democracies, was a clumsy phrase for Don Juan to use – with his own past studying Fascism in Mussolini's Italy.

The British government was assured by the Pretender that he had "categorically" refused Franco's conditions for a restoration – the demand to identify himself with the regime's principles. But in a passage revealing as to Don Juan's innermost disposition he declared: "Don Juan is not opposed to a restoration brought about in concert with General Franco." The Pretender in fact wrote late November to Ventosa, the Catalan monarchist leader, observing that "according to many people the restoration could only take place with Franco's approval".[10] That notwithstanding, a summary of the programme for a return to constitutional government, drafted by López Oliván, was included with the Pretender's memorandum.

Don Juan had blundered and, as in 1943, was appealing to the Allies while being willing to accede to the throne with the Spanish dictator's aid. The Pretender was far from seeking to forge conditions which might have obliged Britain and the US to respond because there already existed the basis for an alternative regime. How could the Allies be expected to take a pretender seriously when he even talked of considering abstaining from all political activity? His clumsiness was an embarrassment for Hoare, long suspected in the Foreign Office for encouraging the monarchists against the Caudillo. This appeal too got no reply.

In contrast to the appeals of Aranda and Don Juan kept secret, Franco was able to intervene publicly as well with an "interview" in the Anglo-Saxon press. An innovation for the regime engineered by Lequerica, it proved eminently successful – judged by the notice abroad it caught. The vehicle adopted was the United Press, seen by the Foreign Minister as the more pliant of the US wire services. Franco never spoke any of his "replies", the answers to previously submitted questions had been supplied by Lequerica. The red carpet treatment accorded a senior executive of UP, who flew the Atlantic for the occasion, was part of Lequerica's campaign to cultivate American business interests. UP later obtained a contract to supply its service to EFE, the regime's news agency.

Spain, Franco declared,[11] was expecting a place at the peace conference which would end the Second World War. Such a brazen claim by a self-styled neutral state simply could not be ignored by Britain. Grasping the changing fortunes of the world, Lequerica had attempted in the interview to re-position the regime internally. Spain was no longer a Fascist-inspired regime but, the astonished outside world was told by the dictator, now an "organic democracy". Franco wrapped Don Juan's knuckles yet again, insisting in the answers on his disposition to install a monarchy based on Falange principles.

An Alternative for Spain

Two days before Franco made his approach via Alba to the British Prime Minister, Hoare had urged London to undertake a full review of the Spanish question in consultation with its American ally. It was Hoare's despatch which made it impossible for London simply to ignore Franco's démarche via Alba, let alone his intervention in the press. In an attempt to strengthen his plea, Hoare came to London for what proved a lengthy and frustrating stay. Franco, the envoy-politician informed London,[12] was apparently still convinced that he could successfully maintain what Hoare dubbed "the double policy of totalitarianism within Spain and friendly relations with the Allies outside it". "Are the Allies prepared to accept this double policy?" Hoare asked, issuing what was effectively a call to Churchill, and the coalition government he led, and to the Roosevelt administration, to face up to Allied responsibilities – as he had come to see them after four years in Madrid.

"With the elimination of other totalitarian governments in Europe the Spanish anomaly becomes more and more conspicuous," Hoare's memorandum began, pointing to the mood in France after the liberation from Vichy. There was a rising tide of resentment against any regime tainted with Fascism. "We may be forced into action by public opinion," the envoy warned. Should not the Allied governments consider "the expediency of some further pressure on the Spanish government?" Hoare recommended that British and US economic experts should study the necessary measures should Franco fail to respond. The measures should be applied gradually and not in sudden, dramatic blows. A propaganda campaign should also be launched by the Allies. While not telling Spaniards what form of government they should adopt, the campaign should nonetheless aim to bring influential people in Spain to see that "a country which does not conform with the basic principles of law and order cannot expect to be regarded as a member of the community of European nations. We should concentrate on broad principles, on certain basic rights for individuals," he advised. "If Spain wishes to be a member of the European 'Club' General Franco should be clearly told that these are the rules that Spain must keep." These issues – what in today's language would be called human rights – Hoare had publicly raised addressing his Chelsea constituents that May and previously in 1943; he was consistent. His last meeting with Franco as Britain's special wartime ambassador, Hoare proposed, should be used to deliver such a "solemn warning" by the British government, and, fully co-ordinated beforehand with the US, Washington's envoy should undertake a parallel step.

Hoare's personal evolution during 1944 helps to explain the thinking behind his memorandum. In March the envoy had told Eden, when the row over the Allies' suspended petrol shipments to Spain was at its height, of his expectation of the regime's demise. "What is it that makes the deathbed of the regime so unconscionably protracted an affair?" he asked.[13] It was only lack of leadership among military and civilian opponents of Franco, and the divisions of both the monarchists and Republicans in exile. But Hoare had concluded: "If our invasion plans succeed, the various oppositions will be forced into action, General Franco's last card will have been trumped." The Spanish generals did not move that summer after the D-Day landings in France, though Franco did, unleashing a fresh wave of political executions "on a considerable scale" as Hoare informed Eden[14]. Franco's repression and contempt for appeals to show mercy – "destroying ideas by executions" as Hoare once put it – appalled the English statesman with a conservative belief in "good government". For Eden's benefit, Hoare instanced the case of the mayor of a small town near Toledo, a well-known doctor, who had been imprisoned with the Nationalists' victory in the Civil War, though he had no personal responsibility in any act of left-wing violence. Kept without trial for five years, he was condemned to death by a military tribunal and shot at the beginning of August 1944, after a wait of seven months under sentence of death. Hoare's despatches kept the Foreign Office well informed on Franco's repression, now heightened, he pointed out, to prevent any opposition from organizing itself.

From July several Spanish Army divisions, dispatched on Franco's orders, were in action in the Pyrenean frontier region against incursions by left-wing guerrillas to prevent the liberation of France being followed up by Communists and other left Republicans attempting to topple his regime as well. This "Red" menace was exploited unceasingly by Franco as portent of a "second round" of Spain's Civil War. The guerrillas' invasion attempt was an unmitigated disaster with serious boomerang effects. They never encountered the widespread welcome they anticipated. But, worse, it caused the generals to swing, at what might otherwise have been a critical juncture, behind the dictator more firmly. De Gaulle's provisional admin-istration seconded in reality the regime's "law and order" operations, but the fact that De Gaulle's War Minister was a Communist was a godsend for Franco's propaganda machine. Hoare, who perceived – as Churchill never did – Franco's interested obsession with "the Communist danger", had already alerted London to this ploy.[15]

A shock greeted Hoare when he reached London in October to play a difficult role in deciding what to do about Spain. An ambassador can go no further than offer new ideas, as Hoare did in the memorandum, without risking being suspected of seeking to make policy – and already many in London did just that of the former Foreign Secretary. Hoare quickly grasped how for London the war had swept on elsewhere – Eisenhower and Montgomery were disputing how the final assault on Germany should be mounted – and Spain had ceased to concern the Allies as a military factor. "Week alone in London: no great interest in Spain," Hoare noted glumly in one of the personal notes[16] he began making. These hand-written notelets, grouped to cover a few days each time, are an invaluable record of Hoare's private feelings at the time; they were a part of his preparations for *Ambassador on Special Mission*.

The Big Debate Begins

When the debate began things turned essentially on the conflict between the wartime expectations and ideals of British public opinion and the demands of national interests. These were however as perceived by profes-sional diplomats and by the Prime Minister and the Foreign Secretary, as and when they took up the dossiers. Both Churchill and Eden gave only intermittent and often superficial attention to Spanish affairs. The Foreign Secretary now also carried the time-consuming role of Leader of the House of Commons, travelled much and was, not infrequently, ill during crucial weeks of policy-making on Spain and Franco's future. The role of their offi-cials inevitably grew. The dictator's approach via Alba showed that he knew a hinge moment had come. But with those "kindly words" from the Prime

Minister, interestedly repeated and repeated in Madrid, Franco might think that his approach to London was not wholly without prospects.

Cadogan's being first to see Hoare indicated the permanent head's desire to set the Foreign Office's tone. Cadogan's minute afterwards was another near-classic expression of nineteenth-century nation state diplomacy. "I told him [Hoare] that however much one might dislike a particular regime one ought to think twice before departing from non-intervention in the internal affairs of another country."[17] Cadogan, who had jostled Chamberlain in 1939 into recognition of the Nationalists' victory in the Civil War, had of course a complete grasp of all the ambiguities and advantages of non-intervention in that conflict. Hoare jotted in his weekly notelet: "Discussion with Cadogan as to the future [of Spain], my memorandum and his doubtful attitude."[18] Cadogan, *grand commis de l'état* and ever-vigilant keeper of the state's "national interest", was countering Hoare's offer of a politician's input for future policy towards Spain.

Roberts nonetheless supported Hoare's memorandum when he wrote what proved to be the key policy paper[19] until Churchill intervened. Roberts too wanted the direct involvement of both Churchill and Roosevelt in what he clearly intended would be a shift in policy regarding Franco. It would be "unrealistic", Roberts contended, not to face up to the ideological considerations – Cadogan detested ideologies – which would be raised by the Franco regime in Britain, France and the United States over the next few months in a victorious war for democracy. "If we do nothing now we may well be risking worse trouble for ourselves later on," Roberts maintained, observing: "We do not wish the moderate opposition to Franco, whether monarchist or Republican . . . to lose sympathy for this country – an important consideration." Such forces should be kept in play, he contended, "so that if and when opposition to Franco comes to a head it is they, and not the Communists and anarchists, who take over. An even worse possibility would be a renewal of the Civil War." Roberts represented a new generation of diplomats; he was not an aristocrat, his father was in business in Argentina.

To have effect Hoare's strong warning to Franco must be accompanied by a message from Churchill; at all events Hoare must be empowered to speak, Roberts argued, "on the direct and personal authority of the Prime Minister". To correct the perception still in Madrid of British support for the regime, Churchill's August homily to the Italians on democracy ought to have a place in his message to Franco. Roberts again referred to the demoralizing effects Churchill's "kindly words" had had on opposition elements inside Spain – "a severe blow" he called them. "Action as above would show the red light to Franco and," Roberts added, "enable HMG to satisfy critics here that we are not appeasing an unpopular regime in Madrid." Roberts, however, rejected Hoare's proposal that British and American experts should study eventual economic sanctions, reiterating the position on the need of Spanish iron ore and pyrites. As to co-ordinating policy with Washington, Roberts allowed there was "always some danger" consulting the Americans about a tougher policy towards Spain. "But this is a risk we must run." The US embassy in London had been repeatedly pressing Roberts,[20] emphasizing State Department concern over how Franco was stepping up the repression of opponents and extending the ugly powers of the Falange – exactly Hoare's submission.

Eden was Hoare's ally as drafting began for a reply to Franco. The Spanish dictator's "double policy", as Hoare had called it, was highlighted in a memorandum on "The Unsatisfactory Situation in Spain".[21] The Foreign Secretary was to tell the War Cabinet that Franco was showing no disposition to alter the "objectionable characteristics" of his regime, in spite of the imminence of a United Nations victory and grossly exploiting the guerrilla "menace" in the Pyrenees. As final aggravation, there was his "insolent suggestion" that Spain should have a seat at the peace conference. "I have therefore come to the conclusion that HMG should reconsider its attitude to Spain." Hoare had rightly drawn attention "to the strong and growing feeling of public opinion that an unfortunate anomaly continues with the existence of a totalitarian regime in Spain".

"Some action" must now be taken, the paper submitted, awaiting an input from Britain's wartime political leaders. Spaniards must be told that genuinely friendly relations with Britain would be "impossible so long as internal conditions remain in complete contradiction to the principles for which the United Nations stand". However diplomatic the language, this was the crucial issue for it referred to Franco's tyranny. The Foreign Secretary wanted full consultations with the US government, Hoare's essential point.

Feeling was indeed rising in London against Franco. Clement Attlee, deputy Prime Minister and Labour leader in the coalition government, now spoke out, urging the Cabinet to make the shift of policy on Spain. "There is not one of our allies who would not wish to see this regime destroyed; we are running the danger of being considered to be Franco's sole external support," Attlee warned in a paper[22] for the Cabinet, clearly opposing Churchill's attitude in his Commons speech. Attlee was unambiguously on Hoare's side, praising the ambassador in the paper to the Cabinet for "the great skill" he had displayed in Madrid. The Labour leader, who had visited Republican Spain in 1937, had disliked Hoare intensely pre-war. But, unlike Churchill, he was prepared by 1944 to judge fairly how Hoare had grown in stature during the war years, with an intellectual evolution while in foreign parts.

Attlee had been a careful reader of the envoy's Madrid despatches. "Lord Templewood has frequently pointed out in the strongest terms the incompetence, corruption and oppression of the Franco regime which the Spanish people have had to endure for so long . . . Franco owes his position to our enemies, who used Spain as a practice ground. He continues to keep in prison many thousands of Spaniards and he executes a number of his prisoners every month," Attlee declared with feeling. Owing to the divisions among the Spanish people, the deputy Premier held that it was unlikely that a democratic government could be established swiftly enjoying general support. "We should aim," Attlee submitted, "at getting in Spain a government which would be inclined to toleration and which would prepare the way for a development towards democracy. To this end we should stiffen our attitude towards the present regime and make it very clear that its disappearance would bring definite advantages to the Spanish people. We should use whatever methods are available to assist in bringing about [the regime's] downfall. We should, especially in the economic field, work with the United States and France to deny facilities to the present regime." In view of the Spaniards' xenophobia, Attlee discarded any overt action inside Spain [by British agents]. But he concluded: "Short of this there is much that can be done."

Here was an input of fresh thinking by a political leader. Attlee's recommendation was sober, realistic and well ahead of the Labour party's public rhetoric on Spain. Aranda's appeal to the Prime Minister, Hoare's suggestions to the Foreign Office and Attlee's proposals, taken together, constitute indeed a yardstick for what might, at this juncture of the war, have been attempted in a bid to loosen the Franco regime's grip on Spain. With Franco's lust for absolute power there is no guarantee that such measures, even applied with sufficient skill, could have obtained Attlee's goal of a less brutal successor regime. But, due to Churchill's intervention, they were never tried.

As the Foreign Office waited for Eden to obtain Churchill's approval of his proposals for the upcoming Cabinet on Spain the two politicians travelled to Paris to meet De Gaulle's provisional government. But so little did the FO anticipate any difficulty, a telegram went to Washington instructing Halifax to seek assurances that Hayes would, under instruction, take similar steps with Franco. If joint warnings proved insufficient to shake the dictator, Halifax should urge the Americans to consider "further measures". These would "show the Spanish people even more clearly that the United Nations is no longer prepared to condone General Franco's policy". We are back with Hoare's suggestion of setting up a party of British and American experts to examine eventual economic sanctions. The telegram to Washington explicitly mentioned the possibility of suspending oil shipments to Spain, as happened at the beginning of the year, and included mention of Churchill's August homily to the Italians – hardly a prelude to appeasing Franco's regime. Eden, overworked, had left drafting that Washington telegram to his principal private secretary, but Roberts had minuted the moment had now come "to turn the heat on General Franco".

Ending in Blood

Four pages long, the Prime Minister's reply[23] was dictated the same day as he received from Eden the Foreign Office draft, the product of weeks of departmental debate, consultations with Hoare and study of all the latest Madrid despatches. Churchill, it seems, consulted no one before reacting. All his prejudices and ignorance of the Spanish situation are laid bare. The Prime Minister rejected outright the Foreign Office plea for "some action" against Franco's regime. "What you are proposing to do is little less than stirring up a revolution in Spain," the Prime Minister thundered at the Foreign Secretary. "You begin with oil [a reference to eventual sanctions which the record shows Eden had already discounted], you will quickly end in blood . . . If we lay hands on Spain I am of the opinion we shall be making needless trouble for ourselves and very definitely taking sides in ideological matters. Should the Communists become masters of Spain we must expect the infection to spread very fast through both Italy and France." Churchill dispatched Hoare's solemn warning to Franco with contempt. "You need not, I think, suppose that Franco's position will be weakened by our warnings. He, and all those associated with him, will never consent to be butchered by the Republicans, which is what would happen." No reports from British diplomats in Spain at that time had suggested any such thing was remotely possible by any Republicans. No observer on the spot doubted the Spanish military's resolve. Churchill's lurid and arbitrary imaginings were similar only to the Franco propagandists' utterances. They, of course, had an interest in playing up Spaniards' fears of an eventual "second round" in the Civil War.

In full flood, the Prime Minister accused the Foreign Office of left-wing sympathies. "I certainly was not aware the FO nursed such sentiments . . . I can well believe that such a policy as you outline would be hailed with delight by our left-wing forces, who would be very glad to see Great Britain [on] the left wing of a doctrinal war." Churchill's intemperate language revealed the party leader: "I doubt very much whether the Conservative party would agree once the case was put before them, and personally I should not be able to seek a fleeting popularity by such paths."

Churchill's attack on members of his own government team was one of the most violent outbursts recorded of him during the world war. It reveals emotions bordering on a paranoia about Spanish unruliness and bloodshedding, whether they derived from his own fantasies or those fed him by his "cousin" the Duke of Alba, in their brandy-laden get-togethers. Churchill's war memoirs of this period – *Triumph and Tragedy* – give an inadequate account of his making policy towards Spain or of the debate on how to deal with Franco with selective references and important omissions. Aranda's letter and Don Juan's plea go unmentioned. It is in an appendix that we learn of the Prime Minister's reply to Franco on behalf of the coalition government. Hoare in his memoirs was to give the British public the first full text. Churchill's reticence over this period contrasts with his personally involved, lurid account of the run up to the Spanish Civil War.

Returning obsessively to the theme of Spanish violence, Churchill told Eden: "A river of blood flows between the two sides in Spain and there is hardly a family which does not nurse a blood feud. Might I venture to beg you to consider the three principal tenets to which I hold?" Here followed a very wide-ranging input by Britain's wartime leader for the policy-makers at the Foreign Office to heed, going far beyond Spain. It went, indeed, just about everywhere that Britain was then perceived to have interests and influence – unless Churchill himself should rule otherwise. "*A*: Opposition to Communism, *B*: Non-intervention in the domestic affairs of countries which have not molested us, *C*: No special engagements in Europe requiring the maintenance of a large British army, but the effective development of a world peace organisation thoroughly armed." The memorandum is initialled WSC in red ink and reveals how many issues were then on his mind and at the mercy of his ever-fluent pen or dictation.

Maybe Churchill was not so completely carried away, but calculated that the broadside would assist Cadogan, who had clearly lost the initial debates to Eden and Hoare. The Prime Minister spoke of the dangers of "interference, yet Churchill was to take "a more direct control", as he described it, the next month in Greece, flying to Athens to do so. Spain, he maintained, had done "us much more good than harm in the war". He clearly had not budged from his May speech despite all the outcry.

"I should, of course, be very glad to see a monarchical and democratic restoration [in Spain], but once we have identified ourselves with the Communist side, which, whatever you say, would be the effect of our policy, all our influence would be gone for a middle course. It would be far better to allow those Spanish tendencies to work themselves out, instead of precip-itating a renewal of the Civil War which is what you will do if you press this matter," Churchill reiterated aggressively to the Foreign Secretary.

The Prime Minister was displaying his complete unawareness of how the Franco regime responded, and would continue to respond, to any "working out" of alternative tendencies inside Spain. Churchill, in effect, was signalling to such tendencies that they could not expect to obtain from him any help, even verbal or moral protection, against systematic repression. As for a move jointly with the Americans, the "Former Naval Person" dismissed the idea in stinging tones. "I do not see why we should go and try and work up the United States," he told Eden.

It is worth emphasizing the gulf which existed at that time between Churchill's imaginings and the reporting by the Madrid embassy on the situation prevailing in Spain. British diplomats' estimates could, of course, err so it may be appropriate to note a remarkably similar analysis of the rela-tion of forces, military and police, and the disorganized opposition elements, being given at that time by an Italian observer exceptionally well-informed on Spain, Cardinal Gaetano Cicognani, Papal Nuncio to Spain since 1938. Bowker had just reported[24] that November the stepping up of arrests of those suspected by the regime – monarchists and moderate Republicans as well as the usual left wingers. More sinister, "Our Man in Madrid," said, selected Falangists were undergoing armed training. "All the evidence suggests that all members of the party from Franco at the top to the lowest thugs at the bottom are determined that the Falange should continue to exist, come what may outside Spain," the chargé told the FO Franco had realized an eventual restoration of the monarchy, engineered by pro-royalist generals in the army – the first pillar of his regime – would mean his own eclipse. The Falange – the second pillar – thus became even more important for the Caudillo's survival.

The chargé reiterated his personal estimate that a majority of Spaniards presently opted for the evil they knew, suffering the vexations of the existing regime. But Bowker offered a highly important proviso for London's atten-tion. "As soon as it is evident that moderate elements in France and Italy have gained control, a vast body of public opinion hostile to the present regime will inevitably make itself felt [in Spain]." Paradoxically, Churchill's efforts at that time were directed to ensuring that moderates had control in precisely those two European countries, that was why he had been in Paris endorsing of General De Gaulle. Roberts, as yet unaware of Churchill's outburst to Eden, noted[25] of Bowker's telegram: "This despatch shows how very necessary it is to make a frontal assault upon the regime as has been proposed. In attacking the Falange we can be sure of the sympathy of the great majority of Spaniards." Churchill's reaction was to throw the Foreign Office proposals completely off course.

Naturally nothing of Churchill's astonishing attack on Eden and his department as a "nest of lefties" emerged in the public domain in wartime Britain. "The policy of the Foreign Office has never tended towards the fostering of Communism. The policy which I am now advocating is designed to avert the danger in Spain which you fear" Eden was recommended by his officials to tell the Prime Minister when they learned, astounded, the contents of Churchill's note. By late 1944, after the Red Army's advances in eastern Europe, Churchill was becoming obsessed with the dangers of a Communist great power upsetting the traditional balance of Europe. Britain's Prime Minister and General Franco apparently shared such fears. But the Spanish dictator had a personal stake in parading such fears; affecting such a stance offered the best chance that other powers would tolerate the survival of his regime. Churchill's views were, in a word, coloured by that quality Cadogan so detested in the conduct of foreign affairs – a lack of realism; anti-Communism was for Churchill a twisted kind of ideology.

Ruling out consultations with the United States, and the reasons he gave for that, form, however, the gravest error in the Prime Minister's stand. Key elements in the Roosevelt administration by that winter felt that Churchill was backing all the most conservative forces in Europe – and in Spain as much as in Greece. Many in Washington did not hesitate to use the word reactionary.

Churchill Makes His Own Policy

The question still outstanding in the policy debate about Spain was whether Churchill after his outburst against the Foreign Office might calm down and heed the advice offered him. Above all, would he perceive that Spain's position had changed, that is weakened, after the Allied successes that autumn against Nazi Germany and the liberation of France? Why go on placating Franco Spain? As the cool-headed Roberts had already argued,[26] as the marches and counter-marches over the oil embargo proceeded with the Americans earlier in the year: "Once the Second Front has been established we can, I am sure, get everything we want in Spain either from the present regime or by changing it." A head of political steam had undoubtedly built up. Hoare, a cautious statesman, held extra pressure could now be safely applied to a deeply compromised regime; so did the British and American Service Chiefs and there was Attlee's call to the War Cabinet that

Britain should not isolate itself among its wartime allies by continued support of Franco.

Before the Cabinet tackled the matter a rare question on Spain in the Commons suggested strikingly how things were moving. An Independent MP sought to learn the coalition government's position on Franco's demand for a place at the peace conference. Richard Law, Eden's deputy at the FO, answered, reversing, as the FO wanted, Churchill's blundering approval of Franco's wartime conduct the previous May. "So far as HMG are concerned," Law stated,[27] "they see no reason why any country which has not made a positive contribution to the United Nations' war effort should be represented at any discussions on the peace settlement." The Minister contemptuously dismissed Franco's claim in the pseudo interview that Spain now enjoyed "organic democracy", observing: "I think HMG are more wide-awake than some people suppose." The notes which Roberts had prepared for Law's reply[28] show the thinking behind a policy shift on Spain under consideration at the FO. "If we wished to do so, these questions would give us an opportunity for encouraging the present wave of criticism of General Franco and thus opening an offensive against his regime," the cautious diplomat advised his political master. Law had seized the opportunity and the FO had subsequently to take note how the shift which he had foreshadowed made a considerable impression in both Madrid and Moscow. But Law's approach was not kept up.

When Eden replied to Churchill the two politicians' basic difference about Spain emerged: whether stronger pressure for a possible re-alignment of political forces inside Spain was needed to avoid a Communist advance or, as the Premier had trumpeted, would only provoke "a revolution in Spain". "It is certainly not my desire to provoke a revolution, nor indeed is this at all likely at the present stage," the Foreign Secretary observed,[29] putting the debate back into the realms of reality. Franco was now bolstering up the discredited Falange more than ever. If Britain did not give Franco "a straight warning" moderate forces in Spain, civilian and military, would, Eden feared, lose all influence. The Foreign Secretary spoke, in passing, of the monarchist leader Ventosa who had, he said, "talked the last few days to friends in London" and even noted Don Juan's sending a message to George VI. But that was the closest the Catalan politician or the Pretender got to Churchill's attention. As Hoare wanted, Eden urged the Prime Minister to write personally to Franco – "Your own position is such that our warning has most chance of being effective if it is made personally by you." Fact and flattery were excellently mingled in Eden's reply.

Churchill agreed to reply. "In any case I should wish to write my own letter," he told Eden.[30] "I doubt very much whether the Duke of Alba will be capable of making this communication verbally with the necessary precision," Churchill observed intriguingly of his "cousin". But the reply must be after hearing the Cabinet discussion on Spain, and the Prime Minister mentioned the wish of Selborne, Minister of Economic Warfare, to speak. Once again, Churchill rejected consulting with the Americans, despite Eden's flattery. "I deprecate opening these matters to the United States. The State Department do not, I think, need any urging from us to hostility against Spain," he told him bluntly.

Hoare met with an identical response. "Lunch with Winston – non-intervention argument. No threats or USA intervention," the envoy-politician jotted down in one weekly note after their meeting.[31] Telegraphic, but abundantly clear: no heightened pressure on Franco would receive the Prime Minister's backing, nor would the Roosevelt administration be asked to support a British initiative. "Winston, pomp and power" Hoare also noted of the occasion, revealing something of his feelings towards the now all-powerful leader. Hoare judged that taking any further Ventosa's talks in London would be "useless". In another of those notes, the envoy had previously summarized the Spanish monarchist leader's message as "Only exterior pressure [on the regime] will be any good."[32] Churchill's all-prevailing sway ruled that out. Nor evidently had Hoare, when he saw the Prime Minister, pushed for considering Don Juan's message to the King – perhaps because of its constitutional ineptness.

Hoare made another bid to get the Foreign Secretary to secure the Prime Minister's involvement, still anticipating that the Cabinet would hold to Eden's line on Spain. "Nov. 17 – my letter to Eden: I won't go back [to Madrid] without a message," Hoare wrote in another note.[33] "My curious position of being anti-appeasement," he added, in his frankest judgment of how he saw Churchill appeasing the dictator whom the envoy had watched at close hand in Madrid. Here, too, were some of the scars Hoare still carried from Churchill's campaign against the pre-war Chamberlain government of which the envoy had been so prominent a member. In that hand-written letter Hoare insisted[34] to Eden that the British government "must instruct me definitely as to what I should say to Franco". Otherwise, the dictator would exploit the absence of a clear stand "as a sign that we do not disapprove of his regime". Churchill otherwise would be appeasing, and thereby strengthening, Franco, Hoare implied correctly.

In a display of the virtually untrammelled power he by then enjoyed in government Churchill trumped everyone at the War Cabinet meeting on Spain on 27 November. The Prime Minister's personal preferences were to determine Britain's policy towards Franco Spain for the crucial months as the world war was ending. The position on the key issue of Spain's internal situation painstakingly worked out by Eden and the FO was swept aside. "I agree with Lord Templewood's recommendation that a solemn warning should be delivered to General Franco that Spain cannot expect to have the place she deserves in the post-war world, nor maintain really friendly relations with this country so long as internal conditions in Spain remain in complete contradiction to the principles for which the United Nations stand," ran the Foreign Secretary's advice[35] for the Cabinet. Knowing such principles were shared by the State Department, Eden reiterated this line in spite of Churchill's resistance to obtaining US support for Hoare.

No invitation could be issued, the Foreign Secretary submitted, to join the future world organization "until Spain genuinely embraces the basic tenets and principles for which the United Nations are now fighting and which will be reaffirmed by their victory". This was the cardinal point, and Eden's defeat in the Cabinet meant its substitution by Churchill's crude decision for an unconditional boycott of Spain, which played so much into Franco's hands. The Prime Minister's friendly stance in his Commons speech of May was contrasted by Eden with the "fact" that for the greater part of the war German influence in Spain had constantly been permitted to embarrass the war effort of Britain and its allies. Churchill, in his reply, should give Franco a long list of Britain's grievances to remind the dictator of his pro-Axis stance and, not least, the Blue Division's fighting for Nazi Germany "against our ally Russia". The reply should also include the Prime Minister's August message to the Italian people – so much for the dictator's talk of "organic democracy". Once, when asked by an intimate what he would do in the event of an Allied victory, Franco had replied with complete, or feigned, equanimity: "Render them the bill."[36] Eden was rightly anxious that Churchill should not pay that "bill".

The Prime Minister's interest in Selborne's addressing the Cabinet was simple. The Minister of Economic Warfare would serve to counteract the impact of Attlee's warning that Britain must not be isolated supporting a regime shunned by all the other democracies. "I venture to deprecate the counsel tendered by the Lord President," Selborne, a grandson of Queen Victoria's last Prime Minister, Salisbury, and an old ally of Churchill's, had declared in a counter-memorandum to the Cabinet.[37] "Whatever we may think of the "incompetence, corruption and oppression of the Franco regime," Selborne observed taking up Attlee's words, "there is plenty of evidence that they are less than under the regime it displaced." The Economic Warfare Minister, who directed Britain's blockade of Europe, dismissed any economic measures against Franco Spain. "The people who would primarily suffer would be British traders and the people of Spain, whose resentment we should arouse and deserve," he went on carefully repeating Churchill's words of gratitude to Franco in the Commons speech. Franco, had he known of these remarks, would have felt well served. The Cabinet left Churchill to decide the terms of a reply to Spain's dictator.[38]

A crucial opportunity had been lost. Beforehand Eden's advisers had pleaded for seizing "a heaven-sent opportunity provided by Franco's approach" to Britain to take a stand against what would undoubtedly become "an anachronism after the defeat of Germany". The Cabinet's failure to obtain from Churchill the requirement of parallel action from the US government swiftly got its deserts. The day after their deliberations the British chargé in Madrid reported that Franco was "discounting Britain's dissatisfaction in the conviction that he and his regime enjoy the goodwill of the United States".[39] Hayes, the American envoy in Madrid, was the real source of the problem, Roberts commented, sensing now how America's policy over Spain was beginning to "slip". Roberts contrasted the Prime Minister's stubborn resistance to bringing in the Americans with the Foreign Office's growing perception that it was Britain which most needed that collaboration: "If we do not [collaborate] the Americans may well take the contrary line," he warned. The US embassy in London was again pressing for coordination of the two governments' policy on Spain. Eden noted: "I agree" on Roberts' minute. But the Foreign Secretary had let himself be outshone in Cabinet.

Churchill continued to refuse to see Washington as an ally on Spain. Yet Halifax was still reporting the State Department eager to support any communication by the Prime Minister "to shake General Franco out of his present complacency".[40] Roberts noted the "five times in six weeks" that the American counsellor in London had been on to him asking whether HMG was "ready" to discuss future policy on Spain. The FO could only string along the Americans.

Two days after the Cabinet on Spain Hoare saw the Foreign Secretary before leaving for Madrid. There had been no move from the Prime Minister. "Pressure for answer from P.M. Talk with Eden – too much on his back," Hoare noted.[41] (As leader of the House of Commons, Eden was occupied the same day with the opening of a new session of Parliament.) On arrival in the Spanish capital Hoare immediately sent off a signal[42] showing his unease: "I greatly hope I shall have the P.M's answer as soon as possible. Franco is exploiting 'the Red peril' and completely complacent as to his position." The tussle of wills between Churchill and Hoare was there for everyone in government circles to see.

"I shall do my best to write your insulting letter to Gen. Franco over the weekend, but I cannot give any guarantee," Churchill minuted Eden on 2 December.[43] That single word "insulting" reveals much, almost too much, about the Prime Minister's attitude towards Spain's ruler. Churchill was incensed by Hoare's pressing to get a message to Franco out of him. Against Hoare's nervousness, Churchill thundered: "The relations between England and Spain have undergone many vicissitudes and variations since the destruction of the Spanish Armada and I cannot feel that a few hours more consideration on my part of the letter are likely markedly to affect the scroll of history." It was Churchill's romanticized idea of history at its worst. Churchill's irony cannot disguise the tense personal relationship between the two men, but it also showed the Prime Minister's reluctance to back any "solemn warning" by Hoare to the dictator. Hoare was indeed scorned in Churchill's minute: "I really cannot see why Lord Templewood's anxiety should be balanced against the efforts I make to discharge my duties."

Looking to Britain

On the morning Churchill dictated that unbridled minute to Eden a long despatch appeared in *The Times* entitled "Spain in the Doldrums – Peaceful Change or Revolution". The special article, written by John Marks, the newspaper's Madrid-based correspondent, was accompanied by an editorial which called on the British government to keep up "a firmer tone" towards the Franco regime which the paper had sensed in Law's answers in the Commons on 15 November. *The Times* proceeded to state publicly the Spanish problem, bringing it out of government closets at what appeared a propitious moment. The paper accorded its Madrid man the prime position beside the leading articles, habitual practice in those days when it wished to lead public debate on a major issue facing the government of the day. Unless Britain brought to bear a strong influence now, Marks argued, Spain might once again see violence just as peace came elsewhere in Europe. "A good article," Eden observed; the piece stated "very well the case the Foreign Secretary has been making to the P.M. in recent weeks," Roberts added. [44]

The Foreign Secretary underlined Marks' observation: "The continued domination of Spain by the Falangists in a Europe in which the democratic cause has been victorious is a possibility which public opinion in other countries can not afford to regard with indifference." *The Times* correspondent allowed that "the unorganized state . . . of the opposition, inevitable under a dictatorship, and the bitterness of feelings generated by an unintelligent policy of revenge give some appearance of truth to the dilemma: Franco or civil war." But, Marks went on, and here Eden for a second time underlined in his habitual red ink the passage: "It seems certain that the longer change is postponed the more violent it will be, and many responsible Spaniards believe that the continuance of the present regime will inevitably lead to civil war." It was, *The Times* man suggested, to Britain that "nearly all Spaniards seeking to avoid the calamity of a 'second round' [of the Civil War] looked as symbol and embodiment of a middle way". Britain, Marks recommended, should now seek to exercise a strong influence so as to contribute to a peaceful solution of the "Spanish dilemma".

The extent of the unabating political repression, with special tribunals, firing squads and detention camps for political prisoners was well exposed in Marks' article. There were, he reported, "hundreds of thousands arrested and tens of thousands" who had been executed. It was sufficient for a Spaniard to be liberal-minded to be sent to gaol. The piece also branded the regime's widespread corruption. The black market had become "the cornerstone of the Spanish economy", with profiteering in Catalonia and Galicia – Marks had in mind the wolfram trade – concentrated in very few hands. Here was a cool, brave look at the reality of Franco's Spain more than five years after the Civil War had ended. It was an example of what the British press, for so long restrained by the demands of war, could contribute to informed public debate in a country committed to fighting, and sacrificing life and substance, for a freer post-war world. Moreover, it underscored why Churchill's false hope for a "working out" of Spanish tendencies was impossible. Marks told his foreign editor that in Barcelona, where he found himself the evening of the day the article appeared, "everyone was agog over it, mostly highly delighted and few finding fault". The BBC had broadcast excerpts in its Spanish language service. Marks estimated only 30 to 40 per cent of "the disillusioned Spanish people" still supported the Franco regime. *The Times* was to be described later that month by Cambó as "the symbol of English good sense" – *seny*, that quality so prized by Catalans.[45]

The Times editorial was first interpreted by the regime in Madrid as a sign of approaching stormy weather. Hoare had, however, to warn the Foreign Office on 6 December that any further delay would be grasped at eagerly by Franco and Lequerica as a "a sign of hesitation" over the stance to be adopted towards the dictator. The ambassador had already requested the interview's re-scheduling because he had no message from Churchill. There could be "no question of pressing the Prime Minister, who has told us that he does not intend to be hurried", Eden's aide replied.[46] In an encounter with Hoare on 4 December Spain's Foreign Minister sensed the envoy had returned without precise instructions to indicate the policy shift Madrid feared. Alba reported he found Eden likewise uncertain.

On the eve of Hoare's re-scheduled interview with Franco on 12 December, six days after the envoy's warning signal, the Foreign Secretary regretted to Hoare that Churchill's message would not now be ready in time for him to use.[47] The Prime Minister was procrastinating. Furthermore, Hoare was instructed that he must not "prejudge" the lines of a Prime Ministerial reply, nor give a briefing to his American colleague. Roberts found this abandoning of Hoare shabby. "There is not much we can tell him, but he might have a legitimate grievance if we said nothing at all," he advised Eden, showing how the Foreign Secretary's cowed reaction before Churchill's inroads was sensed by his officials. Churchill's non-consultation of Washington helped the "flirtation" by the American ambassador and the US business community with Lequerica and the regime to grow. Despairing of Hayes, the State Department was now looking to his successor, a professional diplomat this time who would carry out instructions.

While waiting for his instructions Hoare, in a disillusioned mood, made his diplomatic farewells in Madrid. Their restricted character conveys his sense of personal failure in Madrid. Hoare wanted nothing to do with Lequerica who had outsmarted him. It was at a farewell dinner, given by his oldest and most trusted colleague in the Spanish capital Theotonio Pereira, the Portuguese envoy, that Hoare said goodbye to some of the leading monarchist figures with whom he had close contacts. It was also goodbye to the hopes he once had of their forming the nucleus of a political alternative for Spain. Hoare, who had kept up a steely self-discipline during his last December days in Madrid, finally unburdened himself. He expressed his regret "at leaving Spain in the same uneasy condition" as he had found it four years before, and spoke openly of his "unfulfilled hopes that the monarchy would have been re-established by now". Hayes, who did not give his British colleague any send-off party, reports in his memoirs[48] Hoare's remarking to him sadly: "I have never known so many professed monarchists who didn't really want a king." The US envoy, who was by now well seen by official Madrid, added that Franco had been "immensely annoyed" by Hoare's after dinner remarks. It was only thanks to Britain's wartime censors that the Foreign Office learned of Hoare's speech. The censors had opened, and passed to the FO, the private letter *The Times* correspondent had written to his foreign editor, giving the contents of the speech.[49] Hoare had reported nothing of it to London; long experience had taught him that Eden would disapprove strongly of his expressing such sentiments – but he was leaving the foreign service shortly anyway.

Franco Challenged

Hoare's two hour-long audience with Franco at the Pardo palace was the most remarkable episode of his whole ambassadorship for, after the initial diplomatic niceties, the English politician took up directly with the Spanish dictator his repressive regime. Here was the essence of the difference between Hoare's approach and Churchill's *Realpolitik*, which shunned an ethical basis for foreign policy. In the dictator's den Hoare was coherent with those ideas for a better Spain which he had expressed to his Chelsea constituents the previous summer. Hoare attacked the methods of Spain's military courts, the number of executions and the repression adopted generally.[50] Franco was aroused from his habitual complacency, Hoare reported to London the same day. An argument ensued between the two men whether the military tribunals had stepped up their activities and particularly whether the executions of political prisoners had increased of recent weeks. Franco's purpose was that a heightened wave of repression would subdue an increasingly expectant population as the war's end neared. "Executions starting again in the cemetery [near-by]" Hoare had jotted in one of his notes covering the days around his interview.

"I gave him a very serious warning the time was overdue for still persisting in Civil War hatreds. Informed British opinion was above all concerned by the recrudescence of executions and by the lack of publicity surrounding such cases," Hoare said. Abandoning his usual phlegm, Franco made an astonishing reply: Spain, he said, was *un pais liberal*, countries had differing views of the same political principles. There were still many crimes outstanding from the Civil War, the dictator maintained, cases where individuals had shot up to 15 or 20 persons; many wanted criminals had been long in hiding. The British ambassador could rest assured that all the death sentences carried out would have also resulted in executions "in any other country". All such sentences were closely studied beforehand by the Cabinet, Franco said. A few days after Hoare met Franco *Arriba*, the Falange's daily, in an article entitled "Propaganda Against Spain", gave what amounted to a public admission that death sentences were being carried out on political prisoners. Spaniards were assured, however, that there were "in fact far fewer [executions] than in many European countries".[51] Spain was supposedly at peace.

There was a surreal element to the encounter: Hoare, the pre-1939 Home Secretary who had introduced a liberal Criminal Justice Bill, who had a long family tradition of penal reform – Elizabeth Fry was a great great aunt – was being "re-assured" by the victor of a bloody civil war about the continued shootings of Republican civilians for retroactive political crimes. By contrast, Hoare held it a politician's duty to give the citizenry good governance, and not impose order by hangings and other forms of state terror. "I had seen in the raw the devastating effect of fear

on human nature," Hoare had noted earlier in his Madrid years. In a letter to London in 1942 he had looked to helping Spain "towards normal
life and humane government".[52]

A further irony in the encounter lay in the former British Foreign
Secretary making a stand against the dictator – in the absence of any support
from Churchill and the government – on the ground of British public
opinion, the very force which had swept Hoare from office in 1935. As
Hoare had put it in one of those intimate weekly jottings, here indeed was
his "curious position" of being by 1944 anti-appeasement over Spain while
Churchill, no longer out of office but Britain's Prime Minister, was now
appeasing Franco. "I left him in no doubt as to the state of public opinion,"
the envoy-politician reported, recounting how he had criticized the regime
to Franco – high posts in the ministries, police and the armed forces still
occupied by persons appointed when the Axis powers' influence over Spain
was at its height. The absence of friendly relations between Britain and
Spain was due to "Spanish Fascism", Hoare said bluntly. This had "continually impeded Britain's conduct of the war and prevented Spain from being
genuinely neutral." As such a hostile influence continued to hold sway,
Hoare went on, "it could not be a matter of surprise that the British people
regarded Spain as a Fascist stronghold". Franco tried to argue that
Falangism was "completely different" from Nazism and Fascism. "I
answered that we could not be blamed if we associated Falangism with
Fascism when Falangism continued to adopt Fascist methods."

The exactness of Hoare's account of his words to Franco can not be
doubted: there exists a full Spanish version[53] of the audience, taken down
by a Spanish Foreign Ministry official present. The two versions tally
remarkably, the official taking down Hoare's remarks quite unvarnished.
Hoare emphasized, the Spanish version notes, that it was British diplomatic
practice not to interfere with the internal affairs of another country.
"However, collaboration among the nations of Western Europe in future
would be *incómodo* with a country which maintained Fascist methods. Until
British opinion came to perceive a more radical change in the methods and
internal attitudes in Spain there would be no alteration to the deeply-held
belief that influences and methods copied from Germany continued." Hoare
contrasted this with a situation where citizens' rights were respected by all
countries in Western Europe, whatever their different historical traditions.
This would become "a very important question," the British statesman was
reported by the Spanish official warning Franco, from the moment the war
ended. Hoare closed his remarks making one crucial distinction: he stressed
the friendly relations existing between the British and Spanish peoples, but
avoided any words suggesting an identification of Spaniards with the

present political regime in their land. It was a difference Churchill's *Realpolitik* could have no interest in making as we shall see.

But Franco for his part had not quite finished the meeting. What happened only became public knowledge half a century later when the Public Record Office rules allowed. Professing to regret the ambassador's leaving Madrid, the dictator pressed Hoare to accept Spain's highest civilian honour, the Grand Cross of the Order of Isabel la Católica. Franco had the award in his hand, Hoare told London.[54] He declined politely, observing that Britain's ambassadors customarily did not accept foreign honours. The attempt by Franco to decorate Hoare was, had he accepted, to be exploited as a display of the good relations the Franco regime supposedly enjoyed with the Allies. Exactly why the Foreign Office "weeders" decided the episode must be withheld from public knowledge for an exceptional 50 years can only be conjectured. Not, sadly, for Hoare's sake, for public awareness of his refusal of the honour would rather have helped the Conservative politician's standing. Hoare was to tell a more sympathetic Gerald Brenan after the war of Franco's attempt to decorate him, and of his refusal. The long hiding of the episode was in all probability for the sake of Eden and Cadogan, one-time masters of the house, because of comments they both committed to paper at the time. "Lord Templewood should not want to accept an order from Franco," the FO's permanent head minuted – when he already knew Hoare had refused. To this the Foreign Secretary added: "I agree – absurd man – or perhaps I should write men!" Lumping Franco and Hoare together reveals once again Eden's intense personal distaste for Hoare. The day after the interview Lequerica, accompanied by senior Foreign Ministry officials, went to see Hoare off from Madrid.[55] The opportunity to stage a public appearance of good relations with Britain for Spanish internal consumption was too good to be missed.

London fog, winter cold and continuing German V2 bomb attacks met Hoare as he returned home after more than four years in foreign parts. Hoare's initial intention, matured in Spain, was to seek to exploit his success for Britain during the years of war for a future again in politics. He was soon to discover, however, that he had precious few political friends left in London and none currently in high places. Churchill's influence was all-pervasive. Pursuing that initial idea however, Hoare sought to launch a public debate from the House of Lords with a wide-ranging motion on Spain and its future. He was nervous and felt unsettled by what he sensed as the Churchill government's animosity towards him. The debate was a complete failure, and ended all hopes of re-entering the upper reaches of Conservative politics. Hoare spoke of Franco Spain being "a morally-occupied country" when Axis power was at its zenith, but, surprisingly, refrained from seeking to obtain a public condemnation by the Upper House of the continuing repressive practices of the regime – as he had condemned them when he confronted the dictator personally. Hoare would, without doubt, have better served his own purpose, and immediate reputation, had he spoken out about the Franco regime's repression and not given heed to the Prime Minister's appeasing shadow behind him. Hoare opted for what he evidently calculated to be more future-oriented and capable of securing wider approval. Spain must take her place in a post-war Europe "where European citizens should be ensured of certain fundamental rights and liberties", the ex ambassador and politician insisted. Even that approach did not secure any support from the government benches, nor did any Labour peer speak during the debate. Attlee was well ahead of his party's thinking on Spain and grasping what Hoare had achieved in Franco's pro-Axis Madrid and was now sketching for the future.

It was as an elder statesman, and nothing more, that Lord Cranborne, another of Churchill's hard-line allies, welcomed Hoare back from Madrid when he spoke in the debate. He poured cold water on Hoare's plea for governments to take a stand of principle against an undemocratic regime in Spain – interfering in other states as he put it. Yet the Conservative peer went on in that debate to defend the British government's action – controversial at that time on both sides of the Atlantic – intervening in Greece to uphold in Churchill's words "power, law and freedom in the western world". Cranborne, the future fifth Marquess of Salisbury, was out of sympathy with the hopes for a more democratic post-war world.

Hoare saw that he had no alternative, if he was to exercise any influence on British policy towards Spain, but to concentrate on writing a book to bring to public attention the "anomaly" if Franco should survive the war's end. The book would also show the extent of his contribution to Britain's war effort serving in Spain as kind of rehabilitation. With Churchill so much the towering figure, Hoare retired to Templewood in his native Norfolk and started to write *Ambassador on Special Mission*. It took him one year. The task was not an easy one: he had to brand Franco and yet conceal his fundamental disagreement with Churchill over Spain, otherwise his mission would not appear a success.

Churchill Lets Franco Off

The reply to General Franco was Churchill's most important act concerning Franco Spain of the Second World War – not excluding that clear intervention in Spain's internal affairs, the Prime Minister's involvement in the secret operation to bribe leading Spanish generals to stay out of Hitler's war in 1940–41. Churchill's letter was to have far more lasting consequences for all Spain. It was not, of course, Eden's "insulting letter" that emerged, but one which conformed to what the veteran British statesman perceived to be his country's strategic interests. Churchill's treatment in his war memoirs of his major intervention in the Spanish Question is to say the least curious. His crucial note on 11 December to Eden,[56] justifying the way he would reply to the dictator's letter, is confined to an appendix. There is no outlining there, or anywhere else, for the enlightenment of any reader of the memoirs of any other viewpoints in a debate about Spain which had been going on in government for over two months.

"I do not think the balance of help and hindrance given us by Spain in the war is fairly stated," Churchill observed of the Foreign Office's draft which he wanted amended. "The supreme services of not intervening in 1940 [on the Axis side] or interfering with the use of the airfield and Algeciras Bay in the months before Torch in 1942 outweigh the minor irritations which are so meticulously set forth. Therefore I should like to see the passages reciting our many grievances somewhat reduced," the Prime Minister ruled. Churchill objected to Eden's proposed reply saying, as he expressed it, "the most freezing things" to General Franco. The Prime Minister was writing in terms of Franco Spain's "supreme services" the day before Hoare had his encounter with the dictator. The two statesmen's differing approaches could hardly be more vividly portrayed than by their own words.

Eden, after his defeat in the War Cabinet in November, made a second attempt in the New Year to overcome the Prime Minister's persistent refusal to work with the Roosevelt administration over Spain. "I very much hope that you will be willing to reconsider your view," the Foreign Secretary pleaded,[57] urging a simultaneous démarche by the Allies if Franco was to be shaken. He gave Churchill a cogent warning: if nothing were done to bring Madrid to see both Allies had an agreed stance now on Spain the effect of the Prime Minister's reply "will be much less than it should". If Washington was not brought into play, Franco would go on maintaining that he had the approval of the US government and discount Britain. Eden coupled this with the latest despatch from Halifax reporting that State was "ready to go along with us in any communication calculated to shake General Franco". Churchill's riposte was without any subterfuge. The Americans were "very anti-Franco", and, he added, "I have not the slightest intention of starting an anti-Franco crusade any more than I wish to walk down the street with him." Then, calming down somewhat – Spain seemed to make both Britain's war leaders irascible –

the Premier observed: "Perhaps we ought to ask the Cabinet what they feel about going beyond my letter."

Washington, it must be said, had only been given on 18 December the contents of Franco's 18 October letter and what would be the Prime Minister's reply. The Americans had been informed only in the sketchiest terms of Hoare's final interview with Franco. Sending off these papers to Washington, a junior Foreign Office man artlessly revealed the lack of consultation between the two capitals prevailing about Spain. "Perhaps the P.M's reply should be deferred for some days," he suggested in a minute , "to give State time to consider the matter".[58] The US counsellor, who had for so long been pressing Roberts for joint consultations on Spain, deserved to see Churchill's reply too, the junior diplomat ventured. Oliver Harvey, Eden's trusted aide, added caustically that Halifax would hardly be able to carry out his instructions from London effectively unless he were brought more fully into the prevailing British – that was now essentially Churchill's – view. "Please explain to State that it has not been possible to make an earlier communication on this subject because the preparation of a reply to General Franco has necessarily had to give way to more pressing problems of war," the Foreign Secretary excused himself to Halifax.[59]

The Foreign Office was hamstrung: it was striving to secure some kind of US endorsement , but it was all too aware that Churchill was utterly determined to decide alone how to handle the Spanish dictator's future. A note from the Prime Minister to Eden late December[60] expressed his personal approach with an almost brutal clarity: "I do not consider that we should make suggestions to the State Department to beat up the Spaniards. It is sufficient that we communicate to them the answer we have made to General Franco's approaches." So much for Allied consultation; Churchill by speaking of "the Spaniards" fails again to distinguish them from the Franco regime.

Churchill's letter did not get off until mid January due to a bungle at the FO. This wrong-footed Eden *vis-à-vis* No. 10 and angered the Prime Minister considerably. "What astonishes me is that neither my letter to General Franco, nor a copy to Stalin, has gone off although three weeks have passed . . . I am not prepared to go beyond my already written and signed letter of late December," Churchill curtly told Eden.[61] The Prime Minister may have offered Eden to sound the Cabinet about "going beyond my letter" to Franco. But having got his way over excluding the Americans from any prior consultations, which was in defiance of the original Cabinet decision on Spain of 27 November, Churchill knew the sway he had acquired over his colleagues: there were no changes made to the Prime Minister's reply. Churchill made the fullest use in his letter, now dated 15 January, of the broad authorization accorded him to deal with Franco.[62] The two crucial passages which had the Foreign Secretary's express endorsement were missing: the first on Spain's internal conditions; the second warning that an invitation to Spain to join the future world organization would be impossible "until Spain genuinely embraces the basic tenets and principles for which the United Nations are now fighting, and which will be re-affirmed by their victory".

It was thus without having specified what the barriers were preventing more friendly relations that the Prime Minister informed Franco that it was "out of the question" for Britain to support Spain's wish to be present at the future peace settlement. Nor was it likely, Churchill added, again without supplying the reason, that Spain would be invited to join the future UNO. The vital element of conditionality was jettisoned by Churchill about Spain's embarking upon a course to align her more with the basic principles of the victorious Allies, which Hoare had worked hard to get emphasized. When Alba was shown the text of the reply by Cadogan the ambassador immediately objected that Churchill's "Spain" ought to have read "the Spanish government" which was now faced by exclusion from the councils of nations after the peace – an elementary distinction evidently to all Spaniards. By skirting around why the Franco regime would be ineligible for UN membership the Prime Minister's reply meant, most seriously of all, that Franco was handed the opportunity in 1945 and into '46 of whipping up the Spaniards' sense of patriotism and quick indignation that all the world was "against Spain". Churchill's blunder helped the dictator postwar to obtain the identification of his discredited regime with the Spanish nation in its entirety. The potential significance of the element of conditionality for Spain's evolution had been well highlighted by Lord Perth in the Lords' debate on Hoare's motion. The future UNO was to be "open to all peace-loving nations", Perth emphasized, going on: "I very much doubt whether a nation that consistently persecutes its own subjects can be brought into the category of peace-loving." Ambassador in Mussolini's Italy until the outbreak of the Second World War, Perth had plenty of opportunity to grasp the distinction between regime and people to which Churchill's imperial strategic thinking left him oblivious. As Sir Eric Drummond, Perth had served before Rome as Secretary-General of the League of Nations.

If such a conditional approach had been enunciated by Churchill in the closing stage of the war, Franco's repressive regime would have been seen excluding itself by its nature from the new world body. All influential and informed Spaniards would have had borne in upon them the growing disadvantages, above all political and economic, for their country of self-imposed isolation. Opportunism was the second name of the regime. Yet at a juncture when Franco, by approaching Britain's wartime leader, had revealed himself aware of his regime's uncertain future Churchill ignored the best available advice, setting a course by his reply which benefited only the Spanish dictator.

8

A Wringing of Hands
January–July, 1945

To grasp the full import of Churchill's intervention in the winter of 1944–45 over the policy to be pursued towards Franco Spain it is necessary to follow events both inside the country and in London up to the end of the world war in Europe. Looked at superficially, the period after Britain's great war leader had spoken might seem to be only a postscript, yet in reality these were still vital months when Britain's influence was at its zenith throughout Europe and the Franco regime most vulnerable. But that influence had to be employed swiftly if it was to have effect. In reality, too, the problems about Spain's future Hoare had striven to get heeded in London worsened in this period dramatically.

The problem of Franco's "White Terror", as Jacques Maritain had first labelled it during the Civil War but now employed with renewed fierceness as the regime sensed its vulnerability with an Allied victory, was highly awkward for the Foreign Office. But what ground was left for them to react after the Prime Minister's January letter to the dictator had omitted any mention of Spain's internal condition? Hoare's challenge to Franco's face on the "recrudescence of executions" had gone without the British government's support at the highest level. Could Britain now only wring her hands? The period after Hoare's departure was the most humiliating for British diplomacy towards Spain of the entire war. Churchill had ruled for non-intervention, appeasement in a word, and the diplomats themselves proved highly unimaginative; perhaps they were simply tired out by the long haul of the world war.

Don Juan finally roused himself as the war's end neared, but his Lausanne Manifesto in March proved more of a last fling than a last, best chance. He had made no preparations beforehand when the mood in Spain was changing. More important, the Spanish generals, who professed to being monarchists, again made no move against Franco. It was thus too easy for British diplomats to shrug their shoulders and claim the Pretender wanted them to pull Spanish chestnuts out of the fire and hand him the throne. More significant were the approaches made to London by realists such as the Marqués de Santa Cruz, Spain's second man in the London Embassy, Miguel Mateu Pla, the Barcelona industrialist and business leader and Franco's Mayor, and by Don Alfonso de Borbón, the Pretender's representative in Spain. Unlike Churchill, they each in their own way sensed the unique occasion that the war's ending offered for a public shift in Britain's policy towards Franco and his dictatorial regime. Once again, in the spirit of C.V. Wedgwood's caution quoted at the beginning of this book, it is essential not to allow the knowledge that the Franco regime was to survive after 1945 to prevent us from appreciating the deep uncertainties in the spring of that year. Remarkable though they were, all these appeals by influential Spaniards were ignored by Eden who devised a pitiable policy of "cold reserve" towards Franco. Some of his aides even professed to hope that by ignoring the dictator he would somehow go away. Thus unmolested by Britain, Franco could concentrate on the two tasks most close to his heart – repression at home and, abroad, seeking a new protector in the United States.

Relief and Repression

The inner circle of Spaniards in the know in the Franco regime had no doubts whatsoever about the import of Churchill's January letter. Alba, Spain's ambassador in London on leave in Madrid, told Franco the Premier's letter was "the best he could possibly have hoped for in the circumstances".[1] There could hardly have been a more penetrating indictment of Churchill's leniency towards Franco – and it was from the Prime Minister's "cousin" who knew well British wartime feelings about Spain. The Foreign Minister on reading the reply commented to Alba that it was "much milder than he had expected".[2] But, above all, Lequerica quickly saw that under Churchill's chosen course there was going to be no real pressure exerted by Britain against the regime's fundamental dictatorial nature. And that was the essential point.

It was thanks to Alba, talking to the chargé Bowker, that the British government learnt of Franco's professed reaction to London's attitude as set by Churchill. At the audience with the Duke on 8 February the Caudillo of course showed no relief, striking an attitude to his own advantage – and it was hardly a flattering one for England. Franco talked almost continually for two hours, Alba told Bowker, brushing aside completely the envoy's warning that Spain faced a growing isolation with the Allies' victory. It was Britain, the dictator insisted, who would need Spain's assistance against Russia after the war with Germany was over. The only thing, Franco maintained, was that Spain should remain "strong" under his leadership. Yet a second consecutive year of bad harvests had in fact crippled Spain's national economy, then still overwhelmingly dependent on agriculture and foreign petrol. There must be no modification to his regime as that would only weaken "Spain". Franco was putting on his customary display of supreme confidence to Alba, of whose monarchist tendencies at this juncture the dictator was especially wary. But Franco could hardly be expected to be pleased by Churchill's declaration that there could be no place for Spain *tout court* in the future United Nations Organisation – even though he was able later to exploit Churchill's blunder masterfully. The essential point for him was his regime's survival internally. Britain was "always making difficulties," the dictator told his incredulous ambassador to London; that was why it was easier to make "concessions" to the USA – they were "much more understanding".

Franco had stepped up the repression to prevent any attempt by opposition elements to come together. His approach for the monarchists was relatively kid-gloved, though in one nocturnal swoop by the police just before Christmas some 300 sympathizers with Don Juan, all people from the professional classes and including some moderate ex Republicans convinced a restoration offered the best way ahead for Spain, had been rounded up. They were soon released, but after they had all been suitably chastened. Prominent among those arrested at home after midnight was Gregorio Marañón, the prominent doctor and man of letters. The family knew the Interior Minister, however. When reached, while attending a dance at the Pardo for the coming out of Franco's daughter, the minister personally ordered Marañón's freeing. With the less moderate Republicans and left-wingers of all kinds the regime proceeded with its customary arbitrariness and severity.

The British embassy was being kept exceptionally well informed of what was going on in the country. Opposition elements made a special effort, manifesting a courage in the face of police surveillance born of the hope, and the belief, that change in Spain would be the inevitable accompaniment of Allied victory. The principal conduit was Bernard Malley, Hoare's interpreter who had become almost his tutor on things Spanish. A sympathizer with the Nationalists' cause during the Civil War and a strict Catholic, Malley was by now disgusted by the Franco regime's unabating vindictiveness and brutality. Malley enjoyed excellent contacts inside the regime – which even included the Interior Ministry's director of prisons. Officially there were 22,000 persons admitted as held in Spanish jails five years after the Civil War had ended. These came under the Justice Ministry and were classified as common criminals. But a far larger number, estimated at not less than 100,000 and possibly as many as three times that figure in January 1945, were held by the general directorate of security, which came under the Interior Ministry. Reported by Bowker to London, these figures are in the first of four bulky Foreign Office files[3] on "Political Arrests and Executions" covering solely the issue of Franco's repression during 1945. It is over 200 pages long with the comments the London end. The second file is 400 pages long. The Interior Ministry detainees were all held on suspicion of having committed acts which Franco's police state affected to regard as crimes relating to the Civil War. These were often offences made punishable under the retroactive Law of Political Responsibilities of 1939. Here heavily punishable "crimes" could have been committed even before that conflict broke out. Those in this second category, unlike those in the "normal prisons", were unambiguously political prisoners. Frequently they were detained for years, and tortured, while awaiting trial. To be arrested it was sufficient to have been denounced by a member of the Falange as opposed to the regime. The Justice Minister, Eduardo Aunós, paraded a reformist image to the outside world, pointing any foreign inquirers to the building of more modern prisons. But the unflinchingly tough Falangist Interior Minister, Blas Peréz, kept in place all the "reforms" which Heinrich Himmler had recommended to the Spanish police when he visited Spain in the autumn of 1940.

The director of prisons at the Interior Ministry told Malley in February that death sentences were coming at a rhythm of about 350 verdicts handed down by the courts every six weeks.[4] These then went before the Cabinet for that "close study" the dictator had told Hoare about. About 300 were usually commuted, and the rest confirmed, the director said, and executed forthwith. Franco was the leading spirit, this Spanish high official asserted, insisting that the purge should continue. A group of Spanish bishops, at the urging of Mgr Cicognani, the Papal Nuncio, had appealed to the Justice Minister for clemency but, on Franco's orders, been rejected. In Madrid in one day alone, 17 January, 1945, 23 executions had been carried out, a relation of Julián Besteiro, the Socialist leader of the 1930s, reported to the embassy. Besteiro, perhaps the most moderate of the Second Republic left-wing leaders, had died in gaol in 1940 while serving a 30-year sentence. Relations of those executed had, in another case, followed the lorries taking their loved ones' dead bodies away until they found many blood stains in the winter snow. "There is no reason to disbelieve these reports," the British chargé told London. "A gruesome picture," the desk officer for Spain had to admit,[5] recalling Hoare's reporting of renewed executions the previous autumn. The question of the continuing executions in Spain had been "rather pushed into the background while the correspondence between General Franco and the Prime Minister was under consideration" was all the FO man could minute.

A group of Spanish exiles, all living in the UK, addressed an appeal to the British Prime Minister towards the end of February denouncing "the growing terror" in their country.[6] They asked him to seek of Franco an amnesty for all the political prisoners who were being detained so long after

the Civil War. After the appeal had been sent by No. 10 Downing Street to
the Foreign Office, it was only a junior diplomat who was left to deal with
it: "I do not think we can acknowledge this," he wrote. When Norman
Armour, the new United States ambassador to Spain, told the British chargé
that he had Washington's instructions to raise the issue of the continuing
death sentences and executions when he saw Franco, Bowker, who could
only be seen by the Foreign Minister, suggested to London that the time
had come for "sober and objective" publicity to be given the matter by the
British press.[7] The dictator's failure, six years after the Civil War's end, to
seek to heal the wounds of that conflict might be the appropriate angle, he
thought. Yet London discarded even that idea. Though connected by
marriage with the owners of the *Yorkshire Post*, a leading provincial daily,
Eden went along with the departmental view. He minuted, astonishingly,
that the British press were "always lying in wait for Franco".[8] When a few
days later the National Council of Civil Liberties called on the British
government to protest in Madrid against the continued execution of Spain's
political prisoners, all the Foreign Office did was to acknowledge the
London-based organization's letter and "note" its contents.

It was the Spanish Foreign Minister who took the initiative, telling
Armour and Bowker that he had been instructed by Franco to inform them
that from now on there would be no further death sentences passed on
charges arising out of the Civil War.[9] The special tribunals for political
responsibilities, set up in Febuary 1939 to try those deemed "guilty of
Marxist rebellion", were abolished by the Justice Minister a few days later.
But these concessions, made in evident recognition of the changing international climate, were more apparent than real. Franco's machine of
repression continued with its grim tasks. The Falange still kept its special
powers to bring dissident Spanish citizens before the military courts. Even
the executions of political prisoners still went on: 72 political prisoners were
taken from local jails to the Carabanchel cemetery in Madrid on a single
day, 27 April, and all shot. "In spite of the assurances given by Lequerica I
have reason to suspect that executions for political offences are still taking
place," the British chargé was reporting in June.[10] A survivor among the
condemned men in those April shootings who, because of the inefficiency
of Franco's police, had managed to escape just before the firing squads
started, had informed British embassy staff.

Uneasy Equilibrium in Spain

It was the British government's passivity which allowed Spain's Foreign

Minister, to make the diplomatic running. Lequerica, the consummate opportunist who had served the monarchy of Alfonso XIII before he sided with Franco, judged that the Allies' approaching victory did require some changes of Spain even if it was for him, like the Prince of Salina's nephew in the Lampedusa novel, *Il Gattopardo*, so that everything in the Spanish set-up, economic and social, could stay the same. Lequerica was a master of finessing and had never underestimated his own abilities. At that time he secretly nursed an ambition he might succeed the dictator at the world war's end. But before Lequerica launched his initiative an intriguing meeting occurred mid February between Santa Cruz, the second man in Spain's London embassy, and Derick Hoyar Millar, the new departmental head who had replaced Roberts. A dour unimaginative Scot, Hoyer Millar was manifestly the inferior in his professional skills to the Spanish aristocrat. Santa Cruz put Britain's diplomatic posture on the rack. If the UK really wanted to see General Franco disappear then, he argued, they should make that perfectly clear by some kind of public announcement.[11] And, he suggested, not only that Franco should go, but what kind of regime should take its place. When Hoyer Millar, sticking to his brief, referred to the brazen attitude Franco had struck with Alba in Madrid, the Spanish diplomat deftly replied that Franco had probably failed to understand what Churchill's letter was intended to convey. Speaking, he said, off the record, Santa Cruz said he believed people in Britain were making a mistake if they thought the Franco regime was likely to collapse by itself in the near future. Large numbers of Spaniards, of varying political persuasions, would indeed be glad to see General Franco go, but they were also afraid of doing anything which might run the risk of starting another civil war. All these elements were at sixes and sevens with each other and there was no real organized opposition. It was therefore only if Britain made some clear announcement, Santa Cruz roundly declared to Hoyer Millar (as the latter minuted), that the present uneasy equilibrium prevailing in Spain would be upset. Santa Cruz got in the last word when the Scot argued, in the hypocrisies of routine British diplomacy, against telling Spaniards "how they should settle their internal affairs" observing that intervention in the affairs of other countries "seemed rather fashionable these days".

Here was a clear assessment of the juncture things had reached in Spain by the last months of the war by a high-ranking Spanish diplomat with keen political antennae, just returned from visiting his country. Above all, he put his finger on Britain's inertia regarding Spain. "For goodness sake, don't let's get involved in any responsibility for a particular regime in Spain," Cadogan had exploded in his hidebound way when reading Hoyer Millar's account of that remarkable conversation. The exchange, and Cadogan's reaction, showed that it was not principle, not even the ever-ambiguous diplomatic principle of non-intervention, which in the last analysis moved the Foreign Office's permanent head but national interests as he conceived them. Cadogan had once again laid down the law for the department and his subordinates obeyed. Eden merely endorsed Cadogan's view without any politician's input.

But the "Spanish Problem" posed by Franco for western governments as the war's end came in sight would not go away. So unimaginative diplomats such as Hoyer Millar were reduced to hoping it would somehow resolve itself. When Hoyer Millar heard that General DeGaulle had in early February discussed Spain's future in Moscow, and that the Russians had indicated they would be raising the matter as soon as the war was over, the British diplomat actually minuted: "I hope Franco goes before the Russians have time to get around to Spain." [12] The Foreign Office was well aware of time pressing, but bereft of any policy befitting the hour on how to deal with Franco Spain. It was unwilling to do anything to disturb an "uneasy equilibrium" or to gainsay the dictator's will to stay.

Santa Cruz was formally sent by Spain's Foreign Minister on 1 March with a message to Eden inquiring what steps Britain would like to see the Spanish government undertake to improve relations between the two countries. An opportunity was there to outsmart Lequerica if, of course, exercised in an adroit way. It was not taken. There was not even a British ambassador in Madrid as successor to Hoare, who might have spied out the situation at the highest level; there was no policy, only much suspicion of Lequerica's motives. There was little interest in Spain by the Foreign Secretary after Churchill had taken policy-making on Spain so firmly in hand. Eden was busy elsewhere anyway. There was to be no substantive political input from him on Spain that final spring of the war. From a position demanding of the War Cabinet that "some action" must be taken over Spain in December '44, Eden had swung to one of complete inaction two months later. Churchill alone knew what he wanted and, aided by Cadogan, kept everyone to his course.

Eden opposed making public the text of the Prime Minister's reply to Franco,[13] though *The Times* had already published an accurate summary in February. This was another error since it suggested a British government keen to shield the dictator from adverse happenings abroad, and from an eventual decanting of informed opinion in Spain away from the regime, if what was coming to their country – exclusion from a post-war UNO – had become widely known. Churchill's letter had, without giving reasons, made this plain. Eden proposed the pursuit that decisive spring a tactic of "keeping Franco at arm's length" to justify to Churchill his opposition to making the letter public. "I do not think we want to let Franco think that his fate is really a matter of great concern to us," the Foreign Secretary wrote. The less said in British newspapers about Franco the better for some time to come, he thought. What more at that juncture could the Spanish dictator realistically have asked of one of the victorious Allies? He would be left unhindered to strengthen his regime's hold on Spain.

Eden's stultifying policy had another ill consequence however. Publication of Churchill's reply – as both Bowker in Madrid and Halifax in Washington had recommended – might have dispelled the Americans' suspicion about just what Britain's real intentions were towards the dictator. Halifax was well aware of the Prime Minister's reluctance to consult the US about Spain and of Washington's suspicions of what he had been up to in Greece.[14] Britain's man in Madrid had wanted publication "to strengthen friendly elements" inside Spain.[15]

Another fig leaf British diplomats devised was so-called "cold reserve" towards Franco. But would not Britain, they began worrying, be prejudicing its own national interests in Spain, especially if the Americans did not pursue that cold reserve themselves? The FO came quickly round to consultations about Spain. A reply by Franco to Churchill's January letter had aroused the Roosevelt administration's suspicions even farther. The US press asked whether some behind-the-scenes deal was going on between the British Prime Minister and the dictator? Underlying this tension was the two nations' growing rivalry over Spanish markets. What was seen as an American trade "flirt" with Franco Spain induced a British tendency towards yet further appeasement of the regime – not a trick must be lost commercially. Bowker was kept busy informing London of signs of American and Spanish rapprochement. Lequerica had told the French Minister, the chargé reported, that it was essential to get on well with the Americans "as they were now everything" for Spain.[16] Another of the Foreign Minister's reported "confidences", bitter for English ears retailed to London, was how easy it was to work with the American Commercial Counsellor, in contrast with his British opposite number, "because of his ambitions". Warren Butterworth would soon become a highly influential No. 2 in the Madrid embassy – the American had a head start with helping American businessmen penetrate Spanish markets, having been in charge of the US Commercial Corporation which financed and supervised US purchases at the height of the wolfram battles. When a new head of the Western European department at State met Halifax he again urged publication of Churchill's letter to Franco to clear the air.[17] It would put pressure on the Franco regime. Hoyer Millar was cautious: the two governments, he agreed, ought to settle upon a joint policy towards Franco, but, the British diplomat added disarmingly: "We must be clear in our own minds what our policy should be."[18]

The presence of the new and active US envoy in Madrid made it more than ever essential to ensure that his instructions did not conflict with British views, deeply inhibited those these now were. London was solely bent upon obtaining Washington's acquiescence to its stance. It must be made plain to Franco, the Foreign Office theorized, that playing one country off against the other "will not pay him". The Americans, Halifax was instructed to argue, should make their government's position "equally clear" to Madrid. "Please get quick State reactions as we'll be seeing Santa Cruz soon," the British envoy was told, indicating the importance given the Spaniard's move in London. In deference to Churchill's line, no reference was made to the regime's continuing repression. The FO draft, like Hoyer Millar, looked to the happy eventuality of his regime either falling or being replaced "as a result of some peaceful combination of Spanish opposition parties". There was no input from Eden before this parade of pious hopes was sent off to Halifax with which to make the best he could.

When the new US ambassador actually met the British chargé he was quite forthcoming. The American government maintained diplomatic relations with Spain but, Armour said, his instructions from Washington were that this was "not to be taken as implying, in any sense, approval of the [Franco] regime".[19] Armour assured Bowker that he personally would "remain unimpressed by any special demonstrations of friendship" by Spain and had every intention to keep in step with the British. Straight down the line, it might seem by the State Department. But again the trouble was at the Madrid end. A few days later Bowker felt he had to tell London of his suspicions of what exactly Britain's ally was up to. Franco was staking everything now on American *de facto* support but, the chargé reported, he had "the definite impression he is not being discouraged in this" by the Americans. "The atmosphere here between the Spaniards and the Americans is definitely 'honeymoonish'," Bowker complained.[2] Highlighting the drawbacks of Eden's line the chargé wrote: "We must face the fact that we shall not be able to count on the Americans' support in any issue where their economic interests and 'Big Brother' ambitions are concerned. We are left to apply the 'cold reserve' here, getting all the kicks and none of the half pence."

This was frank speaking on inter-Allied relations, but Hoyer Millar's reaction was only mulish: "We could do with a good deal less publicity about Spain in our newspapers and on the BBC and in Parliament."[21] British officialdom was striving to muzzle the media, and even Parliament, just as the Franco regime became more anachronistic. There was as clear a rebuke for its ally as diplomatic custom permitted when the State Department did reply to the British position paper. American public sentiment was "profoundly opposed" to the present Spanish government founded on undemocratic principles, London was told.[22] There had been no acts of the US government, or public utterances by its officials at variance with that attitude on the matter, nor could General Franco be under any misapprehension. "In the circumstances the State Department is at a loss to understand," the statement went on, "why the UK government would take seriously enough to include in its memorandum the reported allegations of the Spanish government that US feelings towards it are less hostile than those of the UK government." America's diplomats refrained from pointing out that Britain still had no ambassador in Madrid to obtain information first-hand. The US reply expressed the hope that a successor regime in Spain would be based on democratic principles and not indebted to any outside influences. Here was a dig by servants of the great republic at the British Prime Minister suspected of seeking to put back monarchs on the throne all over Europe, as well as at Soviet expansionism.

When the day set for the interview with the Foreign Secretary, but delayed in accordance with "cold reserve", finally came Eden had to fly off to Washington for President Roosevelt's funeral. British diplomats had been so puzzled by Santa Cruz that they put intelligence agents on to finding out what the Spaniard's "real views" were in the diplomatic bag when he reported to Lequerica. Hoyer Millar made a note on this point, but it was suppressed as too embarrassing for public knowledge under the 50-year rule.[23] Lequerica, while waiting, sought to play the British chargé in Madrid. Bowker was bluntly told that he must not become involved while the interview with Eden was "under consideration".[24] The Foreign Office feared the Basque was laying a trap while buying time for the regime. Essentially what was happening was a continuation of what Hoare had urged the British and American governments to confront once and for all – Franco's double policy of continued repression at home while seeking to wring an appearance of good relations from the Allies.

So the Spanish chargé only got to see Eden's aide, Harvey, who shirked confronting Santa Cruz on the repression and continuing execution of political prisoners even though Eden had indicated in a minute he wanted to speak of the British government's "shock" at the continued executions – a return, however weak, to Hoare's line. The Spanish diplomat easily put his finger on an awkward point, remarking that he hoped that Britain and the United States would "speak with one voice in Madrid".[25] This was important, Santa Cruz underlined, owing to the tendency in Madrid to read "different shades of meaning" into the Allies' actions. The new American ambassador had spoken firmly and frankly, and a new British ambassador should go to Spain soon and, Santa Cruz urged, "speak out clearly on his arrival". A servant of the Spanish government could hardly have given British diplomats sounder advice. It was, however, not until July 1945 that Hoare's successor, the mediocre professional diplomat Victor Mallet, reached Madrid. The decisive eight months in Spain from December 1944 for Franco's survival passed with only a British chargé *en poste*. Churchill had yet again exercised his sway. Eden sought several times to press him to fill the gap. The Prime Minister had read a memorandum prepared for him on the Santa Cruz interview and caught the Spaniard's well-directed remarks. "I cannot vacate Stockholm at the moment," he minuted the Foreign Secretary.[26] The transfer of German troops near the war's end through neutral Sweden, where Mallet was then Minister, was more important for Churchill than Spain's future. Two senior British diplomats, including David Kelly, the man Hoare had recommended and ex Minister in Berne, were both passed over. Another month passed so Eden minuted the Prime Minister: "We have been without an ambassador in Spain since December last. Our interests there are consequently suffering. Mallet is regarded as adequate for Madrid, but he is not so exceptional for Stockholm. In the circumstances I must ask you to let me go ahead."[27] Churchill was being stubborn; Spain now had no interest for him.

The Pretender Outsmarted

It was thus with the Allies in disarray, though with each government now effectively pursuing policies which shored up Franco's regime, that the Pretender issued his Lausanne Manifesto.[28] Don Juan believed that he was seizing a last chance before the Allies' complete victory. Advisers like Gil Robles had long been urging him to speak out. "The worst is the King continues without any sign of life. I am seriously thinking of going to Switzerland to try and get him out of his suicidal inactivity," the exiled politician had confided to his diary[29] at the end of 1944.

The manifesto called on Franco to recognize the failure of his totalitarian state and to abandon power in order to allow a return to what Don Juan called, with studied ambiguity, Spain's "traditional regime". Based on the Christian concept of the state and the rule of law, this set up would permit, he asserted, "the realization of a harmonious synthesis of order and liberty". Alone the "Traditional Monarchy" offered a way to reconcile all Spaniards, the Pretender was even at this juncture still maintaining. By contrast, Franco's Spain risked plunging the nation into a new civil war, he said. It had pursued foreign policies inspired by the Axis. A new republic would mean lurching to extremes and end up, he predicted, in a further round of fratricidal battles. "I incite no one to rebellion, but I want to remind those who support the existing regime of the tremendous responsibility they incur by contributing to the prolongation of a situation which will inevitably bring the country to an irreparable catastrophe," the Pretender proclaimed dramatically. The manifesto was been given to the press on 19 March, with a copy handed beforehand into the Spanish embassy in Berne.

Don Juan promised all Spaniards constitutional rights under the new regime, an elected Parliament and a wide-ranging political amnesty – though vaguely expressed, all elements intended for the Anglo-Saxon powers' ears. But insistence still upon a "Traditional Monarchy" was, as clearly, intended to appeal to his right-wing supporters inside Spain. The manifesto reflected well the contrasting advice Don Juan had been subjected to in exile in Switzerland. It was an amalgam of the views of López Oliván, the Republic's ambassador in London when the Civil War broke out, and those among his small entourage in Lausanne like Eugenio Vegas, a Catholic Traditionalist and uncompromising opponent of a constitutional monarchy with limited powers, who had fought against the Republic and written against democratic ideals for Spain. The Pretender's most direct appeal was evidently to those monarchists whose support he most needed, those who had thrown in their lot with Franco. He pleaded with them to understand his patriotic motives: events, he told them – meaning the Allies' complete victory over Hitler – would soon show how well timed was the step he was now taking for Spain. The reception of the manifesto, both inside Spain and abroad, in fact only laid bare the weakness of Don Juan's position. López Oliván had been in London in February, where the professional reserve of a former Registrar of the International Court at The Hague had only been increased by his soundings with Foreign Office advisers. He was under no illusions, but he did pointedly tell the British official to whom he got nearest: "Without intervening you can help us."[30] Even this encounter, with only a member of the FO research department, was suppressed by the "weeders" under the 50-year rule. London was "less favourable" to Don Juan than previously, López Oliván subsequently told Gil Robles.[31] The subtle plea for help by a former Spanish ambassador in London never found its way to the Foreign Secretary – Cadogan would have stamped upon the idea anyway. Hoyer Millar, however, on learning of the contact noted that "great anxiety" existed among the advisers about Don Juan's apparent resignation.

There was a more resolute voice trying at this late hour to get through to the British. As the manifesto was launched the Infante Alfonso, the

Pretender's official representative in Spain, wrote to Hoare saying that it was now "imperative" that the British and American governments should make absolutely clear their repudiation of the Franco regime. "If this attitude became widely known all law-abiding elements in Spain would side with a constitutional monarchy," Don Juan's man maintained. "Time is getting short, the collapse of Germany seems near. You often told me: 'You will miss the boat if you still have the Falange regime when peace comes'," the Infante quoted Hoare as saying. "Here we continue in a fool's paradise. Is there no means by which you could induce your government to make its position clear towards our present regime?", Don Alfonso urged of the former British ambassador and friend. We are back to the call for a public stand by Britain urged the previous October of Churchill by General Aranda and ignored. The Infante spoke of a Spain with an all-powerful police and the courts cowed. The press and radio trumpeted only that the Franco regime enjoyed the firm friendship of the United States. Monarchists and those who expressed a desire for a change of regime faced fines, imprisonment and confinement. Don Alfonso, a one-time businessman, judged that Spain would not be strong enough economically to confront a hostile world if the Franco regime were really put under concerted pressure by the victorious Allies. This was a fundamental point which had been always overlooked by the Foreign Office men, poorly equipped to grasp economic facts. That kind of economic weakness was no longer a matter of "high politics" when Britain's crisis of survival had passed. It was now sufficient, as Hoyer Millar had routinely done, to "alert" the Board of Trade to counter America's drive for markets in Spain.

A copy of Don Alfonso's letter[32] exists among the correspondence in the Templewood Papers. Uncertain whether it had ever reached Hoare, because of the Spanish police state, Don Alfonso repeated the contents in a second letter to the ex ambassador. Hoare, out of office, evidently judged it useless to show the appeal to the Foreign Office given the line Churchill had adopted towards Franco Spain. When the Infante doggedly made another attempt via the British chargé in Madrid to get his appeal heard Hoare's judgment was confirmed. Hoyer Millar, on receiving Bowker's despatch on his seeing the Infante Alfonso, minuted: "We must be careful not to give advance pledges of support to the monarchists."[33] "Certainly, especially as Lord Templewood was inclined to go rather too far in this direction," Harvey added.

The Foreign Office reaction to Don Juan's manifesto was negative. With the inhibition imposed by Churchill, and now seconded by Eden, the diplomats would have been deeply embarrassed if the response from inside Spain had been at all encouraging for the Pretender. "Don Juan has at last decided to chance his arm, but I doubt if it will have much effect," Hoyer Millar commented without even waiting to receive an assessment from the Madrid embassy.[34]

What lay behind Don Juan's issuing the manifesto is revealed in a letter the Pretender wrote February to Kindelán.[35] It offers a better insight into the Pretender's real sympathies than those professed publicly in the manifesto. "Spaniards should know that I guarantee the fundamental ideals of the National Movement, freeing them, on the one hand, from the dictatorial institutions which now oppress them and, on the other, I bar the road to fresh unrest and a return to power of the Marxist extremists," Don Juan unblushingly told the general. The "National Movement" was the regime's preferred term for the Falangists. Don Juan claimed in the letter that Spain's well-to-do classes now wanted to see a restoration of the monarchy. Only Franco was stopping this from coming about. Don Juan was apparently hoping for a putsch that spring from the professedly monarchist generals against Franco to topple the regime. But, as in 1943, this move never came. The Pretender in his letter had asked Kindelán whether the generals had "an important project" on hand which might be prejudiced if he issued a public manifesto. Kindelán had nothing on foot to report and backed the manifesto move.

Many monarchists were taken by surprise by the manifesto. The Pretender, it seems, had not even alerted the Infante, his representative inside Spain, that it was about to be launched. Civilian monarchists like Ventosa, who had pleaded discreetly when in London for at least a gesture of sympathy from the Allies, took refuge in silence. The sharpest commentary on the Pretender's move came from Cambó: "Everything makes me believe the Manifesto one more failure [of Don Juan]. If that's so, and this is more serious, it would gravely compromise the monarchist cause in Spain."[36] The Catalan politician observed that good sense would have required Don Juan to prepare his closest supporters in Spain before putting out the manifesto. The Pretender's additional problem was how to make Spaniards aware of what he was offering them. Monarchists did circulate handbills cautiously, giving the gist of his manifesto. Cambó, who enjoyed the advantage of a relatively free press in Argentina, commented in his diary that brave young monarchists, defying Franco's police and the risk of imprisonment, could at least succeed in making the handbills' contents known. It was once again the BBC's Spanish Service which informed politically-aware people best and most swiftly.

Franco was "greatly angered" by Don Juan's launching the manifesto publicly from Switzerland, Aranda told Bowker.[37] The dictator claimed he had only recently been assured by Spain's envoy in Berne that a manifesto would not be made public and so immediately picked up by the international wire services. Franco's promptly ordered a press campaign against the monarchy. The most prominent "collaborationist" monarchist, Antonio Goicoechea, who enjoyed a fat prebend as Governor of the Bank of Spain, was put up to lead the attack on Don Juan's manifesto. *ABC*, Madrid's professed monarchist daily, led the rest of the press in attacking the Pretender's advisers in exile. This was the sole "coverage" of the manifesto inside Spain, with nothing of its text permitted by the propaganda machine run by the Falangists.

The dictator once again browbeat the generals successfully at a meeting of the army's high command a few days after the manifesto's release. He had President Roosevelt's personal support for the regime, he told them. Relations with America were, he boasted, "excellent" and "only America would count after the war".[38] More substantively, Franco was pursuing his practice at critical times of "fattening the generals" – in the Mexicans' phrase – to make sure they were kept too contented materially by promotions and emoluments to countenance any change of regime. Many army officers had lucrative jobs normally discharged by civilians, and often with "black market" opportunities as well. Franco's wrath over the manifesto came down on the two leading generals who were the sincerest in the monarchist cause. The Infante Alfonso was stripped of his Air Force command in Seville and put under house arrest, which lasted for several months, and Kindelán was dismissed from his post as director of the Army's Higher Military Academy. He had foolishly told a gathering of colonels there that "the illustrious exile of Lausanne, King Juan III" would soon ascend the throne after the defeat of Germany.[39]

As a follow-up move to his manifesto Don Juan, in phone calls from Switzerland, called upon all monarchists to give up their official posts under the regime. Only the generals were exempted from the call – to facilitate the putsch Don Juan waited for in vain. The Duke of Alba proved to be alone in obeying "his king", though he was reluctant to give up wartime London and did not formally depart from the embassy until the autumn of 1945. All other senior ambassadors in capitals like Washington, Buenos Aires, and Berne, who professed to be monarchists, simply ignored the Pretender's call and carried on serving Franco – enjoying their tax privileges as well. "All very Spanish," Eden sneered after reading Bowker's despatch on that fiasco.[40]

Franco's own assessment of Don Juan's call – or, at least, that part convenient to a strong man who so rarely revealed himself to others – came when Alba was given an audience. Lequerica simply refused to accept the London envoy's resignation. This Franco–Alba interview on 5 April was important:

the dictator knew that Spain's premier aristocrat was at the time consulting all the leading Spanish generals – Orgaz, Varela, Asensio, García Valiño, Kindelán and Martínez Campos, the army's chief of intelligence. But Franco also knew that he had got in first: the generals might plot, but they were unwilling to move to get Don Juan on the throne. Franco affected a brutal confidence to Alba, telling him that he was sacrificing himself in a cause that was "a vain one". After years of stringing the monarchists along, Franco felt able to be unambiguous. The Duke replied saying that he could not continue as Spanish ambassador to London unless he got an assurance from the dictator that he intended to restore the monarchy and abolish the Falange. Churchill's letter, Alba maintained, made plain the impossibility of good relations unless things changed. England was not important, Franco replied. Spain's external relations in future would be based on America, and he could afford "to ignore England entirely". Churchill, Franco added, was anyway "a slave of Freemasonry and head of a corrupt and decadent country". It was the duke who kept the British embassy in the know, this time reporting his encounter with the dictator[41] over lunch with the military attaché, Torr – after Hoare's departure the best-informed man in the Madrid embassy.

Such were the "guidelines" Franco offered his envoy. Alba expressed his resentment, observing that such expressions made it impossible for him to continue as Spain's ambassador in London. Franco had made it clear that he was at all costs determined to prevent a restoration – this was the message the dictator, at that delicate juncture, wanted to convey to a leader among the monarchists. Franco had ignored Alba's suggestion that he (Franco) should negotiate with the Pretender, by sending an emissary to Lausanne to work out a "constitutional compromise", Alba informed Torr. Franco's truculence that spring of 1945 holds an important paradox: it was his determination to stay in untrammelled power which, while it prevented Don Juan from ascending the throne, saved his reputation. During 1944–45 the Pretender was, in reality, prepared to accept Franco's assistance to get the throne. It would have been the kiss of political death. It was only what was to become Franco's long "reign" which allowed Don Juan to evolve and take up the stance of a democratic and constitutional would-be monarch, which became his subsequent claim to respect. It was however a very late conversion.

The dictator had easily won the battle of wills with the Pretender. Having seen that the Allies were not going to undertake any steps to favour a restoration, Franco got down to building up Spain's armed forces and cultivating aspiring young colonels loyal to his person. By 1945 the armed forces, and the political and security police, were absorbing an estimated

50 per cent of the national budget. In the last months of the world war Franco watched closely Generals Aranda and Kindelán for any moves against his position. The Army's chief of staff, General Rafael García Valiño, still young at 46 after a meteoric career in the Civil War, might also have been a challenger. He expressed outright disapproval of Franco and the Falange on one occasion to Brigadier Torr.[42] But Franco's superior manoeuvring skills – and the essentially bureaucratic nature of the Spanish Army – saw the Generalísimo through. The appointment of General Agustín Muñoz Grandes as Captain General of the crucial Madrid region, a rival to García Valiño and no less ambitious, was typically astute. As the first commander of Spain's Blue Division fighting for the Germans against the Soviet Union, Muñoz Grandes had every reason to seek the dictator's protection. The Russians after the war's end sought to have him put on trial at Nuremberg as a war criminal. Torr well summed up the situation prevailing at that time: no grouping around the rival generals held "sufficient key positions to enable them to carry through a coup on their own". Franco was keeping "the most influential posts for adherents of his that he can rely upon", the attaché observed. The dictator, moreover, did nothing to cut back the power of the Falange, which by now owed everything to him for its survival. It was more than ever the second pillar of his regime. Franco' supreme political luck was to have a strength of personality and of will surpassing that of any of the brother generals around him. He was the head of what the soldiers liked, sentimentally, to call *"la familia militar"*. With the years of experience in office that distance grew. Franco was an outstanding manipulator of all kinds and conditions of men, exploiting their ambitions, weaknesses, vanities, jealousies and fears. Alone among the soldiers, he was the consummate politician.

Don Juan, by contrast, had singularly failed during the long years of the world war to build up a group of gifted-enough men to form the kernel of a future political organization, and not mere courtiers, for the time when the Allies achieved victory. Vacillating in his thinking and self-indulgent in his personal life, Don Juan possessed none of the iron qualities of leadership or belief in self required of an exiled prince bent on recovering a father's throne. The Pretender was unlucky in the men he had around him in Switzerland: the too subtle caution of López Oliván contrasted with the anti-democrat and impatient Vegas. Don Juan allowed himself to be constantly buffeted by the interested advice of collaborationist supporters inside Spain. Perhaps that was a reason for his poor sense of timing. Don Juan had only a limited choice of men willing to serve him. The Infante Alfonso was prevented by his royal background from becoming the real leader required and Gil Robles, the political figure who aspired to such a role with a future king, failed to grasp whatever opportunities were presented him. Early in 1945 Aranda urged the political leader of pre-1936 days to go to London to attempt to raise the monarchists flag but Gil Robles dithered – and for no less than 12 months, though he had a Home Office visa in his pocket. The Foreign Office was relieved at his inaction. "I can't see why Gil Robles can't stay where he is," Hoyer Millar minuted disingenuously.[43] A Spanish monarchist politician in London as the war was ending was actually felt by British diplomats as risky *vis-à-vis* Franco. An attempt by Harold Nicolson, that fair-minded man, writer and ex diplomat, to help Dr Juan Negrín, Spain's last Prime Minister under the Republic who spent the entire war in exile in London, to see Eden the same month was brushed aside.[44] "It is essential for us to keep right out of Spain's internal politics," was how, yet again, Cadogan advised Eden. Britain's policy thus had the effect of leaving Franco undisturbed and in control of events inside Spain as the war ended.

Yet Britain was seemingly Don Juan's only hope of outside assistance, even though he had seen Churchill dash such possibilities, first with his "kindly words" to General Franco in May 1944 and then with the Prime Minister's correspondence with the dictator. The Pretender could hardly look for help from the United States with its republican traditions: all the Infante Alfonso could report from inside Spain was America's burgeoning trade invading England's old markets. Franco's November '44 interview criticizing the monarchy to an American wire service had been yet another blow.

Don Juan could only pick himself up after all these defeats, in public and in private, and launch his Lausanne Manifesto. Two semi-official emissaries of Franco came afterwards to Switzerland to see the Pretender. Both Kindelán and Aranda warned him against receiving them, but they were messengers from Franco and they got in. Don Juan tried to justify the manifesto, Alberto Martín Artajo, the Catholic Action leader who was soon to accept from the dictator the post of Foreign Minister, and one of the emissaries, reported when back in Madrid. He subsequently also briefed the British embassy.[45] The manifesto had been primarily directed at opinion abroad, the Pretender had told them, claiming to have been following secret British advice. It was naïve duplicity.

The Opportunists and Franco

Apart from his own lack of leadership qualities, what militated against Don Juan's chances was the attitude prevailing then among most of the upper echelons of Spanish society. A ruling class which had gone to war against a widening democracy, as the Republic threatened to become, was unlikely to provide a nucleus of men feeling a pressing need in the winter of 1944 and the spring of '45 to end an authoritarian regime. The regime was still protecting their interests and personal safety, whatever the wider social price. Apart from the landed aristocracy, the financial elites in the big cities and the Catholic Church, which had blessed the Nationalists' "crusade" and was soon to come to Franco's aid with some of its leading lay figures, felt doubts about the Pretender's promise of "order and liberty". None of them could be sure what a monarchy in the person of the uncertain Don Juan might bring. Franco's regime was indeed irksome to many of them, but personal connexions and the balm of corruption offered the well-to-do a way to prosper and get around indignities and inconveniences.

It is, however, important not to allow our knowledge that the Franco regime was to survive the world war's end, and the dictator to rule Spain for no less than 30 years more, to lead us into failing to appreciate the deep uncertainties which prevailed in that spring of 1945. Opportunists after all reigned supreme in that regime. No less a figure than Miguel Mateu Pla, one of the rare personal friends of the dictator and a rich Barcelona industrialist, voiced the uncertainties at that juncture felt among the influential inside the regime. He was simply more outspoken than most. The occasion was a lengthy talk with Harold Farquhar, the well-entrenched British Consul-General in Barcelona. Mateu Pla urged, like others as we have seen, the British and American governments to shake Franco's position by threatening him that they were about to make public their dissatisfaction with his regime. The argument he used was striking – and moreover in tune with the values the Allies then proclaimed. "Maintenance of normal relations with the present Spanish government was tantamount to misleading the Spanish people who could not understand why we maintained friendly with a Fascist regime," the Spanish business leader, who also owned the *Diario de Barcelona* and thus was well aware of trends of informed opinion, was reported by Farquhar as saying.[46] Franco was at that time attempting to get his hand-picked Mayor of Barcelona accepted by the French as Spain's ambassador to Paris, the most important capital for Spain after Washington and London. Mateu Pla's attitude suggests vividly what influence Britain might have exercised, acting together with Washington, upon Spain's influential opportunists had Churchill not already decided otherwise. Mateu Pla, one of the leading monarchists who helped Franco during the Civil War, had prefaced his appeal to the Allies with frank remarks about Spain's troubled condition. The Catalan industrialist was typically fearful of working-class unrest and a revolutionary situation coming about if the

Falange continued with its present powers. It would be fatal for Spain if General Franco and Don Juan continued to adopt an attitude of "mutual hostility". Franco was now "living in a vacuum", the dictator's close acquaintance reported, with General Vigón almost the sole person to whom he really listened. Lequerica simply refrained from passing on to Franco whatever was unpalatable that the American ambassador or the British chargé conveyed to him.

Like the Infante Alfonso, Mateu Pla talked subsequently in identical terms to Bowker in Madrid so that it can hardly be doubted he was making an attempt to move things on. He urged the chargé to recommend to London the diplomatic isolation of the Franco regime. Taken with the remarks of Santa Cruz of the Spanish embassy in London about an "unstable equilibrium" in Spain, caution in making judgments about Spain's prevailing mood at that time is obviously recommendable. The sullen attitude among the bulk of the working classes, and especially in Catalonia, and their expectations of what an Allied victory would mean, can be taken for granted. Voices such as Mateu Pla's were certainly significant: were leading supporters not now turning away from the Franco regime in a mixture of fear and opportunistic self interest?

The Foreign Office did not react to this latent crisis within the regime manifested by men of economic dominance until 23 May, more than one month after Bowker reported on his interview with the Catalan industrialist. "We are doing all that is necessary to show our disapproval of the Spanish regime. There is no call for us to go any further. What Mateu really wants us to do is to support the monarchist cause," the desk officer for Spain minuted unimaginatively, but in accord with the line laid down by his superiors.[47] "There is no reason why we should pull the Spanish monarchists' chestnuts out of the fire . . . by putting increased pressure on Franco." Hoyer Millar simply initialled that minute as if he were by now bored by the whole matter. He saw no reason to put the fundamental issue raised at a critical juncture before his political masters.

It was, of course, Franco's chestnuts that the Foreign Office had long been pulling out of the fire. Inactivity by the Spanish royalists made things very easy for routine-minded British diplomats. Don Juan, who had started out enjoying a certain measure of official British sympathy – certainly Churchill's, by Hillgarth's account – had failed to prepare a political alternative. If an alternative, one with a minimum of appeal for moderate Republicans, had taken form it might, by creating a fait accompli, have obliged the Allies to take heed of Don Juan and his supporters and to accord them at the least a degree of moral support under the impetus of victory.

Eden's zigzagging course over the years on Franco Spain was to end in total self-contradiction. The Foreign Secretary finished up advocating selling arms to the regime. There had been several inquiries about purchasing war material and equipment from Britain by the Spanish government, Eden minuted the Prime Minister early April. "If we don't allow from the UK we may find orders being placed in the U.S . . . We know from 'most secret sources' [i.e. British intelligence] that the Americans are already offering certain surplus civil aircraft to the Spaniards," the Foreign Secretary argued.[48] In January '43 it was Eden who had stopped any talk of military sales to Franco. In 1945 Eden appears from the record to have been willing to accept an official's cunning formula, which would have permitted all but Bren-gun carriers and anti-aircraft guns to be ordered by Madrid. Eden sought to settle the matter between himself and the Prime Minister without further ado. It was Churchill who ruled: "I am shy of this. Better raise at Cabinet."[49] That the Yanks were already doing it, or about to do it if Britain hesitated, became the stock argument in a battle for Spanish markets. With the long absence from Madrid of an ambassador the British service attachés felt free to make British policy in that sphere.

A timely book by Salvador de Madariaga, the distinguished Spanish liberal Republican, written that spring from his Oxford retreat, denounced what was really going on. In *Victors Beware!* Madariaga pointed out that the Franco regime now "rests on little if any national assent". The dictator must therefore at that critical juncture rely on foreign support. But instead of the Anglo-Saxon powers bringing about the end of the Franco regime, by making clear that its survival was incompatible with a peaceful Europe, the two victorious powers were engaged in carrying out business deals in Spain. "Hardly a day passes without some more or less veiled revelation about deals with some American (or, at times, English) business agency and there are many more which do not get into the papers at all," he wrote.[50] In Oxford Madariaga spotted the presence from time to time of high ups of the Franco regime being shown around the sights by attentive British businessmen. The book fell on officials' deaf ears. Madariaga was to many Foreign Office minds the epitome of the impractical Spanish intellectual in exile.

In that twilight period as Churchill's caretaker government waited for the results of the 1945 General Election until late July there occurred a distasteful episode: the Foreign Secretary refused to see Pau Casals, the exiled Spanish cellist, who wanted to discuss the situation in his native Catalonia and "the persecution of Republicans [which] still persists". Eden's aides invoked the precedent of his refusing the previous March to see the politician Negrín. What an opportunity, one might think, for a Foreign Secretary to enhance his stature by indicating Britain's repugnance for the Franco regime's still continuing repression, treating with one of the great artistic figures of Spain. "Mr Eden fears it will not be possible to receive Señor Casals," Eden's private secretary wrote.[51] "Anyhow, the S. of S. is much too busy just now," Hoyer Millar officiously minuted his colleagues. Such was the degree of truckling to the Franco regime with which Eden left office.

There had, however, been an even worse occasion when an appeal to stop Franco's reign of terror had been addressed directly to the Prime Minister two days before Victory in Europe Day – and was ignored. As the executions, and threats of executions, continued throughout March and April, a crescendo of protests against the repression built up in both Britain and France. In this country the trade unions, groups of Spanish Republicans who had been in exile during the war, and the National Council for Civil Liberties urged the government unanimously to make a bid to stop the executions by strong representations in Madrid. The Labour party and the Liberal party, whose leaders had served in Churchill's wartime coalition, had already called for the breaking off of diplomatic relations between Britain and Spain. The case of José Vitini Flores brought together, almost inextricably, the democratic and moral elements forged by the world war and the Resistance, shaping it as something of a test of Churchill's personal values in fighting the war. Known as "Lieut. Col. Ernesto" during the Germans' occupation of France, Vitini was one of those Spaniards who had fought with distinction in the liberation of southern France with the Forces Françaises de l' Intérieur (FFI) the year before. With other ex-Republican Spanish members of the Maquis, he had subsequently crossed the Pyrenees into northern Spain to fight a guerrilla campaign against the Franco regime. He had been captured and executed on Franco's orders, in spite of the French provisional government's vigorous protests. A telegram was thereupon sent to Churchill as Europe's supreme democratic wartime leader. "We urge you to get the Franco terror stopped and to re-establish democracy in Spain," it begged of the Prime Minister. The signatories were headed by the writer Jean Cassou, the government's Commissioner for the Toulouse Region. They included 107 delegates to the French Consultative Assembly (the provisional parliament after the liberation), 16 Third Republic former ministers, 59 ex deputies, 21 prefects, 10 Academicians, 39 newspaper or magazine editors, 33 university professors, 22 Catholic clergy, including one cardinal, 12 Protestant pastors, 44 armed services officers and representatives of all the French political parties.

The Prime Minister's office passed the plea on to the Foreign Office apparently feeling it appropriate to deal with such routine foreign matters in the routine way. "Toulouse is, of course, the storm centre of anti-Franco feeling in France, but the number of signatories is certainly impressive,"

Peter Garran, the desk officer, here at least evidently uncomfortable with the Foreign Office line, minuted. There is no evidence that either Hoyer Millar, Cadogan or his deputy, Orme Sargent, considered the telegram. Eden did not move. Yet Bowker had raised in Madrid the matter of Vitini's execution when he saw Lequerica. A state of war existed in Spain, the Foreign Minister replied and Vitini had been court-martialled after confessing to a "double murder". Vitini had been guilty of a common law offence; it was in no sense a political crime.[52] Lequerica was at the time so undisturbed about Britain's sentiments towards Franco Spain that he invited Churchill to cross the frontier and visit his country when he heard the Prime Minister had gone with a holiday party to the French Basque country during the wait for the election results.[53] The Spanish authorities would be "delighted", the Foreign Minister brazenly told Bowker. With the Labour party making an election issue of Franco Spain, though in truth only a minor one, Churchill fortunately did not accept.

Five days before VE Day, it was the Spanish government in an official note on 3 May which declared that "no change of regime" was contemplated. Franco had sufficient grounds evidently for anticipating that he had won the decisive round, and would survive, with his regime intact, the end of the Second World War. The Caudillo chose to make his first public appearance after VE Day at Valladolid, ostentatiously dressed in the uniform of the Falange. Accompanied by José Luis Arrese, the National Movement's secretary-general, Franco reiterated again his emphatic endorsement of the principles of the Falange.[54] "The events which have come to pass in the world only confirm the clear sightedness of the Spanish Movement," was the Spanish dictator's sole, and stunning, reference to the Allies' victory over Fascism in the Second World War. There was thus something melancholy, even macabre, about a little scene played out in Madrid's Yeserías gaol in those days of Allied victory in Europe. A group of men, all political prisoners, was permitted by the chief warder, who sensed that things might be changing even for Spain, to drink from their precious hoard of cheap wine and bread, and to smoke from their saved cigarette butts while toasting to democracy and freedom.[55] But Franco, and Churchill, had already willed that things should be otherwise in Spain.

Epilogue: Hoare versus Churchill over Spain

Hoare

"Why did I not stay longer [in Madrid]?" Hoare asked himself in an intriguing note he left buried among the Templewood papers.[1] The note – amidst the preparations for another book re-working the years he had spent in Spain left uncompleted when he died in 1959 – reveals his sense of unfinished business. But at the time Hoare was keen to return to England to resume, as he then hoped, a political career. On Spain the truth was that by the autumn of 1944 he had made up his mind about the deficiencies of Don Juan and the monarchists. Hoare had also reached a sobering conclusion about General Franco. The little dictator – Hoare once dismissed him to his aide Malley as "this little man"[2] – would be quite unmovable by the ambassador-politician's efforts alone. Only with decisive support from London, above all from Churchill, and with the co-ordinated backing of Washington, might Franco, Hoare had then calculated, be isolated abroad, and thus sufficiently from influential elements in Spanish society, to be vulnerable. The withdrawal of support by these elements would, in the last analysis, be decisive for so opportunistic a regime hinging on Franco's unique personality. After reaching London in the autumn of 1944 Hoare saw that the British Prime Minister was willed otherwise, whether personal animosity between the two veteran Conservatives was a factor or not.

Hoare's wartime memoirs omit, at first sight surprisingly, an account of his efforts while in Madrid to get the Spanish monarchists into a position to forge the basis for an alternative to Franco's authoritarian regime. The reasons for this omission are simple. As Gerald Brenan put it in the Prologue, Hoare's chief purpose was to indict the regime still prevailing in Spain for its *un*-neutral conduct during the world war and to show up its Fascist-inspired and repressive system of government. The former ambassador believed the first was inseparable from the latter and vice versa. But Hoare the politician was also keen to show, by telling his war-time story, his achievements in a foreign country with a regime deeply hostile to

Britain's war effort. His contribution had gone unjustly unappreciated in Britain – and there were former political enemies, he felt, who wanted to keep it so. To recount in any detail the failure of his efforts with Spain's monarchists would have detracted from the picture of a successful Spanish mission. Worse, any full account would have had to reveal his disagreements with the line Eden and the Foreign Office had obliged him to pursue, amidst their growing suspicion and animosity. That would have obliged Hoare to deal in his memoirs with his final, and cardinal, disagreement with Churchill and to justifying publicly the position he had taken up and believed best for Britain's interests. Any such critical account could not have hidden the Prime Minister's very personal responsibility in declining to assist Hoare's final reckoning with General Franco, thus inevitably ending *Special Mission* with a "failure". Hoare's old foe in the Conservative party was far too powerful for Hoare to challenge. Churchill, and his over-willing aides, kept Hoare still tarred by the appeasement brush. Hoare shied away, when writing in 1945, from assaying to "set the record straight". But, in a vividly-written book, Hoare helped notably in the public branding of the Franco regime.

Hoare's efforts to counsel and cajole Spain's monarchists inside Spain, particularly during 1943, are only to be found reflected in the despatches he wrote at the time to an unsympathetic Foreign Office. Hoare's disenchantment with the monarchists finds expression in only the penultimate chapter of the memoirs, and only a paragraph, when he refers to "the other opposition, the monarchists".[3] They dissipated, he wrote, "their very considerable strength in inconclusive discussions, and were without resolute action and careful preparations". The generals, "many of whom were monarchists in theory, remained inert" and the rank and file civilians had neither the power nor the will to move without them. Hoare's punchline was for the Pretender himself: "Don Juan," the politician of long experience wrote, "needed much more than manifestoes" to regain the Spanish throne.

Samuel Hoare is a fascinating, yet often discarded, figure in twentieth-century British political history. The record has been settled – he was the most vulnerable figure among the Chamberlainite appeasers of the era of the European dictators – and with no direct heirs to defend his reputation. Any critic might easily omit to re-examine Hoare's record while far away in Spain. Hoare's failures, including the ultimate failure in Spain, do not, however, detract from his fascination for they do not necessarily mean that he was mistaken in the policies he proposed or in the judgments he made: in the Spanish case, as we have seen, quite the reverse. Rare among his contemporaries of like Cabinet-status and experience of any political party,

Hoare is a British politician who learnt from an extended foreign experience – his four and half years in Spain, far longer, as he himself noted, than his time in Russia and Italy during the First World War. A posting by Churchill to Madrid in that awesome May 1940 was indeed a poisoned gift. Spain's dictator was seriously tempted that summer to throw in his lot with the triumphant dictators. Franco only slowly forged the political skills for the fluctuating balancing act needed for his own and his hybrid regime's survival between the two more powerful belligerent blocks. When Hoare had played his part by late 1940 in mastering that situation, keeping Spain even if only perhaps temporarily out of the German camp, he still nursed an ambition to become Viceroy of India. A far more congenial, and influential, post for a leading British statesman, Hoare had set his heart on Delhi ever since his Government of India legislative battle in the 1930s with Churchill, perhaps even since his pioneering direct civil flight as Air Minister to the subcontinent in the 1920s. Churchill, now Prime Minister, refused Hoare that posting outright. So Hoare stayed on as ambassador in a deeply uncongenial Madrid. A sensitive politician and a cultured man, Hoare learned to adapt, to acquire more understanding of things Spanish – his interests came to range over Spain's Golden Age literature, its rich bird life among the country sports he pursued and daily rides in the Casa del Campo adjoining Madrid's Oriente Palace[4] – and he endeavoured, much to London's disapproval, to give some political input to Spain's monarchists. When this failed, Hoare began to think more critically than ever about Franco's repressive regime. Spain, as he said in the Lords' debate, was "a morally occupied country" alongside those physically occupied by Nazi Germany elsewhere in Europe, all hated regimes destined to disappear as Hoare, undoubtedly though erroneously, believed at the world war's end.

It is striking how European in his political thinking this British statesman, and Norfolk landowner, had become by 1944. In his emphasis on the liberties of the citizen as the basis for European post-war society and states founded on the rule of law, after the disasters and human waste of the dictatorial regimes, Hoare came close to those European Christian Democrats then secretly preparing themselves for their emergence after the war. Principles such as Hoare recommended were to be paralleled, notably in the Germans' concept of the *Rechtsstaat* post-war. Hoare's December '44 House of Lords speech and, above all, his May '44 address to his Chelsea constituents (which goes unmentioned in *Ambassador On Special Mission*, evidently to avoid any suggestion of his differing about policy towards Spain) contain much of his acquired political philosophy: a cautious, but principled liberalism.

Brenan was not the only seasoned observer of the Spanish scene who praised Hoare and sensed his evolution while living in that country. Two other Britons, who both worked in the wartime Madrid embassy, spoke admiringly of his personality and efforts as envoy. The most important for a fair appraisal of Hoare's wartime achievement is the testimony of Alan Hillgarth, the "super spy" naval attaché in Hoare's embassy until late 1943. He enjoyed Churchill's confidence to a remarkable degree yet, as we have seen, when he felt the Foreign Office was hiding behind Hoare's pre-war reputation as an appeaser, in order to pursue a complaisant line towards Franco, Hillgarth did not hesitate to write in Hoare's defence.[5] Churchill confessed himself "impressed",[6] but did not bring himself to any public follow-up. John Lomax, a tough-minded Scot and unconventional diplomat, who supervised much of the economic warfare at the Madrid end in the crucial early years of the war, praised Hoare in his memoirs[7] for his willingness to step out of the routines of diplomacy and seek "to bend local events to his will". It seems those who worked closest with Hoare in wartime Madrid admired most how he had "made amends" for his pre-1939 record and grown in stature during the war. But Hoare's lasting image was made by the powerful in London.

Hoare's description in the memoirs of his position in British politics[8] is convincing, though he did himself no service thereby with his enemies. He had been, he said, "a liberal amongst conservatives and a conservative among liberals" and thus handicapped for party politics. Yet no leading British politician of the period obeyed more strictly party discipline as his resignation from the Baldwin Cabinet in December 1935 over the Abyssinian débâcle testified. The label "Slippery Sam", attached to him by the Churchillians and of which they never let go, came from pre-1939 days. Hoare's efforts in Madrid, the last phase of his political career, were aimed as far as Spain was concerned at reconciling good government and civic principles with nation-state politics. "I was never blind to the over-riding services that he rendered to his fellow countrymen," Hoare wrote,[9] defensively, of Churchill when he returned, ten years after the Second World War's end, to ponder his fortunes serving in one outpost of that conflict: Hoare's observation evidently leaves much unsaid.

Churchill

Churchill, at the zenith of his political power during the closing stages of the war, did not suffer from any of Hoare's inhibiting baggage. Churchill was only ever concerned with Spain, Franco's Spain, in so far as it affected

Britain's strategic and, in his thinking, imperial interests. But the last thing that meant was a position unwavering in its perception of where Britain's national interest lay. Churchill's attitude was changing – according sometimes to his perception of external events and, as often, to his fierce and fluctuating emotions. In *The Gathering Storm* Churchill gives an extraordinarily unguarded glimpse of how he could perceive things Spanish, even when in Spain, shortly before the outbreak of the Civil War. There is a complete identification of himself with what would soon emerge as the Nationalist, anti-Republican side on grounds which can only be called Churchill's class-consciousness. For a statesman it was an inadequate starting point for a balanced understanding of Spain at that moment and for judging the Civil War and its aftermath – the Franco regime. "Naturally I was not in favour of the Communists," the future British Prime Minister wrote,[10] "how could I be when, if I had been a Spaniard, they would have murdered me and my family and friends"? That was in Barcelona in 1935 before the conflict, but, as Harold Nicolson remarked when it was under way, Churchill's views on the country were dependent upon his "personal friendship with Spanish grandees".[11] During the Civil War Churchill actually took up four different, and public, positions – for non-intervention, against non-intervention, for the Nationalists and for the Republic. Initially, and as we have seen by instinct, Churchill was with the Nationalists, then for non-intervention – that was in line with British Imperial Defence Staff analyses the government of the day allowed him to see.

But by late 1937 in an article he wrote in *The Daily Telegraph*[12] he was advocating British support for the Spanish Republic – otherwise, he warned, Britain risked facing a strengthened Germany with Hitler having Franco "by the scruff of the neck". Six months later in a speech in Manchester he was attacking "the despicable cloak of non-intervention". When Prime Minister in 1940 Churchill approved the bribing of senior Spanish generals who were opposed to Franco over joining the Axis in the war. As 1944 turned into '45 Britain's leader considered Spain's geographical position vital in a world he already saw divided between Communist and western blocs, and he overrode others' counsels, insisting upon the appeasement of the Franco regime.

The only possible way to reconcile Churchill's varying stances on Spain is by seeing them all justified, and solely justified, by his changing perception of Britain's interests at any particular time, in a word the abiding relativity of his *Realpolitik*. At no time does Churchill show himself considering Hoare's good governance of Spain, nor troubled by Eden's intermittent fears that a continuance of Franco's repressive regime might strengthen the growth of Communism inside Spain. As in Greece, force would be enough against such a threat.

In the ghostly "divide up" of Europe into spheres of influence Churchill famously discussed with Stalin the Prime Minister had to witness the establishment of totalitarian regimes throughout Eastern Europe, but in the West, where he was accorded, and exercised, influence Churchill made no attempt before the world war ended to influence and perhaps extend the sphere of would-be democratic values to include Spain, as Hoare had sketched. Maybe Franco, by 1944–45, was in a position to withstand whatever degree of pressure the Allies might have brought upon his regime; what is not conjecture is that Churchill, by appeasing Franco, showed that he did accept for Spaniards a tyranny, as General Aranda had put it, which he indignantly rejected for the British people. Churchill, whose historic fame rests upon his refusal to appease Hitler's Germany, became the appeaser of the Franco regime when his potential influence over other European nations as Prime Minister of the leading victorious democratic power in the region, was at its height.

Churchill in his reply to the letter from Franco, which had revealed the dictator's own sense of vulnerability in that last autumn of the war, dropped the crucial phrases which condemned the regime's repressive nature as the ground for refusing Spain a place post-war alongside the other nations of Europe. Britain's imperial interests alone counted for him, in spite of a world fundamentally changed by the world war. Churchill may indeed have seen the advantage for Britain of the prospect of a pariah state like Franco's excluded from the UNO, eager to perform certain "services". These might include defence facilities and intelligence-gathering opportunities – Madrid's importance for tapping into Germany's war-time signal traffic could well have been an additional, though diplomatically unconfessable, reason for seeing disadvantages for Britain in a change of regime in Spain. In return, there would be material support and favour for an unpopular regime – the old-fashioned attractions indeed for an imperialist of pliant local chieftains. Only by 1945 Franco had already settled for his future protector upon the United States.

Churchill, who had celebrated his 40th birthday just as the First World War broke out, fits well the description the distinguished liberal journalist J. A. Spender once gave of the typical nineteenth-century European statesman. "To him the god of nations is the god of battles who has no mercy on the weaklings pleading for the Christian virtues in the dealings of nations. This typical statesman prides himself on being above all things a realist, 'a real politician', who abjures sentiment, recognises in a clear-sighted way that the world is ruled by force and treats all facts and situations 'objectively' and with single eye to their effect on his nation, or group of nations with which it is associated . . . The object he sets before himself is not the settlement of questions according to what in other relations might be called their merits or their rights and wrongs, but to make sure that they are not settled in any way which diminishes the power of his own country or enhances that of a rival."[13] Churchill was indeed a great war leader for Britain, but he was no friend of Spain.

Notes

Prologue

1   Interviews with the author, London, 12.2. and 27.2.1995.

I   In the Hour of Britain's Need, 1940

1   Churchill Archives (CA) CHAR 20/13, p. 40, 29.9.40.
2   CHAR 20/13, p. 27.
3   CA CHAR 20/11, p. 75.
4   CA CHAR 2/405, p. 2.
5   S. Hoare, *Ambassador on Special Mission* (London: Collins, 1946), p. 16.
6   A. Cadogan, *Diaries, 1938–45* (London, 1971).
7   Ibid., entry 20.5.40.
8   Ibid., 23.5.40.
9   Ibid., 21.5.40.
10   FO 371 – 24501 c. 6938 and PREM 4 21/2A, p. 546.
11   M. Gilbert, *Winston Churchill – Finest Hour, 1939–41* (London: Heinemann, 1983), p. 585.
12   J. Godfrey: *The Naval Memoirs*, Vol. V, part I, p. 113, Admiralty Library, Portsmouth (unpublished).
13   Cadogan, *Diaries*, Introduction, p. 21.
14   Templewood Papers (TP) XIII – 17, 6.6.40.
15   FO 371 – 24508 c. 7164, 8.6.40.
16   TP XIII –16, Correspondence with Prime Minister, no. 15.
17   Ibid. , Correspondence with Foreign Secretary, no. 3.
18   Ibid., 18.6.40.
19   Ibid., no. 272, 22.6.40.
20   CA CHAR 20/9A 5, p. 27, 27.6.40.
21   TP XIII – 16, no. 29, 27.6.40.
22   PREM 4 21/2A, p. 539, 21.6.40.
23   Ibid., p. 520, 27.7.40.
24   Ibid., 30.7.40.
25   CA CHAR 20/13, p. 40.
26   TP XIII – 16, 22.10.40.
27   TP XXIII, *My Third Mission*, unpublished typescript, c. 1958, chap. VI, p. 24.
28   PREM 3 405/1.
29   CA CHAR 20/2A, 23.10.40.

30 Hoare, *Ambassador*, p. 99.
31 FO 371 – 24508 c. 11259, 18.10.40.
32 FO 371 – 23168 c. 19707, 1.12.39.
33 Ibid., c. 19131, 25.11.39.
34 M. Broggi, *Memorias de Un Cirujano* (Barcelona: Peninsula, 2001), p. 283.
35 Ibid., p. 309.
36 A. Vinas, J. Vinuela, F. Eguidazu, C. Fernandez Pulgar and S. Florencia, *Politica Comercial Exterior en Espana 1931–75* (Madrid: Banco de Espana, Servicio de Estudios Economicos 1979), vol. I, p. 332.
37 FO 371 – 24502 c. 9630, 6.9.40.
38 FO 371 – 24504 c. 12174, 8.11.40.
39 FO 371 – 24502 c. 8394, 16.11.40.
40 FO 371 – 24508 c. 11573, p. 275, 1.11.40.
41 Ibid., p. 278, 2.11.40.
42 FO 371 – 24505 c. 12495.
43 FO 371 – 24504 c. 11076, 1.11. and c. 11942, 8.11.40.
44 Ibid., c. 12218, 16.11.40.
45 FO 371 – 24509 c. 13008.
46 Ibid., c. 12866.
47 FO 371 – 24505 c. 13173, pp. 358 and 364.
48 FO 371 – 24506 c. 13776, 24.12.40.
49 C. Hull, *Memoirs* (London: Hodder and Stoughton, 1948), p. 875.
50 T. Hamilton, *Appeasement's Child, the Franco Regime in Spain* (London: Gollancz, 1943), p. 215.
51 FO 371 – 24505 c. 12501, p. 115, 18.11.40.
52 Ibid., p. 123.
53 Ibid., c. 13023, 27.11.40.
54 Ibid., 28.11.40.
55 Spanish Ministry of Foreign Affairs (MAE), Leg 985, exp. 8, 9.12.40, author's translation.
56 Gilbert, *Winston Churchill – Finest Hour*, p. 924.
57 Ibid., p. 959.
58 W. Churchill, *Second World War*, Vol. I, *The Gathering Storm* (London: Cassell, 1948), p. 167.
59 FO 371 – 24508 c. 11538, 6.12.40.

2 Spain, a Balancing Country, 1941

1 CA CHAR 20/36, p. 23, 15.3.41.
2 TP XIII – 16 Correspondence with PM, 7.3.41.
3 Hamilton, *Appeasement's Child* (London: Gollancz, 1943), p. 77.
4 P. Sainz Rodriguez, *Un Reinado en la Sombra* (Barcelona: Planeta, 1981), p. 282; and E. Vegas, *Memorias Politicas 1938–42* (Madrid: Actas, 1995), p. 223.
5 Vegas, *Memorias*, p. 239.
6 Ibid., p. 242.

7   J.M. Toquero, *Franco y Don Juan* (Barcelona: Plaza Janes, 1989), p. 41.

8   K.H. Ruhl, *Spanien im Zweiten Weltkrieg* (Hamburg: Hoffmann u. Campe, 1975), p. 69 and FO 371 – 49550 z 10982, 24.9.45.

9   AP (Avon 954 – 27), p. 177, 20.7.41.

10   H. Trevor-Roper, *Hitler's War Directives* (London: Sidgwick and Jackson, 1964), p. 81.

11   TP XXIII –1, *My Third Mission*, unpublished memoirs (c. 1958), chap. VII, no. 11.

12   Ibid., no. 12.

13   W. Churchill, *Secret Session Speeches* (London: Cassell, 1946), p. 44.

14   CA CHAR 20/, p. 35.

15   PREM 4/21/1, 13.1.41.

16   CAB 69/2 DO (41).

17   PREM 3 405/8, p. 230, 7.1.41.

18   CA CHAR 20/36, 12.2.41.

19   Hansard, H. of C., 22.4.41.

20   Hamilton, *Appeasement*, chap. XV.

21   A. Eden, *Memoirs*, Vol. II, *The Reckoning* (London: Cassell, 1968), entry for 16.2.41.

22   PREM 3 –405/6, p. 85, 9.3.41.

23   Ibid., p. 87, 13.3.41.

24   Ibid., 14.3.41.

25   Ibid., 19.3.41.

26   Ibid., undated, p. 71.

27   PREM 4 21/2A, p. 480, 7.1.41.

28   PREM – 3 405/6, p. 62, 9.4.41.

29   Ruhl, *Spanien*, p. 305.

30   J.P. Fusi, *Franco* (Madrid: Ediciones El Pais, 1985), p. 88.

31   A. Cadogan, *Diaries* (London: Cassell, 1971), 4.5.41.

32   PREM 4 21/2A, p. 469, 10.5.41.

33   FO 371 – 26945 c. 4255, 25.4.41.

34   Ibid., c. 4170, p. 130, 27.4.41.

35   Ibid., p. 134, 3.5.41.

36   Hoare, *Ambassador on Special Mission* (London: Collins, 1946), p. 114.

37   C. Foltz, *The Masquerade in Spain* (Boston: Houghton Mifflin, 1948), p. 161.

38   Hamilton, *Appeasement's Child*, p. 222.

39   Hansard, H. of C, 24.7.41.

40   F. Cambo, *Meditacions, Dietari 1941–46* (Barcelona: Alpha, 1982), vol. II, 19.7.41.

41   PREM 4/21/1.

42   FO 371 – 26891 c. 8744, 5.8.41.

43   Ibid., c. 9154, 13.8.41.

44   AP 954 – 27, p. 181, 13.8.41.

45   FO 371 26939 c. 6555, 14.8.41.

46   CA CHAR 20/36, 16.8.41.
47   C. Wilmot, *The Struggle for Europe* (London: Collins, 1959 edn), p. 86.
48   AP, p. 181.
49   FO 371 – 26891 c. 9154, 13.8.41.
50   Cadogan, *Diaries*, entry for 25.4.41.
51   Ibid., c. 8733, 6.8.41.
52   AP, p. 183, 26.8.41.
53   Sainz Rodriguez, *Reinado*, p. 147.
54   AP, p. 195.
55   Ibid., p. 188, 11.9.41.
56   Ibid., p. 193.
57   PREM 4 – 32/7.
58   R. Hodgson, *Spain Resurgent* (London: Hutchinson, 1953), p. 107.
59   Hoare, *Ambassador*, p. 119.
60   PREM 4/21/1, 30.7.41.
61   TP XXIII – 1 *Third Mission*, chap. VIII, p. 9.
62   Hoare, *Ambassador*, p. 121.
63   AP, p. 200, 21.11.41.
64   FO 371 – 26899, 10.11.41.
65   A. Kindelán, *La Verdad de mis Relaciones con Franco* (Barcelona: Planeta, 1981), p. 46.
66   E. Vegas, Personal Archives, letter of 23.12.41.
67   Hoare, *Ambassador*, p. 127.
68   PREM 4 21/2A, 19.12.41.
69   FO 371 – 26964 c. 14354.
70   FO 371 – 26891 c. 12972, 22.11.41.
71   Eccles, *By Safe Hand* (London: Bodley Head, 1983).

3   Ambiguous Assurances, 1942

 1   W. Churchill, *The Second World War,* Vol. IV; *The Hinge of Fate* (London: Cassell 1951), p. 460.
 2   PREM 4 21/2A, p. 452, 5.1.42.
 3   Ibid., p. 446, 20.1.42.
 4   Herbert Feis, *The Spanish Story, Franco and the Nations at War* (New York: Norton, 1966), p. 152.
 5   PREM 4 21/2A, pp. 443 and 426, 20 and 22.1.42.
 6   C. Hull, *Memoirs* (London: Hodder and Stoughton, 1948), vol. II, p. 1187.
 7   PREM 4 21/2A, p. 430, 8.2.42.
 8   Ibid., p. 432, 10.2.42.
 9   CA CHAR 20/70, p. 133, 26.2.42.
10   PREM 4 21/2A, p. 422, 2.4.42.
11   FO 371 – 31211.
12   V. Salmador, *Don Juan de Borbon* (Barcelona: Planeta, 1981).
13   L. Lopez Rodo, *La Larga Marcha hacia la Monarquia* (Barcelona: Noguer, 1977), p. 26.

14   FO 371 – 31227 – c. 180, 5.1.42.

15   Lopez Rodo, *Larga Marcha*, speech of 1.3.42, p. 27.

16   FO 371 – 31227 – c. 3296, 6.3.42.

17   Sainz Rodriguez, *Un Reinado* (Barcelona: Planeta, 1981), p. 351.

18   FO 371 – 31227 c. 6879.

19   TP XIII – 22 no. 215, 1.7.42.

20   FO 371 – 31227 – c. 4567, 2.5.42.

21   AP 954 – 27 p. 247, 13.5.42.

22   Ibid., p. 254, 3.6.42.

23   FO 371 – 31227 c. 6068, 18.6.42.

24   Ibid., c. 6323, 23.6.42.

25   Ibid., c. 6393, 27.6.42.

26   Ibid., c. 6323, 27.6.42.

27   Vegas Archives, dated 17.8.42.

28   CA CHAR 20/83, 15.11.42.

29   Hoare, *Ambassador* (London: Collins, 1946), p. 199; F.H. Hinsley, *British Intelligence in the Second World War* (London: HMSO, 1979), vol. II, chap. 24, appendix 15, p. 719; and D. McLachlan, *Naval Intelligence 1939–45* (London: Weidenfeld and Nicolson, 1968), p. 204.

30   Churchill, *World War*, Vol. IV, p. 473.

31   AP, p. 268, 29.8.42.

32   Hoare, *Ambassador*, p. 164.

33   AP, p. 271, 4.9.42.

34   Lopez Rodo, *Larga Marcha*, p. 29.

35   Galeazzo Ciano, *Diary, 1939–43* (London: Heinemann, 1947), 4.9.42.

36   Churchill, *World War*, Vol. IV, p. 488.

37   Hinsley, *Intelligence*, Vol. II, pp. 19 and 37.

38   D. Hamilton-Hill, *S.O.E. Assignment*, chap. III (London: Kimber, 1973).

39   J.M. Gil Robles, *La Monarquia por la que yo luche* (Madrid: Taurus, 1976), diary entry 25.10.43.

40   FO 371 – 31227 c. 8279, 24.8.42.

41   FO 370 – 31228 – c. 9254, 22.9.42.

42   Ibid., c. 10239, 25.10.42.

43   FO 371 – 31228 c. 9979, 7.10.42.

44   FO 371 –31227 c. 8028, 6.8.42.

45   C. Hayes, *Wartime Mission in Spain*, (New York: Macmillan, 1945), p. 56.

46   Hoare, *Ambassador*, p. 173.

47   Ibid., p. 174.

48   Capt. Harry Butcher, *Three Years with Eisenhower* (London: Heinemann, 1946), p. 97.

49   AP, p. 312, 26.10.42 (PM's message to FDR).

50   Ibid., p. 342, 5.11.42.

51   Hayes, *War Mission*, p. 90.

52   FO 371 –34754 c. 3673, 8.11.42.

53 Ciano, *Diary*, 7.11.42.

54 AP, p. 360.

55 AP, p. 363, 20.11.42.

56 Cadogan, *Diaries* (London: Cassell, 1971) , 14.11.42.

57 MAE Legajo R 1117, ex 13, 31.10.42. Author's translation.

58 MAE Legajo R 869 ex 17.

59 R. Rodriguez Monino, *La Mision Diplomatica del Duque de Alba en la Embajada de Espana en Londres, 1937–45* (Valencia: Castalia, 1971), p. 99.

60 A. Cave Brown, *The Last Hero: Wild Bill Donovan* (London: Joseph, 1982), p. 233.

61 PREM 4 21/2A, p. 376, 16.12.42.

62 Ibid. p. 377, undated.

63 Toquero, *Franco y Don Juan* (Barcelona: Plaza Janes, 1989), p. 58; Lopez Rodo, *Larga Marcha*, p. 33 and FO 371 – 31228 c. 11042, 11.11.42.

64 Gil Robles, *Monarquia*, entry for 1.10.42.

65 FO 371 31228 c. 11282, 16.11.42.

66 Ibid., c. 11529, 21.11.42.

67 Ibid., c. 11695, 25.11.42.

68 Ibid., c. 11737, 26.11.42.

69 FO 371 – 31228 c. 11982, 3.12.42.

70 Kindelán, *La Verdad* (Madrid: Planeta, 1981), p. 32.

4 Franco Toughs It Out, January–October, 1943

1 PREM 3 – 405/8, pp. 218 and 206.

2 FO 371 – 34810 c. 340, 7.1.43 and Hoare, *Ambassador* (London: Collins, 1946), p. 185.

3 FO 371 – 34810 c. 1469, c. 1974, c. 2032 and c. 2236 and AP, p. 376.

4 Ibid., c. 1469.

5 *The Times*, 22.3.43.

6 FO 371 – 34811 c. 3399, 26.3.43.

7 FO 371 – 34787 c. 3897.

8 Cadogan, *Diaries* (London: Cassell, 1971), 7.4.43.

9 FO 371 – 34774A c. 4641, 21.4.43.

10 M. Gilbert, *Road to Victory – 1941–45* (London: Heinemann, 1989), p. 377.

11 K. Philby, *My Silent War* (London: Panther, 1968 edn), p. 67.

12 FO 371 – 34811 c. 3399, 10.4.43.

13 Ibid., 16.4.43.

14 FO 371 – 34796 c. 4481, 14.4.43.

15 FO 371 – 34811 c. 3572, 29.3.43.

16 AP p. 375, 30.1.43.

17 FO 371 – 34819 c. 350, 8.1.43.

18 FO 371 – 34811 c. 5395, 7.5.43.

19 FO 371 – 34752 c. 5497, 10.5.43.

20 CA CHAR 20/110, 26.4.43.

21 FO 371 – 34764 c. 6336.
22 FO 371 – 34787 c. 5313, 11.5.43.
23 Barcelona: Planeta (1944).
24 FO 371 – 34820 c. 8073, 7.7.43.
25 FO 371 – 39806 *Personalities in Tangiers and the Spanish Zone*, June '44.
26 Barcelona: Planeta (1981).
27 FO 371 – 34811 c. 4382.
28 FO 371 – 31227 c. 7247, 7.7.42.
29 FO 371 – 34820 c. 7248, 28.6.43.
30 E. Alison Peers (London: Methuen, 1943), p. 231.
31 Lopez Rodo, *Larga Marcha* (Barcelona: Noguer, 1977), pp. 39–41.
32 FO 371 – 34820 c. 7182.
33 Lopez Rodo, *Larga Marcha*, p. 34 and FO 371 – 34819 c. 3858, 6.4.43.
34 Ibid., p. 35 and FO 371 – 34787 c. 3089, 17.3.43.
35 Ibid., p. 36.
36 Ibid., pp. 37–8 and Toquero, *Franco y Don Juan* (Barcelona: Plaza Janes, 1989), p. 67.
37 FO 371 – 34787 c. 5313, 19.5.43.
38 FO 371 – 34819 c. 2525, 22.2.43.
39 FO 371 – 34819 c. 3303, 30.3 43.
40 AP, p. 390, 19.4.43.
41 Ibid., p. 398, 7.5.43.
42 PREM 4 21/2A, pp. 283–6.
43 AP, p. 402, 24.5.43.
44 FO 371 – 34819 c. 5828, 26.5.43.
45 J. Godfrey, *Naval Memoirs*, unpublished, vol. IV, part II, p. 294.
46 Hoare, *Ambassador*, p. 66.
47 FO 371 – 34820 c. 6426, 28.5.43.
48 Ibid., c. 6430, 6.6.43.
49 Ibid., c. 6729, 13.6.43.
50 AP, p. 403, 1.6.43.
51 FO 371 – 34820 c. 7248, 23.5.43.
52 Sainz Rodriguez, *Un Reinado* (Barcelona: Planeta, 1981), p. 161.
53 Toquero, *Franco*, p. 67.
54 Gil Robles, *La Monarquia* (Madrid: Taurus, 1976), 23.6.43 and 14.7.43.
55 FO 371 – 34820 c. 8388, 21.7.43.
56 Ibid., c. 8302, 18.7.43.
57 Ibid., c. 8205, 16.7.43.
58 FO 371 – 34788 c. 8310 and c. 8602, 17 and 18.7.43.
59 FO 371 – 34789 c. 9379, 2.8.43.
60 Hoare, *Ambassador*, p. 211.
61 FO 371 34788 c. 8919, 27.7.43.
62 FO 371 – 34755 c. 8722, 30.7.43.
63 Ibid., c. 8774, 30.7. and 3.8.43.

64 FO 371 – 34756 c. 12354, 21.10.43 and PREM 4 21/2A , p. 236.
65 Gil Robles, *Monarquia*, 11.8.43.
66 Hansard, H. of C., 4.8.43.
67 Lopez Rodo, *Marcha*, p. 50.
68 PREM 4 21/2A, p. 231, 28.7.43.
69 Ibid., p. 229, 6.8.43.
70 AP, p. 432, 19.8.43.
71 TP XXIII, *Third Mission*, chap. IX.
72 FO 371 – 34788 c. 8919.
73 FO 371 – 34765 c. 8737, 4 and 5.8.43.
74 FO 371 –34789 c. 9712, 21.8.43.
75 FO 371 – 34821 c. 9692.
76 Gil Robles, *Monarquia*, 16.8.43.
77 FO 371 – 34821 c. 9692, 24.8.43.
78 Ibid., 25.8.43.
79 *Ambassador*, pp. 220–22.
80 Vinas, *Politica Comercial* (Madrid: Banco Exterior de Espana, Servicio de Estudios Economicos, 1979), vol. I, pp. 406 and 408.
81 Ibid., table no. 23, p. 442.
82 FO 371 – 34755 c. 9602, 21.8.43.
83 Ibid., 3.9.43.
84 Ibid., c. 10232, p. 118.
85 FO 371 – 34755 c. 10232, 21.8.43.
86 Ibid., 22 and 24.8.43.
87 Ibid., 27.8.43.
88 PREM 3 – 405/8, 27.6.43.
89 Ibid., 9.7.43.
90 FO 371 – 34755 c. 9809, 24.8.43.
91 FO 371 – 34852 c. 11123, 16.9.43.
92 *The Times*, 21.9.43.
93 FO 371 –34756 c. 11179.
94 FO 371 – 34766 c. 10523, dated 13.9.43.
95 FO 371 – 34789 c. 11083, 13.9.43.
96 FO 371 – 34821 c. 10074, 1.9.43.
97 FO 371 – 34789 c. 9994, 30.8.43.
98 Ibid., c. 10190, 4.9.43.
99 Ibid., c. 11000, 11.9.43.
100 Fusi, *Franco* (Madrid: Ediciones El Pais, 1985), p. 88; Toquero, Franco, p. 73; Lopez Rodo, *Marcha*, p. 43 and Jean Creac'h, *Le Coeur et L'Epee – Chroniques Espagnoles* (Paris: Plon, 1958), p. 206.
101 FO 371 – 34821 c. 11895, 30.9.43.
102 Kindelán, *Verdad*, p. 122.
103 Gil Robles, *Monarquia,* 26.10.43.
104 Kindelán, *Verdad*, p. 222.

105 FO 371 – 34821 c. 13103, 28.10.43.
106 Kindelán, *Verdad*, p. 20.
107 FO 371 – 34820 c. 8388, undated.
108 FO 371 – 34821 c. 11895, 30.9.43.
109 Cambo, *Meditations* (Barcelona: Alpha, 1982), 9.11.43.
110 Ibid., 28.10.43.
111 Ibid., 28.7.43 ,.
112 FO 371 – 34756 c. 13123, 4.11.43.
113 López Rodó, *Marcha*, p. 44.
114 FO 371 – 34790 c. 14115, 13.11.43.
115 11.5.43.
116 Augusto de Castro, *Politica Externa Portuguesa durante a Guerra 1939–45* (Lisbon, 1958), p. 47.
117 TP XIII – 16, 14.10.43.

5 The Wolfram War, November–December, 1943

1   Feis, *The Spanish Story* (New York: Norton, 1966), p. 200.
2   FO 371 – 34801 c. 8771, 27.7.43.
3   FO 371 – 34805 c. 11527, 5.10.43 and 34807 c. 13998, O.E.W. message of 7.10.43.
4   FO 371 – 34804 c. 10800, 18.9.43.
5   M.B. Stoff, *Oil, War and American Security, 1941–47* (New Haven: Yale University Press, 1980), p. 209.
6   Vinas, *Politica Comercial* (Madrid: Banco Exterior de Espana, 1979), vol. I, p. 359.
7   FO 371 – 34796 c. 4896, 1.5.43 and FO 371 – 34798 c. 6401, 27.5.43.
8   C.J. Hayes, *Wartime Mission in Spain* (New York: Macmillan, 1945), p. 96 and Feis, op. cit. (1966), p. 198.
9   FO 371 – 34795 c. 3745, 10.4.43.
10 Vinas, *Politica Comercial*, p. 446.
11 FO 371 – 34800 c. 7924, 10.7.43.
12 R. Tamames, *Economia Espanola* (Madrid: Alianza, 1967), p. 189.
13 FO 371 – 34806 c. 12479, 9.11.43.
14 FO 371 – 34803 c. 10430, 25.8.43.
15 FO 371 – 34802 c. 9486, 14.8.43.
16 FO 371 – 34801 c. 8884, 26.7.43.
17 FO 371 34802 c. 9819, 26.8.43.
18 Ibid., c. 9883, 3.9.43.
19 P. Martin Acena, *Los Movimientos de Oro en Espana durante la Segunda Guerra Mundial* (Madrid Ministerio de Asuntos Exteriores, Centro de Publicaciones, 2001), pp. 66 and 88.
20 FO 371 – 34805 c. 12263, 20.10.43.
21 FO 371 – 34809 c. 15328, 4.1.44.
22 Feis, *The Spanish Story*, p. 222.

23 FO 371 – 34809 c. 15216.
24 FO 371 34802 c. 9661, 20.8.43.
25 Ibid., c. 9808, 23.8.43.
26 Ibid., c. 6066, 27.5.43.
27 FO 371 34800 c. 7883, 8.7.43.
28 FO 371 34799 c. 6957.
29 FO 371 – 34852 c. 7107, 18.6.43 and FO 371 – 34799 c. 6957, 14.6.43.
30 FO 371 – 34800 – c. 8550, 9 and 10.7.43.
31 FO 371 – 34801 c. 8668, 30.7.43.
32 Vinas, *Politica Comercial*, op. cit., vol. I, pp. 446 and 442.
33 FO 371 – 34803 c. 10544, 11.9.43.
34 FO 371 – 34794 c. 3561 and 3562.
35 FO 371 – 34789 c. 10701, 20.9.43.
36 FO 371 – 34806 c. 12479, 21.10.43.
37 FO 371 – 34805 c. 11777, 8.10.43.
38 FO 371 – 34807 c. 13488.
39 FO 371 – 34805 c. 11527.
40 C. Hull, *Memoirs* (London: Hodder and Stoughton, 1948), p. 1327.
41 Hayes, *Wartime Mission*, op. cit., p. 192.
42 U.S. Memorandum of 18.11.43 in FO 371 – 34807 – c. 14061.
43 Hayes, *Wartime Mission*, op. cit., p. 185.
44 Hull, *Memoirs,* p. 1329.
45 Hayes, *Wartime Mission*, op. cit., p. 196.
46 Ruhl, *Spanien* (Hamburg: Hoffmann u. Campe, 1975), p. 234.
47 F. Eguidazu, Monetary Aspects of Spanish Neutrality in *Revista de Estudios Internacionales*, April–June issue, Madrid (1984), p. 382 and D. Acheson, *Present at the Creation* (London: Hamilton, 1969), p. 62.
48 Hayes, *Wartime Mission*, p. 203.
49 FO 371 – 34808 c. 14395.
50 FO 371 – 34807 c. 14061, 18.11.43.
51 FO 371 – 34808 c. 14107, 21.11.43.
52 Ibid., c. 14198, 11.12.43.
53 Ibid., minute of 2.12.43.
54 FO 371 – 34806 c. 12905, minute of 3.11.43.
55 FO 371 – 34809 c. 14715, 14.12.43.
56 Vinas, *Politica Comercial*, p. 427, table no. 15.
57 FO 371 – 34809 c. 14665, 15 and 16.12.43.
58 Ibid., c. 15294.
59 FO 371 – 34809 c. 15328.

6 Churchill Intervenes I, January–September, 1944

1 FO 371 – 39667 c. 2237, 12.2.44.
2 AP, p. 467, 14.2.44.
3 Cadogan, *Diaries* (London: Cassell, 1971), 28.1.44.

4 FO 371 – 39666 c. 1414, 1.2.44.

5 Hayes, *Wartime Mission* (New York: Macmillan, 1945), p. 212.

6 FO 371 – 39665 c. 315, 28.12.43.

7 J. Tusell, *Franco, Espana y la Segunda Guerra Mundial* (Madrid: Temas de Hoy, 1995), p. 464.

8 AP, p. 450.

9 FO 371 – 39665 c. 1321, undated.

10 Vinas, *Politica Comercial* (Madrid: Banco Exterior de Espana, 1979), vol. I, p. 372.

11 *The Times*, ex Madrid, February 2 and 3.

12 Hayes, *Wartime Mission*, p. 217.

13 Vinas, *Politica Comercial*, p. 414.

14 FO 371 – 39666 c. 1571, 3.2.44.

15 FO 371 – 39667 c. 2236, 7.2.44.

16 FO 371 – 39666 c. 1953.

17 Cadogan, *Diaries*, 3.2.44.

18 AP, p. 469, 14.2.44.

19 Ibid., p. 470, 20.2.44.

20 Tom Burns, *The Use of Memory* (London: Sheed and Ward, 1993), p. 118.

21 FO 371 – 39665 c. 859.

22 Ibid., c. 1288, 1309 and 1321, 28–9.1.44.

23 FO 371 – 39667 c. 2614, 15.2.44.

24 Ibid., c. 2737, 23.2.44.

25 Ibid., c. 2511.

26 AP, p. 473, 21.2.44.

27 Ibid., p. 476, 24.2.44.

28 Hayes, *Wartime Mission*, p. 219.

29 FO 371 – 39668 c. 3643.

30 Ibid., c. 3645, 20.3.44.

31 Ibid., c. 3646, 21.3.44.

32 Hayes, *Wartime Mission*, p. 220.

33 Hayes, *Wartime Mission*, p. 213.

34 FO 371 – 39668 c. 3646, 21.3.44.

35 Ibid., c. 3940, 25.3.44.

36 R. Garcia Perez, *Franquismo y Tercer Reich* (Madrid: Centro de Estudios Constitucionales, 1994) , p. 473, quoting Dieckhoff's telegram, p. 473.

37 Acena, *Movimientos* (Madrid: Ministerio de Asuntos Exteriores (Publicaciones), 2001), p. 228, Garcia Perez, p. 473 and 488 and Vinas, p. 415.

38 CAB – 120/692, 31.3.44 and AP, p. 490.

39 AP, p. 492, 5.4.44 and CAB – 120/692.

40 CA CHAR 20/164/91, 14.5.44.

41 Acheson, *Present at the Creation* (New York and London: Hamilton, 1969), p. 56.

42   AP, p. 493.

43   Ibid., p. 506, 22.4.44 and CAB –120/692.

44   Cadogan, *Diaries*, 22.4.44.

45   AP, p. 507, 22.4.44 and CAB – 120/ 692 T909/4.

46   Ibid., p. 508.

47   Ibid., p. 508, 23.4.44.

48   Hull, *Memoirs* (London: Hodder and Stoughton, 1948), vol. II, p. 1331.

49   AP, p. 511, 26.4.44.

50   Ibid., p. 512, 26.4.44.

51   Hayes, *Wartime Mission*, p. 225.

52   Hull, *Memoirs*, p. 1331.

53   Ibid., p. 1332.

54   Acheson, *Present*, p. 59.

55   Ibid., p. 61.

56   Ruhl, *Spanien* (Hamburg: Hoffmann und Campe, 1975), pp. 242 and 349.

57   Feis, *Spanish Story* (New York: Norton, 1966), p. 251.

58   Feis, *Spanish Story*, p. 254.

59   Cambo, *Meditacions* (Barcelona: Alpha, 1982), vol. II, p. 1446, 3.5.44.

60   R. Skidelsky, *John Maynard Keynes*, Vol. III, *Fighting for Britain* (London: Papermac, 2001), p. 133.

61   A.P. Dobson, *U.S. War-time Aid to Britain* (London: Croom Helm, 1986), p. 171.

62   Board of Trade BT 11/3068, *Economic Relations with Spain (1942–46)*, 26.3.44.

63   Hayes, p. 225.

64   Ibid., p. 226.

65   H. Nicolson, *Diaries and Letters 1939–45* (London: Collins, 1967), p. 372.

66   C. Foltz, *Masquerade in Spain* (Boston: Houghton Mifflin, 1948), p. 220.

67   Treasury T 160/ 1381 F 18784.

68   Cadogan, *Diaries*, 24.5.44.

69   AP, p. 507, 22.4.44.

70   CAB – 120/ 692 T 962/4, 26.5.44.

71   H. Nicholas, ed. (London: Weidenfeld and Nicolson, 1981), entries for 30.5 and 4.6.44.

72   FO 371 – 39669 c. 7355, 1.6.44.

73   Ibid., c. 7647, 4.6.44.

74   CAB – 120 /692 M 731/4, 19.6.44.

75   FO 371 – 39669 c. 7160.

76   FO 371 – 39677 c. 13568, 12.10.44.

77   Cambo, *Meditations*, entries for 25.5 and 2.6.44.

78   *Nazi Gold: Information from the British Archives, History Notes*, no. 11, September 1996, Foreign Office Record Department.

79   *News Chronicle*, 29.6.44.

80   FO – 371 –39669 c. 7175.

81   Ibid., c. 7456, 2.6.44.

82 Ibid., 2.6.44.
83 Ibid., c. 7595, 5.6.44.
84 Ibid., c. 7954.
85 AP, p. 533, 29.6.44.
86 FO 371 – 39669 c. 8791, 1.7.44.
87 Ibid., 5.7.44.
88 TP – XIII – 24.
89 Op. cit., p. 236–8.
90 FO 371 – 39748 c. 8310, 15.6.44.
91 Hayes, *Wartime Mission*, p. 242.
92 FO 371 – 39670 c. 9418, 13.7.44.
93 Hayes, *Wartime Mission*, p. 259.
94 Hoare, *Ambassador* (London: Collins, 1946), p. 273.
95 FO 371 – 39670 c. 11012, 20.8.44.
96 Ibid., c. 10864, 22.8.44.
97 Ibid., c. 10973, 18.8.44.
98 FO 371 – 39671 c. 13318, 3.10.44.
99 AP, p. 519, 1.5.44.
100 Ibid., p. 522, 5.5.44.
101 Gil Robles, *La Monarquia* (Madrid: Taurus, 1976),14.12.43.
102 Toquero, *Franco y Don Juan* (Barcelona: Plaza Janes, 1989), p. 84.
103 Lopez Rodo, *Larga Marcha* (Barcelona: Noguer, 1977), Annexo 12, p. 520.
104 Ibid., Annexo 13, p. 522, 25.1.44.
105 *La Prensa*, Buenos Aires, 28.1.44.
106 Lopez Rodo, *Marcha*, p. 45.
107 Ibid.
108 Toquero, *Franco*, p. 90 and Lopez Rodo, *Marcha*, Annexo 14, pp. 524–27.
109 Gil Robles, *La Monarquia*, p. 92, 13.2.44.
110 Sainz, *Reinado* (Barcelona: Planeta, 1981), p. 124.
111 Gil Robles, *Monarquia*, 27.10.44.
112 Sainz, *Reinado*, p. 156, 17.4.44.
113 Toquero, *Franco*, p. 96, 6.6.44.
114 Sainz, *Reinado*, p. 290, September 1970.
115 Gil Robles, *Monarquia*, 22.9.44.
116 R. Carr, *Spain 1808 – 1975* (Oxford: Clarendon, 1982), p. 340.
117 FO 371 – 24527 c. 7531, 1.7.40.
118 Pierson Dixon, *Double Diploma* (London: Hutchinson, 1968), 28.8.44.

7   Churchill Intervenes II, October–December, 1944

1   W. Churchill, *The Second World War*, Vol. VI *(Triumph and Tragedy)* (London: Cassell, 1954), message of 28.8.44, p. 111.
2   Hoare, *Ambassador* (London: Collins, 1946), p. 283, full text in translation.
3   Text of the letter re-inserted under the 50-year rule in FO 371 – 39677 c. 13568 in December '94.

4 Ibid., minute 12.10.44.
5 FO 371 – 39678 c. 15660, 7.11.44.
6 FO 371 – 39677 c. 13568, 13.10.44.
7 TP XIII 7 no. 8.
8 FO 371 – 39671 c. 16068, 17.11.44.
9 FO 954 – 28, p. 37, 10.10.44.
10 Toquero, *Franco y Don Juan* (Barcelona: Plaza Janes, 1989), p. 101.
11 *Sunday Times*, ex Madrid, 5.11.44.
12 FO 371 – 39671 c. 14492, 16.10.44.
13 TP XIII – 23, no. 206, 23.3.44.
14 TP XIII – 24, no. 545, 3.9.44.
15 FO 371 – 39669 c. 7954, 12.6.44.
16 TP XIII – 12, 5–16.10.44.
17 FO 371 – 396671 c. 144922, 20.10.44.
18 TP XIII –12, 18–20.10.44.
19 FO 371 – 39671 c. 14492.
20 Ibid., c. 14409, 19.10.44.
21 Ibid., c. 15948.
22 Ibid., c. 15487, p. 79 – War Cabinet Paper (44) 622.
23 Ibid. c. 16068, p. 124 – PM's Personal Minute no. M 1101 , 10.11.44.
24 FO 371 – 39677 c. 15433 1.11.44.
25 Ibid., 11.11.44.
26 FO 371 – 39666 c. 1627, 5.2.44.
27 Hansard, Commons, 15.11.44.
28 FO 371 – 39836 c. 15934 (?), 14.11.44.
29 FO 371 – 39671 c. 16068, 17.11.44.
30 Ibid., p. 139, 18.11.44.
31 TP XIII – 12, 11–18.11.44.
32 Ibid., 1–12.11.44.
33 Ibid., 17.11.44.
34 AP, p. 543.
35 FO 371 – 39671 c. 16069, 18.11.44.
36 Emmet Hughes, *Report from Spain* (New York: Henry Holt, 1947), p. 269.
37 FO 371 – 39671 c. 15974 – WP (44), 14.11.44.
38 FO 371 – 39672 c. 18082, p120.
39 FO 371 – 39671 c. 16466, 28.11.44.
40 FO 371 – 39672 c. 16742, 2.12.44.
41 TP XIII – 12, 27.11–3.12.44.
42 FO 371 – 39672 c. 16599, 30.11.44.
43 Ibid., c. 16882, p. 25.
44 FO 371 – 39678 c. 16898, 3.12.44.
45 Cambo, *Meditacions* (Barcelona: Alpha, 1982), p. 1552, 29.12.44.
46 AP, p. 555, 7.12.44.
47 FO 371 – 39672 c. 17212, 11.12.44.

48 Hayes, *Wartime Mission in Spain* (New York: Macmillan, 1945), pp. 269 and 278.

49 FO 371 – 39678 c. 16898, 12.12.44.

50 FO 371 – 39672 c. 17266, 12.12.44.

51 FO 371 – 39823 c. 17918.

52 Hoare, *Ambassador*, pp. 123 and 137.

53 Memorandum in Ministerio de Relaciones Exteriores (MAE) Legajo R – 1372 e 22, 12.12.44..

54 FO 371 – 39672 c. 17272, 13.12.44.

55 *The Times*, ex Madrid, 14.12.44.

56 Churchill, *Second World War*, Vol. VI, Appendix C, p. 616.

57 AP, p. 568, 8.1.45.

58 FO 371 – 39672 c. 18083, 19.12.44.

59 Ibid., 22.12.44.

60 PREM 8 – 106, 31.12.44.

61 AP, p. 570, 11.1.45.

62 FO 371 – 39672 c. 17827 and Hoare, *Ambassador*, Appendix A.

8 A Wringing of Hands, January–July, 1945

1 FO 371 – 49610 z 2099, 13.2.45.

2 Ibid., z 1420 30.1.45.

3 FO 371 – 49575 z 89, received 3.1.45.

4 Ibid. z 2952, 24.2.44.

5 Ibid., 10.3.45, p. 17.

6 Ibid., z 3194, p. 30.

7 Ibid., z 3783, 21.3.45.

8 Ibid., z 3783, minute on above file, 7.4.45.

9 FO 371 – 49575 z 4874, 17.4.45 , p48.

10 Ibid., z 7167, 4.6.45.

11 FO 371 – 49611 z 2783, 14.2.45.

12 FO 371 – 49610 z 2003, 13.2.45.

13 AP, p. 576, 4.3.45.

14 FO 371 – 49610 z 1678.

15 Ibid., z 1814.

16 FO 371 – 49581 z 3999, 20.3.45.

17 Ibid., z 1907, 2.2.45.

18 Ibid., z 1907, minute on above, 26.2.45.

19 FO 371 – 49611 z 3693, 20.3.45.

20 Ibid., z 4225, 27.3.45.

21 Ibid., z 4656, 9.4.45.

22 Ibid., z 4450, 7.4.45.

23 FO 371 – 49611 z 2712 , 1.3.45.

24 Ibid., z 2972, 5.3.45.

25 AP, p. 586, 21.4.45.

26 PREM 8 – 106, 25.4.45.
27 AP, p. 591, 24.5.45.
28 Lopez Rodo, *Larga Marcha* (Barcelona: Noguer, 1977), pp. 48–50.
29 Gil Robles, *La Monarquia* (Madrid: Taurus, 1976), 12.12.44.
30 FO 371 – 49629 z 2353, 13.2.45.
31 Gil Robles, 10.4.45.
32 TP xiii – 27, repeat 22.5.45.
33 FO 371 – 49611 z 3425.
34 FO 371 49629 z 3742, 23.3.45.
35 Toquero, *Franco y Don Juan* (Madrid: Plaza Janes, 1989), p. 107.
36 Cambo, Meditacions (Barcelona: Alpha, 1982), 23.4.45.
37 FO 371 – 49629 z 4138.
38 FO 371 49611 z 4147, 27.3.45.
39 Kindelán, *La Verdad* (Madrid: Planeta, 1981), p. 254.
40 FO 371 – 49629 z 4138, 27.3.45.
41 Ibid., z 4822, 10.4.45.
42 FO 371 – 49587 z 1595, 30.1.45.
43 FO 371 – 49629 z 4094, 30.3.45.
44 AP, p. 579, 26.3.45.
45 FO 371 – 49629 z 5249, 26.4.45.
46 FO 371 – 49611 z 5974, 17.4.45.
47 Ibid., p. 219.
48 AP, p. 581, 2.4.45.
49 Ibid., undated.
50 S. Madariaga, *Victors Beware!* (London: Cape, 1946), pp. 287 and 289.
51 AP, p. 595, 10.7.45.
52 FO 371 – 49575 z 5996, 16.5.45.
53 FO 371 – 49612 z 8140, 7.7.45 and J. Colville, *The Fringes of Power*, Vol. 2 (London: Hodder and Stoughton, 1987), p. 258.
54 *Arriba* 22.5.45, in Hughes, *Report from Spain* (New York: Henry Holt, 1947), p. 97.
55 Ibid., p. 165.

Epilogue   Hoare versus Churchill over Spain

1 TP XXIII – 3.
2 Ibid., xiii 25/2.
3 Hoare, *Ambassador* (London: Collins, 1946), p. 292.
4 S. Hoare, *The Unbroken Thread* (London: Collins, 1949), chap. Wild Spain.
5 PREM 4 21/2a 28.7.43.
6 AP, p. 427, 6.8.43.
7 J. Lomax, *The Diplomatic Smuggler* (London: Barker, 1965), chap. Sir Samuel Hoare in Action.
8 *Ambassador*, p. 10.
9 TP XXIII – 1 *Third Mission*, chap. XI, p. 12.

10   Churchill, *Second World War*, Vol. I (London: Cassell, 1948), p. 167.
11   Nicolson, *Diaries and Letters 1930–39* (London: Collins, 1966), 16.3.38.
12   *Daily Telegraph*, 30.12.37.
13   J.A. Spender, *Fifty Years of Europe* (London: Cassell, 1933), p. 295.

Bibliography

Official Archives

The National Archives/Public Record Office, London.

War Cabinet CAB.
Prime Minister's Correspondence and Papers PREM.
Foreign Office FO371.
Avon Papers FO 954 – 27.
Treasury T 160.
Board of Trade BT 11.
Fuel and Power POWE.

Ministerio de Asuntos Exteriores, Madrid

Archivo General

Private Collections

Churchill Archives CHAR, Churchill Archives Centre, Churchill College, Cambridge.
Templewood Papers, University Library, Cambridge.

Books

ACENA, P.M., *Los Movimientos de Oro en Espana durante la Segunda Guerra Mundial*, Madrid: Ministerio de Asuntos Exteriores, Centro de Publicaciones, 2001.
ACHESON, D., *Present at the Creation,* London: Hamilton, 1970.
BROGGI, M., *Memorias de un Cirujano*, Barcelona: Peninsula, 2001.
BURNS, T., *The Use of Memory*, London: Sheed and Ward, 1993.
BUTCHER, H., *Three Years with Eisenhower*, London: Heinemann, 1946.
CADOGAN, A., *Diaries, 1938–45*, London: Cassell, 1971.
CAMBO, F., *Meditacions, Dietari, 1936–46*, Barcelona: Alpha, 1982.
CAMPO, R., *El Oro de Canfranc*, Zaragoza: Biblioteca Aragonesa de Cultura, 2002.
CARR, R., *Spain, 1808–1975*, Oxford: Clarendon, 1982.
De CASTRO, A., *Politica Externa Portuguesa durante a Guerra 1939–45*, Lisbon, 1958.
CATALAN, J, *La Economia Espanola y la Segunda Guerra Mundial*, Barcelona: Ariel, 1995.
CAVE BROWN, A., *The Last Hero* London: Joseph, 1982.
CHURCHILL, W., *The Second World War*, 6 vols, London: Cassell, 1948–54.

CHURCHILL, W., *Secret Session Speeches*, London: Cassell, 1946.

CIANO, G., *Diaries, 1939–43*, London: Heinemann, 1947.

COLVILLE, J., *The Fringes of Power*, 2 vols, London: Hodder and Stoughton, 1987 edn.

CREAC'H, J., *Le Coeur et L'Epee, Chroniques Espagnoles*, Paris: Plon, 1958.

DIXON, P., *Double Diploma*, London: Hutchinson, 1968.

DOBSON, A., *U.S. War-time Aid to Britain*, London: Croom Helm, 1986.

ECCLES, D., *By Safe Hand*, London: Bodley, 1983.

EDEN, A., *Memoirs: The Reckoning*, London: Cassell, 1965.

EGUIDAZU, F., *Aspectos Monetarios de la Neutralidad Espanola, Revista de Estudios Internacionales*, April–June issue, Madrid, 1984.

FEIS, H., *The Spanish Story*, New York: Norton, 1966.

FOLTZ, C., *Masquerade in Spain*, Boston: Houghton Mifflin, 1948.

FUSI, J., *Franco*, Madrid: El Pais, 1985.

GARCIA PEREZ, R., *Franquismo y Tercer Reich*, Madrid: Centro de Estudios Constitucionales, 1994.

GILBERT, M., *Winston Churchill – Finest Hour, 1939–41*, London: Heinemann, 1983.

GILBERT, M., *Road to Victory, 1941–45*, London: Heinemann, 1989.

GIL ROBLES, J., *La Monarquia por la que Yo Luche*, Madrid: Taurus, 1976.

GODFREY, J., *Naval Memoirs*, unpublished Admiralty Library, Portsmouth.

HAMILTON, T., *Appeasement's Child*, London: Gollancz, 1943.

HAYES, C., *War-time Mission in Spain*, New York: Macmillan, 1945.

HILL, D., *SOE Assignment*, London: Kimber, 1973.

HINSLEY, F., *British Intelligence in the Second World War*, 4 vols, London: HMSO, 1979–88.

HOARE, S., *Ambassador on Special Mission*, London: Collins, 1946.

HOARE, S., *The Unbroken Thread,* London: Collins, 1949.

HODGSON, R., *Spain Resurgent*, London: Hutchinson, 1953.

HUGHES, E., *Report from Spain*, New York: Holt, 1947.

HULL, C., *Memoirs*, 2 vols, London: Hodder and Stoughton, 1948.

KINDELAN, A., *La Verdad de Mis Relaciones con Franco*, Barcelona: Planeta, 1981.

LAFORET, C., *Nada*, Barcelona: Planeta, 1944.

LIDDELL HART, B., *History of the Second World War*, London Pan Books, 1973 edn.

LOMAX, J., *Diplomatic Smuggler*, London: Barker, 1965.

LOPEZ RODO, L., *La Larga Marcha hacia la Monarquia*, Barcelona: Noguer, 1977.

MacLACHLAN, D., *Room 39 Naval Intelligence in Action, 1939–45*, London: Weidenfeld, 1968.

MADARIAGA, S., *Victors Beware!,* London: Cape, 1946.

MARTINEZ NADAL R., *La Politica Espanola del Foreign Office, 1940–44*, Madrid: Casariego, 1989.

MOLINERO, C. and ISAS, P., *Els Industrials Catalans durant el Franquisme*, Vic: Eumo, 1991.

NAZI GOLD, History Notes No. 11, September 1996, London: Foreign Office Record Dept.

NICHOLAS, H. (ed.), *Washington Despatches*, London: Weidenfeld, 1981.

NICOLSON, H., *Diaries and Letters, 1930–39* and *1939–45*, London: Collins, 1966 and 67.

PEERS, E., *Spain in Eclipse*, London: Methuen, 1943.

PHILBY, H., *My Silent War*, London: Panther, 1969 edn.

PRESTON, P., *Franco,* London: HarperCollins, 1993.

RODRIGUEZ-MONINO, R., *La Mision Diplomatica del Duque de Alba en Londres, 1937–45*, Valencia: Castalia, 1971.

RUHL, K., *Spanien im Zweiten Weltkrieg*, Hamburg: Hoffmann und Campe, 1975.

SAINZ RODRIGUEZ, P., *Un Reinado en la Sombra*, Barcelona: Planeta, 1981.

SALMADOR, V., *Don Juan de Borbon*, Barcelona: Planeta, 1981.

SKIDELSKY, R., *Keynes, 1937–46*, London: Papermac, 2001 edn.

SPENDER, J., *Fifty Years of Europe*, London: Cassell, 1933.

STOFF, M., *Oil, War and American Security*, New Haven: Yale University Press, 1980.

TAMAMES, R., *La Economia Espanola*, Madrid: Alianza, 1967.

TOQUERO, J., *Franco y Don Juan*, Barcelona: Plaza Janes, 1989.

TREVOR-ROPER, H., *Hitler's War Directives*, London: Sidgwick Jackson, 1964.

TUSELL, J., *Franco, Espana y la Segunda Guerra Mundial*, Madrid: Temas de Hoy, 1995.

VEGAS, E, *Memorias Politicas, 1938–42*, Madrid: Actas, 1995.

VINAS, A. with VINUELA, J., EGUIDAZU, F., FERNANDEZ PULGAR, C. and FLORENSA, S., *Politica Comercial Exterior de Espana* vol. 1, Madrid: Banco Exterior de Espana, Servicio de Estudios Economicos, 1979.

WILMOT, C., *Struggle for Europe*, London: Collins, 1959 edn.

Index